The Globally Familiar

Duke University Press   Durham and London   2020

The Globally Familiar

Digital Hip Hop, Masculinity,
and Urban Space in Delhi

Ethiraj Gabriel
Dattatreyan

© 2020 DUKE UNIVERSITY PRESS All rights reserved
Printed in the United States of America on acid-free paper ∞
Designed by Courtney Leigh Richardson
Typeset in Whitman by Westchester Publishing Services
Library of Congress Cataloging-in-Publication Data
Names: Dattatreyan, Ethiraj Gabriel, [date].
Title: The globally familiar : digital hip hop, masculinity, and urban space
in Delhi / Ethiraj Gabriel Dattatreyan.
Description: Durham : Duke University Press, 2020. | Includes bibliographical
references and index.
Identifiers: LCCN 2020006435 (print) | LCCN 2020006436 (ebook) |
ISBN 9781478010159 (hardcover) | ISBN 9781478011200 (paperback) |
ISBN 9781478012726 (ebook)
Subjects: LCSH: Music and youth—India—Delhi. | Hip-hop—Social
aspects—India—Delhi. | Music—Social aspects—India—Delhi.
Classification: LCC ML3917.14 D388 2020 (print) | LCC ML3917.14 (ebook) |
DDC 305.242/1095456—dc23
LC record available at https://lccn.loc.gov/2020006435
LC ebook record available at https://lccn.loc.gov/2020006436
Cover art: B-boy Ashu in SDA Market, South Delhi, 2019. © Vivek Vision.
Courtesy of the artist and Khatarnaak Hip Hop Collective.

Contents

I returned to Delhi in the first week of January 2013 to begin fieldwork in earnest, just in time to bear witness to a fomenting moral panic. A few weeks prior to my arrival, a brutal rape and murder took place, now infamously referred to as *the* Delhi rape case. A young woman and her male friend had attended a film in a South Delhi movie theater located in a garish new mall that opened in 2007, just across the road from where several of the stories that follow in the pages ahead unfold. After watching the film, they went to the main road to find transportation to take them home. Instead of taking an auto-rickshaw, they opted to take an inexpensive minibus, the kind that operates in the peripheries of the city and provides transportation for domestic workers and service laborers whose jobs run into the night. That evening they were picked up by a group of six young men driving a small private bus. The young men operating the bus were all migrants to the city, hailing from various rural villages across the region. They ranged in age from sixteen to thirty and lived in South Delhi's informal housing settlements. To supplement their income, they used the bus to ferry passengers in the late evening. On this night, their entrepreneurial endeavor transformed into a violent encounter. These men, after picking up the young woman—referred to as Nirbhaya (fearless) in the media in the weeks and months that followed—proceeded to brutalize her: raping, torturing, and, finally, leaving her for dead on the side of the road.

Following the incident, candlelight vigils and protests erupted across India. When I arrived in the cold, smog-filled city in early January, India Gate was lit up like it was Diwali. The city's well-to-do as well as those aspiring toward economic and social mobility had turned out in numbers in support of Nirbhaya as she lay in a hospital bed fighting for her life. They also came out to protest. People from all backgrounds and of all ages rallied to decry the toxic masculinity that produced the possibility for such violence as well as rage against the state and its inability to protect women.

Delhi elections were just around the corner and the rise of the Aam Aadmi Party (AAP, Common Man's Party), which had come into being in November 2012 as an official political entity, was portended in the swell of people who rose up just after the Delhi rape case.[1] At the national level, the right-wing Hindu Bharatiya Janata Party (BJP) had not yet ascended to power. It would be roughly another two years before Narendra Modi would assume office as prime minister on the twin platform of development through privatization and the assertion of so-called Hindu values as central to a successful future India. But the discourse that catapulted both Modi and the BJP into power was on display after the violent incident.

The city, depicted through the Delhi rape case as a place of moral dissolution and a symbol of a failed liberal, secular India, offered a platform to voice another politic that had been lurking just under the surface. This discourse—which had emerged in key moments at local and regional levels since liberalization took hold in the 1990s but had not as yet been articulated at the scale of the national—was one that championed an ascendant Hindu Rashtra that would cleanse the country and its cities of their vices. The image of an unmarried couple going to see a film in the garish consumer space of the mall movie theater was part of the BJP's conservative critique, a way to shift the responsibility of the violence onto the victims by purporting a failure to uphold traditional (Hindu) norms. The figure of the young male perpetrator from a minority community was also mobilized to point to urban India's morass and capitalize on the collective rage, anxiety, and desire for action that the case generated.

Over the next several months, the six young men indicted in the Delhi rape case—their images, their testimonies, their histories—circulated in ways that cast the male migrant as a threat to the city's and the nation's present and future, a narrative that has a long history in postcolonial India.[2] The responsibility for the uptick in violence in cities, so the mediatized narrative went, could be squarely placed on young men like them, the poor, undereducated migrant males who preyed on victims in the public spaces of the city. In the wake of the case, the government of India commissioned a report to review and recommend new sexual assault laws. In this report, produced by a committee headed by former supreme court chief justice J. S. Verma, "young and prospectless men . . . fighting for space in an economy that offers mainly casual work" were blamed for the uptick in sexual violence.[3] The report effectively legitimized the media narrative about young migrant males in Delhi. Typified as backward, lacking the skills to participate in or contribute to a globalized Indian economy, and devoid of the right moral values, the specter of the feckless male outsider in the city became a ghost to be banished or reformed.[4]

As this shrill discourse demonizing the young, undereducated, and economically marginalized young men of Delhi was being broadcast far and wide, I began to get to know young men from the urban villages and informal settlements of South and West Delhi involved in Delhi's burgeoning hip hop scene. These young men, for the most part, had arrived in the city with their families as young children in the early years of the twenty-first century, in a period when the city had begun to swell in size, both demographically and topographically.[5]

The young men who populate the pages ahead—whether originally from the rural hinterlands of the Gangetic plains, from the northeastern edges of the country, from the mountain villages of Garhwal, or from Afghanistan, Nigeria, Somalia, or Nepal—all contended in similar as well as in quite strikingly different ways with being cast in the media and in their everyday lives as Delhi's Others, potentially destructive outsiders who live on the peripheries of vital change in the city. Yet as I got to know them, it became evident that these young men, like their upper-caste and well-to-do peers in the gated colonies that surround the informal housing settlements and urban villages where they live, were undeniably all part of the diverse, urban cross section of a millennial iteration of the Zippie generation.[6]

That is, despite economic and biographical differences, they were born in the late 1990s and came of age in urban India almost two decades after the nation opened its borders to capital.[7] They are part of a generation of young people who have grown up in Delhi in an era when malls, the metro, and mobile phones are taken-for-granted lived realities. Moreover, they have come of age in an era where the interjection of global capital into urban India has brought economic, political, and social instability that at once produces the appearance that there are opportunities for mobility even as it generates deep anxiety and, in some instances, calamitous friction. Rather than being out of step or disconnected from processes of globalization and the subsequent intensification of urban development it has wrought, these young men saw themselves at the nexus of a changing Indian urbanity that is predicated on digitally enabled transnational connection, distinctive consumption, and creative self-production as key components of social belonging and the basis for potential futures.[8]

This book focuses on these young dancers, rappers, and graffiti artists and offers a different entry point to think through masculinity in Delhi than that of the common mediatized narrative that positions young men like those I got to know as lumpen and surplus labor that, at best, "timepass," waiting for an otherwise seemingly foreclosed urban future to rupture and yield opportunity and, at worst, prey on those more vulnerable than them.[9] To be clear from the outset, this book will not focus on their perspectives on sexual violence in Delhi, a city that has in recent years gained the dubious distinction of being called the rape capital of the world. Nor will it focus on the problematic debates that pit (Hindu) traditionalism in opposition to a secular (urban) modernity when it comes to prescribed gender roles in the city.[10] Rather, the pages ahead offer an account of how a diverse cross section of young male migrants growing up in a globalizing Delhi become gendered, racialized, and classed subjects within a social, economic, and political context marked by uncertainty, anxiety, threat, and possibility—and the profound role that digital communications and media technology has in shaping them.

As importantly, this book tells the story of how these young men mobilize hip hop's creative arts as a means to refashion their embodied difference and their spatial communities' marked Otherness as productive sites of distinction. Throughout the book, I discuss how their creative endeavors in the offline and online worlds they frequented created new social and economic possibilities for them that make visible an alternate mapping of the city in ways that complicate the cloistering rhetoric of fear and threat that animate media depictions of Delhi. In so doing, I show how the top-down world-class city discourse that has reshaped Delhi's spaces in the last decade is being unexpectedly inhabited and interrupted in the second decade of the twenty-first century.[11]

While sexual violence is not at the center of the narrative that follows, the Delhi rape case unavoidably framed my interactions with the young men I met in the Delhi hip hop scene. In the pages that follow, I show how the rape case was explicitly deployed by the young people I got to know as a critique of their cohort living in their spatial communities. In other moments, I discuss how my interlocutors evoked it as a way of marking their own distinction, a way of narrating a masculine subjectivity that could never be like the men who committed such an atrocity.

The young men who populate this book, of course, were not the only young people in Delhi who grappled with the rape case and its implications. As Tara Atluri suggests, the case reframed how young people in the city and the nation talked and thought about gender, age, and classed power in twenty-first-century India.[12] The case also opened up public discourse about urban in-migration, processes of dispossession, aspirations for the good life, and the ways in which these phenomena are linked. These conversations, as they were simultaneously staged in the media and during the everyday interactions that make up the life of the city, made evident the disjuncture between discourses that posited Delhi as a site of moral dissolution and social disintegration, and those that framed Delhi as a world-class city-in-the-making. They also brought to the foreground the fact that young people are crucial actors in the drama to define the present and future of Delhi and India, not in small part because the under-thirty-year-old demographic comprise a sizable and growing number of the city's and nation's population.[13]

It is my hope that this book, as it offers a take on contemporary Delhi as a site of masculine becoming and digital transformation, captures something of this historical moment and its unfoldings into the present. In the account that follows, the imagined and inhabited Delhi that I was privileged to witness emerging in the young men's articulated dreams, embodied practices, and audiovisual representations is inextricably linked to urbanities elsewhere and otherwise through digital hip hop.[14]

Acknowledgments

It has taken me six years to write this book and many folks have helped me along the way. First and foremost, many thanks to the b-boys, graffiti writers, and MCs I met in Delhi for their openness, enthusiasm, and willingness to share their lives and creative work with me. I hope, if they choose to read this book, they find something of value. This book has been shaped by a number of diligent readers and sharp interlocutors who pushed me to rethink my first assumptions. I owe a great debt to Jaspal Naveel Singh for his thoughtful and critical engagements during fieldwork and for reading my manuscript countless times and, each time, patiently offering his incisive feedback. This book would not exist without him. Many thanks to all the artists, activists, and educators I met while in Delhi. They inspired and instigated thought and brought much joy into my life during my time in the city. Amardeep Kainth, Pooja Sood, Tenzin Lekhmon, Juan Orrantia, Priya Sen, Sitara Chowfla, Radha Mahendru, Aastha Chauhan, He Ra, and the many others I met and learned from during my years in South Delhi: thank you for all your warmth, generosity, and critical feedback.

Radha Hegde, during a South Asia Media Conference held in London in 2014, offered me sage advice and encouragement on my then nascent ideas on digital mediations from below. Faye Ginsburg helped me think through how to articulate the collaborative aspect of this project just before I headed off to Delhi. I received wonderful feedback when I attended the Yale Modern South Asia Workshop in 2015. Special thanks to Kasturi Gupta, Rohit De, Kathryn Hardy, Tariq Thachil, and Tejaswini Ganti for facilitating the event. While I was a graduate student at the University of Pennsylvania, several friends helped me develop my thinking around gender, race, space, digitality, audiovisuality, and ethnography. Many thanks to Arjun I. Shankar, Mariam Durrani, Sandra Ristovska, Krystal Smalls, Savannah Shange, Roseann Liu, Sofia Chaparro, Tali Ziv, Shashank Saini, and Andrew Hudson, for all their brilliant insights that continue to shape my work.

    While at the University of Pennsylvania, a few key mentors shaped my thinking and helped me articulate my commitments. Throughout the development of this project, John Lester Jackson Jr. and Deborah Thomas have offered me steady, unwavering, and enthusiastic support, advice, and critical engagement. Thank you both for your friendship. Kathy Schultz, Kathleen Hall, Stanton Wortham, Lisa Mitchell, and Sharon Ravitch: thank you for all your support. I owe Jesse Weaver Shipley a great debt for providing an intellectual home at Haverford College just after graduate school to develop this project and start others. Several of my colleagues at Goldsmiths, University of London have generously read and commented on my chapters. As importantly, during casual chats in the pub, they have pushed me to articulate my investments and critiques of anthropology in wonderfully productive ways. Special thanks to Isaac Marrero Guillamón, Martyn Wemyss, Alice Elliot, Elena Gonzalez-Polledo, Les Back, and Emma Tarlo for all their feedback and support along the way. Many thanks to Sareeta Amrute and Debanuj Dasgupta, who read versions of the introduction to this book and helped me strengthen it. A huge thank you to Sahana Udupa, whose warm and vivacious intellect has sharpened my own over the years since we first met in Philadelphia. A big shout out to H. Samy Alim, who read some of the earliest drafts of chapters from this book and has been a champion of my work since. Brent Luvaas, thank you for helping me think through the relationship between co-optation and cooperation. Thanks to the Wenner Gren Foundation for funding my research, on which this book is based. This project owes a great debt to Ken Wissoker, the Duke University Press team, and the two anonymous readers who reviewed this manuscript. All their hard work and thoughtful feedback and guidance helped me immensely. I am grateful.

    To my heart, Karin, for holding me down while I did this thing: all my love.

Picture a young man, about seventeen years of age. His family originally hails from the agrarian heartlands of eastern Uttar Pradesh but moved to Delhi to find work in the early twenty-first century. They live in a diverse and dense urban village in South Delhi, a place where migrants reside.[1] At his age, he would normally be attending senior secondary school or college, or working as a driver, a construction worker, or in a shop in one of the many malls that have cropped up all over the city, like the other males in his immediate and extended family. Instead of attending school or working, he practices his b-boy moves in the park close to his house with other young men from different ethnic, caste, and national backgrounds. He walks around his neighborhood and the city "battle ready," striding with an arrogant confidence— almost as if a soundtrack that we cannot hear and he alone can affords him a different embodied relationship to the streets he frequents.[2]

He and his friends write graffiti on the cement walls of their neighborhood and in other parts of the city. They spend their time traveling across the city on the Delhi metro, doing spontaneous dance performances in malls, parks, and historic ruins across the city. They rap in Hindi and English to each other and, occasionally, to an audience, microphone in one hand, the other pointing outward toward the crowd. They take photos and make videos of these performances and their other acts of creation and post them on social media.

Some people who witness their creative performances (and social media circulations of them) are excited and enthusiastic as they come across a familiar representation of youthful urban life from elsewhere laminated onto the urban terrain of Delhi. For them, these young men's hip hop play offers the opportunity for a quick news story about globalization in the so-called slums of the city.[3] Their performances also provide a viable image for a marketing campaign to promote a global sneaker brand in India or a narrative of political valence that could support an ongoing activist project.

For others, it is strange, unsettling. An old man in a South Delhi urban village mutters, "*Kya fyda?* What is the value?" under his breath as he stands in front of a graffiti mural painted by this young man and his friends. A former government school teacher of his says, "What will he do in the future? How will he earn money? He is already disadvantaged and poor. What will he do with this singing and dancing?" His parents are uncertain that this will lead anywhere. "Dress normally," his mother says. "Stop wearing your pants so low. Why this music?"[4]

In his recent monograph, D. Asher Ghertner argues that Delhi has been remade through the elites' (the planners', developers', politicians', and entrepreneurs') aesthetic vision of the future that places Delhi in comparison to, say, Paris or Singapore.[5] He suggests that urban development projects in Delhi that began soon after economic liberalization policies in India were enacted in the 1990s and that picked up pace in 2006 after the Delhi Master Plan 2021 was drafted have been mobilized through an image of these idealized world-class cities rather than by surveys, synoptic maps, or demographic data.[6]

This hegemonic image of a future Delhi, he contends, valorizes familiar scenes of urban life elsewhere toward the goal of making Delhi, to quote the authors of the Delhi Master Plan 2021, "a prime mover and nerve centre of ideas and actions, the seat of national governance and a centre of business, culture, education and sports."[7] Ghertner contends that, as this top-down aesthetic regime becomes policy and practice and taken-for-granted doxa, it generates the city's spatial everyday, its subjects, and its futures. It makes, if we play with the old anthropological adage a bit, the familiar of a Delhi past strange and the strange of a Delhi future familiar.[8]

The diverse young men who populate the pages ahead also use imaginaries of an urban elsewhere to conceptualize and produce sonic, visual, and embodied representations of themselves, the city they live in, and the potential futures of both. However, the key resource they utilize to imagine a different city and self, steeped in the familiar images and sounds of an urban elsewhere, are found in hip hop. This book is about these young men—the children of newcomers, ethnic or caste others, and laborers in the city—as they come of age on the margins of Delhi's economic and social transformation with the promise that through transnational media consumption *and* production, they can fashion themselves and the worlds they inhabit.

Throughout this book, I use the synthetic term *globally familiar* to describe and theorize how smart phones and social media platforms offer these young men the means to reimagine and remake self and city through hip hop practice. The globally familiar, broadly speaking, is the technological infrastructure that facilitates connection across place and time as well as the diversity of media these technologies can be made to conjure. These mediations offer those from "below" an opportunity to reimagine the city and themselves on different and productive terms.[9] Perhaps more importantly, the globally familiar is a feeling of connectedness made possible through media-enabled participation and practice and the affective economy and structure of aspiration this feeling produces.[10] It suggests that by cultivating the self through the consumption, production, and circulation of transnational popular culture, a different present and future, replete with unanticipated participation and opportunity, is possible.[11]

Since the 1990s, media consumption has become a key site to track the effects of what was somewhat faddishly (in both hopeful and pessimistic ways) called globalization—a term used to describe not only the economic but the social, cultural, and political changes that arrived in the post–Cold War era in national contexts, like India for instance, which were previously economically "protected."[12] As Arjun Appadurai argues (as does Stuart Hall, in a different moment and context), by listening to, reading, and watching the "popular," people are not simply interpellated as docile subjects.[13] Rather, the explosion of access to TV, films, music, and the news—whether produced elsewhere or "locally"—offers people a site by which to understand, engage, and even contest changes that the flow of capital, in its myriad forms, produces in a particular place as it reconstitutes livelihoods, lifestyles, and personhood.

I pick up this idea in the contemporary, digital moment when a clear distinction between media consumption and production of media forms has collapsed.[14] The availability of inexpensive smart phones that allow for the possibility to access and repost (and remix) existing media and creatively capture our everyday experiences profoundly shapes how we come to know ourselves in the world. In this moment, media is not simply something to consume and imagine with but a way to actively create oneself and the world anew and communicate these understandings to others.[15] As Donna

Haraway presciently argued almost three decades ago, "communications technologies . . . are the crucial tool recrafting our bodies."[16] In the present moment, digital communication technologies hold the potential to remake bodies *and* places precisely because of the speed of continuous and recursive connectivity and comparison they facilitate.

I deploy the globally familiar in this book to specifically engage with "digital hip hop" as a site of gendered becoming and spatial transformation in Delhi. The globally familiar, in the close ethnographic reading that follows, is Black American masculinity as it is digitally broadcast, received, and retrofitted for rebroadcast through hip hop's sonic, visual, and kinesthetic sensibilities. I draw from a range of research that has engaged with hip hop as a global phenomenon and that recognizes the reach of American Blackness beyond African diasporic circuits to explore how digital hip hop becomes the key *global familiar* by which the young men I met in Delhi's hip hop scene come to understand and creatively mobilize their perceived and experienced gendered (classed, and racialized) difference in ways that produce new relations in and with the city they call home.[17] To focus on digital media circulations as a site of gendered becoming in Delhi is, as Joshua Neves and Bhaskar Sarkar argue, to move away from "normative imaginations of global technoculture" that center Europe and North America.[18] To engage with hip hop in urban India is to recognize the reach of African diasporic arts as they are amplified through digital means to produce unanticipated subjects and places.

In the last decade, feminist hip hop scholars working in the United States have paid close attention to how hip hop envisions, articulates, and shapes normative and deeply problematic ideas about gender and sexuality as well as offers opportunities to interrupt them.[19] However, while there has been plenty of research on hip hop's "global linguistic flows," there has been little work on how hip hop's aesthetics, in its global travels, have shaped gendered subjectivities elsewhere.[20]

As importantly, there have been few close engagements with contemporary embodiments of working-class masculinity in the complex social worlds of postliberalization urban India. As Sareeta Amrute argues, contemporary scholarship on India has tended to focus on either the so-called urban middle class or on the rural caste, religious, ethnic, and tribal subject.[21] The urban and peri-urban poor and working class, as a result, tend to get subsumed into one analytical project or the other or are left out altogether. With regard to the study of masculinity, this tendency has resulted in two strands of scholarship. The first strand has engaged with colonialism's impact on the male gendered body, with an analytical focus on caste Hindu male sexuality, bodily cultivation, semen conservation, religious-nationalist identity formation, and consequent sectarian violence.[22] The settings for these engagements, with some notable exceptions, have been either in the village or in one of India's many second-tier cities or large towns.

The second strand has delved into "middle-class" masculinities and sexualities in the postliberalization period, touching upon the impact of consumerism, national and regional mass media, and a newfound sense of publicness.[23] The settings for these studies have included cities but have, with few exceptions, failed to differentiate male subjects based on their laboring opportunities, racialized positions, or spatialized conditions.[24] In other words, there has not been a close engagement with how in-migration and expropriative development have impacted how the male children of workers, as they come of age in urban spaces of transformation, imagine and perform themselves as men.[25]

In the pages ahead, I foreground how transnational media circulation influences the aspirations and everyday gendered performances of a diverse group of young working-class men growing up in urban India as well as think through the ways in which media *production* becomes a site of transformation and opportunity. In particular, I push for an attention to the ways the miniaturized screen—as it brings notions of personhood and place from elsewhere into immediate and productive conversation with the here and now—provides a diverse cross section of working-class men in Delhi the opportunity to self-fashion themselves *as* men in the context of the city they call home.[26]

I engage with masculinity in my participants' social (media) play, physical embodiments, conceptual understandings of gender, aspirations for the future, and their opportunities for work. In each case, I look at the ways in which their social performances and gendered aspirations are influenced as much by the context they live in as by the media content they consume and emulate in their online productions and everyday hip hop embodiments. By situating my account among a diverse group of working-class young men living in the city, I push against readings of masculinity as regional (South Asian) or national (Indian). Rather, I focus on the fluid and complex assemblages of gender in relation to class, caste, race, and ethnicity within the context of Delhi but linked to transnational circuits of becoming.[27]

By engaging with Delhi as a spatial field of transformation made optical, audible, and visceral not only in the ethnographic *cut* I inhabited with these young men who generously included me in their cipha but also in their audiovisual productions, I offer an alternative narrative to the ways in which urban place-making is often discussed in South Asia—as a project that is ruled by experts and ratified by the desires of the so-called middle class.[28] Brian Larkin poetically argues that "the quotidian landscapes of life—posters on the walls, shop signs, dancing girls, bestsellers, panoramas, the shape, style, and circulation of city buses—are all surface representations of the fantasy energy by which the collective perceives the social order."[29] In the pages ahead, I show how digital hip hop offered these young men the opportunity to claim and reimagine the spaces of their city—the parks, the malls, the historical ruins, the cement walls surrounding the streets of the slums and urban villages where they reside—in ways that productively disrupted normative understandings of twenty-first-century Delhi's social order.[30]

In their renderings and inhabitations, contemporary Delhi was reimagined as global or world class not because of the new roads to accommodate the surge in privately owned automobiles; the new glass, steel, and concrete private housing developments; the shiny international airport; or the countless shopping malls and private hospitals that have come to dominate the city's built environs.[31] Rather, the young men I met in the city utilized hip hop to reimagine their city as global because of its slums, its graffiti murals across the city's expanses, and its regular hip hop events. Their hip hop–inspired self-fashioning projects in the city, in this sense, not only indexed their gendered becoming but was constitutive of *Delhi as a place*.[32]

Consider that much of the scholarship on twenty-first-century Delhi has focused on either a top-down reimagining of the city or on the urban poor and their plight as a result of slum clearances and the like.[33] In each case, Delhi's urban poor and working class are depicted as homogenous and either passive recipients or, at best, as examples of anachronistic resistance to an urban Indian present and future that, ultimately, does not include them in its imaginaries. This book provides a different entry point to engaging with Delhi than those offered by scholars, literary writers, or the mainstream media, who portray the city in terms of clear demarcation and division where the cosmopolitan elite have access to the global—literally and metaphorically—while the masses do not.[34] What emerged—in the images, videos, and social media narrations of the diverse young male hip hop dancers, MCs, and graffiti writers' everyday border crossings and relational entanglements in the city coupled with my ethnographic deep dive into the contexts of their production—was a picture of Delhi that did not seem so clearly divided on some counts but was deeply unequal (and segregated) in others.

This doubling, where the young men I got to know deployed hip hop to spatialize Delhi as a site of productive mobility and recalcitrant inequality, at once challenged and reinforced the logics of a top-down aesthetic vision of Delhi as a world-class city. In this sense, the pages that follow will not offer a simple tale of celebratory subaltern resistance against the dominant aesthetic that has in the last twenty years transformed many of India's urban spaces into what media theorist Ravi Sundaram has argued are "middle class utopias."[35] Rather, the story that unfolds centers on how these young men negotiated the changing economic, social, and spatial conditions around them through hip hop–influenced modes of consumption and performances of distinction that did not, for instance, critique their economically and socially privileged peers but were meant to productively grab their attention even if that sometimes meant calling into question the structural forces that produced their shared reality.

Nor does this book offer a dismal narrative of digital subjectification, global consumerist interpellation, and capitalist dispossession: the kind of ethnographic account that Sherry Ortner has described as "dark anthropology" and that Jodi Dean argues exemplifies the (digital) communicative turn in capitalism.[36] The mere fact that these young men have taken up the hopeful, creative, and vitally embodied and spatialized practices of hip hop, with its political history of representing racial capitalism and its effects, would make that impossible.[37] Rather, I endeavor to explore and unwind the stories of how my participants' digital hip hop practice in Delhi reflects the complicated relationship between their desire to participate in global capital's reworking of the city and the opportunities and exclusions they encounter *as* marginal male subjects otherwise in the shadows of globalization's transformation of the city and the country.

If the anxieties their elders and parents have about their hip hop practice reflect the limits linked to these young men's economic and social futures in the city (*Kya fyda?* What is the value?), my participants' insistence on pursuing hip hop art forms and developing digitally enabled transnational communities of practice reveals the ways they imagine the transformative potential of digital technology and hip hop to create new possibilities for life otherwise. Taken in this spirit, my analysis of masculinity, urban space, and digital hip hop in Delhi offers something akin to what Lila Abu-Lughod describes as a "diagnostic of power."[38] This diagnostic concerns itself, in large part, with the ways in which the young men who let me into their lives positioned themselves (and were positioned) as gendered subjects in the fast-changing urban terrains of the city more than two decades since economic liberalization changed the country and its cities irrevocably.

In this sense, this book—with its focus on transnational (digital) media, hip hop praxis, masculine becoming, and urban change in India's capital city—offers the latest "digital take" on a body of literature concerned with how economic liberalization in India in the 1990s and the consumptive flows it has since let loose have transformed public space, understandings of gender, and aspiration for young people.[39] Anthropological work that has focused on the liminal category of youth in the postliberalization era has carefully engaged with the ways in which access to global circulations has ushered in tastes, desires, aspirations, and political sensibilities that anxiously reconstitute gender roles, reimagine public space, and, in some instances, fatally mark aspiration as future death.[40] These accounts have offered opportunities to critically reflect on how young people living in India, as they reimagine and reposition themselves through sartorial choice, consumptive habits, and articulations of their hopes and dreams, at once transgress and reinforce class, religious, caste, and gendered difference in the lifeworlds they inhabit. Some of this rich corpus of scholarship on youth in postliberalization India has highlighted mass mediation as a key element in the reformulation of gendered subjectivities, social practices, and spatial relations.

For instance, Filippo Osella and Caroline Osella's account of young men in small-town Kerala going to the cinema and Sarah Dickey's theorization of film-star fan clubs in a second-tier city in Tamil Nadu provide a way to think about how national and regional cinema shapes everyday life for young men in India. In their accounts, what emerges are the kinds of gendered relations, political sensibilities, and spatial inhabitations produced through the act of watching together in an era marked by a consciousness of elsewhere and otherwise.[41]

I also think of Devan, the young low-caste college student based in small-town Kerala who appears in Ritty Lukose's work on youth transformations in postliberalization India. In Lukose's account, Devan, in part by watching the Tamil film *Kaaladan* (Loverboy), began to shop for and dress in what Lukose describes as a Ragga-inspired style (baggy pants, loose shirts, sneakers, and a ponytail) in an effort to be "*chethu,*" cool or sharp in Malayali. Global Blackness, mediated through Tamil cinema, offered a different gendered and racialized possibility for Devan and, in turn, produced different social practices and aspirations for him and his peers.

In more recent ethnographic work, there has been a focus on reality television shows like *Indian Idol* and the ways in which youthful aspirations for national fame are sparked and cultivated by the promise and possibility of televisual appearance.[42] Simply watching the show—modeled after an American show by a similar name—sparks the desire in young people to fashion themselves as musical performers, even if the possibility to access the requisite training to become one is limited based on gender, class, and caste and the particular aesthetics of the show favor the reproduction of a dominant aesthetic.

These ethnographies of youthful media practice have not (and, in some cases, could not have, given their timing) paid close attention to the ways in which transnational, networked media connectivity has become a taken-for-granted horizon of possibility that shapes desire, personhood, relationships to space, and dreams for the future.[43] As with previous shifts in media infrastructure in India—for instance, the cassette tape boom in the 1980s or the advent of satellite television in the 1990s that caused the proliferation of a broad variety of local, regional, and globally circulating media forms—the post-2008 digital explosion has opened up the possibility for new modes of consumption, communication, and production.[44]

For instance, as of 2019, India has the largest number of regular Facebook users in the world (approximately 269 million people).[45] These users are concentrated in India's urban centers, particularly first-tier cities like Delhi, Mumbai, and Bengaluru where there has been a rapid creation of digital infrastructure in the last decade, especially after 2008, when 3G and 4G spectrums were auctioned by the government to private interests that rapidly expanded internet connectivity.[46]

The globally familiar takes up this new spatialized media ecology and the concomitant social practices, acts of self-fashioning, and unbridled aspiration it motivates among India's diverse youth—an under-twenty-five-year-old demographic that comprises more than half the nation's population.[47] The globally familiar pushes us to think what happens when the silver screen is miniaturized, when media of all sorts can be evoked with a swipe or a click of the button, and when collective viewing practices consist of a group of young people (in the case of this book, young men) gathered around one small blue-lit screen in public space.

In the current moment, quite literally, the global can fit in one's pocket to be summoned in an instant. This emergent digital infrastructure has provided young people across various social divides in urban India with, among other things, access to popular cultural content from around the world: global news (fake and otherwise), English Premier League football, K-pop, Naija pop, Japanese manga, and, of course, hip hop, all of which supplement their previous diet of the popular produced by national and regional mass media industries as well as web-based media directed at "Indian" youth.[48]

The globally familiar, in this sense, demands a recognition that in the age of social media, the popular, in its various media manifestations, is more diversified than ever before. Amateur YouTube videos shot by youth living in cities around the world are just as likely to be accessed as corporate-produced media depictions, and the ways young people in India gain access to what they consume is increasingly a function of the online and offline web of relationships they find themselves enmeshed in.[49] These media forms, taken as a whole, are constitutive of how young people in urban India make sense of who they are and where (and when) they live. In this sense, the globally familiar suggests that transnational circulations of media content open up a site by which to understand how places and subjects are produced that are neither global nor local but in excess of both.[50]

Why Hip Hop?

"Why hip hop?" was a question I asked b-boys, graffiti writers, and MCs quite frequently early on in my stay in the city. The response I got was an affectively charged one: hip hop is freedom; hip hop is life. Hip hop, as these young men described, allowed them to create a feeling of connection and belonging through stylistic play and embodied practice that exceeded their conditions of possibility as the children of laborers, refugees, and caste Others.[51] For these young men, digital connectivity offered access to youth cultural worlds beyond what they deemed "Indian" popular culture, which they argued they felt no connection to because they were outside the dominant narrative these popular representations portrayed. In their accounts, they imagined regional and national cinema and TV as local, even though they too were in global circulation within and beyond diasporic circuits.[52]

"Bollywood films. I hate them. They are horrible," said Jay, in a mixture of Hindi and English. Jay was eighteen years old when I first met him in 2012. A talented MC and b-boy, he moved with his father from Garhwal district in the mountains of North India to South Delhi in 2003 but claimed Nepal as home. "*Ghazals*? Filmy music? That is not for me. That is for Indians. *Aam aadmi*.[53] Ordinary man. *Main alag aadmi hoon*. I am a different man." For Jay and his peers, their positions as *alag aadmi* could only be articulated and aestheticized through hip hop. Their reclamation of *alag* (difference) through hip hop transformed their outsider positionality in Delhi into a globally familiar one—where a creative embodiment of spatialized, gendered, and racialized difference becomes a resource and strategy for realizing social and economic mobility. As such, hip hop fulfilled itself in Delhi as it has throughout its forty-year history since its inception in Black and Latinx neighborhoods of urban America: as a technology of creative bricolage that opens up opportunities to self-fashion as a response to processes of disenfranchisement, and to generate new social and economic possibilities as a result.[54]

In this sense, practicing hip hop in Delhi reveals what Achille Mbembe describes as the "manifest dualism" of Blackness as it circulates across the world. Mbembe argues that "Blackness was invented to signify exclusion, brutalization, and degradation, to point to a limit constantly conjured and abhorred." And yet, he argues, Blackness, in its travels across the world as art and merchandise, also "becomes the symbol of a conscious desire for life, a force springing forth, buoyant and plastic, fully engaged in the act of creation and capable of living in the midst of several times and several histories at once."[55]

The dual nature of Blackness—its capacity to generate vitality, relationships, and economic value while indexing or becoming synonymous with violent exclusion—has been foundational to hip hop's aesthetic and its success globally and was on display in Delhi. Through hip hop, the young men I got to know in Delhi were able to first imitate and then embody the circulating image of Black masculinity clothed in hip hop's bravado and rebellion to make sense of themselves, individually and collectively, as marginalized subjects in the capital city of India.[56] Blackness vis-à-vis hip hop became a political category of possibility and inclusion for these diverse young men, an incipient possibility for solidarity and friendship across ethnic, religious, caste, and racialized difference.

Yet hip hop's practices, styles, and embodied ways of being, especially when coupled with the potential for social media circulation, also offered them the means to frame their unequal experience as a global hustle: a way to get by, even succeed, in a city striving to become world class precisely because of hip hop's capacity to signify subversion and sovereignty in its public affect and its embodied experience as socially and economically valuable. Which is to say, digitally enabled hip hop offered these young men a means to self-fashion themselves as unique, creative, even entrepreneurial individuals who could participate in urban India's aspirations for world-class status.[57]

By remaking themselves and the city, even if uncomfortably and unevenly, to fit the narrative capital has produced about a world-class Delhi through their claims to Black masculinity, (some of) these young men made friends they would otherwise have never met, found unanticipated work, explored the breadth of the city, and (in some cases) were even able to participate in activist-driven initiatives in ways that would have otherwise been foreclosed to them. Yet despite the opportunities that arose for some, the potential for fracture and dislocation lurked in the background, linked to a postponement of a prescribed reproductive future of marriage, children, and a steady pay-check (likely from a casual service labor job, which is all they would be able to obtain given their social backgrounds, access to education, and so on).

These potential and delayed futures evoked a specter of normative masculinity in Delhi's migrant and working-class neighborhoods that the young men explicitly pushed against through hip hop praxis, even as some of them had to succumb to living a dual life of being a wage laborer and a hip hop artist to help their family pay the bills. The promise of fame and fortune also created competition, disagreement, and hostility between Delhi's aspiring young hip hop artists in ways that fractured solidarity as it became evident, over the course of the several years that I have known these young men, that only some would succeed financially as digital hip hop artists—in part because their claims to an authentic "Indian" hip hop urbanity stuck better than others.

The globally familiar, as it manifests American Black masculinity in Delhi, is thus an ambivalent optimism (rather than a cruel one).[58] Why? Because it offers a hip hop otherwise that is always already saturated in racialized capitalist realism of the Atlantic world.[59] It feeds aspiration by providing the resources for the self-cultivation of an affectively charged and globally manifest gendered and racialized subjectivity that promises a different (economic and social) future. It delivers on its promise in the moment when vital embodied practice and the thrill of digital documentation offer a way out of the everyday and a chance to connect with unanticipated others. Yet over time, it only partially, at best, lives up to the expectation it generates, even if social media promises something more.

Throughout the book, I think through and theorize hip hop practice for social media circulation within and beyond one's existing networks as a key aspect of the globally familiar. The relationship between media consumption and production in the digital age is recursive.[60] What one consumes shapes what one produces and vice versa. The do-it-yourself (DIY) media content one produces beckons, cajoles, invites, and, invariably, offers the potential for new relations as it travels through the digital circuitry of social media: #dmforcollab.[61] The content that gets ratified on social media through "likes" intensifies the circulation and production of particular gendered, classed, and racialized subjectivities laminated onto space and place. One never knows how far what one makes will travel. One's affectively charged audiovisual self-productions on platforms such as Instagram, as Alice Marwick teasingly and tantalizingly writes, might even create "instafame."[62]

As Kathleen Stewart explains, affects do not work through explicit meaning but rather "in the way they pick up densities and texture as they move through bodies, dreams, dramas, and social worldings of all kinds."[63] The globally familiar, in this sense, asks us to pay attention to the ways in which digital content channels and organizes affect through circulation as well as during the behind-the-scenes work that needs to be done to produce the audiovisual artifacts in the first place. It also asks us to pay attention to the sign-concepts that travel in the media that are consumed and reproduced as citation in everyday interaction and in subsequent social media representations.[64]

In the chapters ahead, I explore the ways in which aspiring b-boys, rappers, graffiti artists, and DJs in Delhi's margins evoked and deployed gendered, spatial, racialized, classed, and kin concepts linked to their hip hop media consumption but also animated in other transnational popular discourses—friend, swag, racist, nigga, nation, race, slum, and bro, to name a few—and the ways in which these concepts both disrupted previous and generated new understandings and embodiments of masculinity, reimagined the city's spatial coordinates, and indexed their aspirations as well as the uneven social and economic opportunities available to them.

The globally familiar, when theorized as a tracking of mediatized moving concepts as they shape life in a particular place and time, animates what Michael Lampert argues is the role of contemporary "global" anthropology as it "prides itself on critically pluralizing concepts that purport to be the same across contexts . . . to work as connoisseurs of the 'not quite' rather than peddlers of the strange."[65] To engage with the hip hop–inflected concepts these young men use to understand, theorize, and aestheticize their situated subject formation is to recognize that media consumption generates new ways of seeing, hearing, understanding, and articulating difference as well as opportunities for producing place.[66] It also pushes us to recognize how moving concepts, held together and intensified in hip hop's aesthetics, produce social, economic, and political value for the young men who remade themselves in and through them.

Indeed, if I could go back in time and respond to the old man who looked at the graffiti mural and wondered aloud about the value of such an endeavor, I would tell him that the mural, when made into an image that can travel with a caption that might read *Delhi swag*, opens up worlds of deferred possibility and potential capital.[67] If he gave me the time, I would explain that hip hop's technologies of practice, as they have been picked up across the globe, have always been about productive appropriation of concepts, materials, and technologies to, as James G. Spady argues, "loop link," or "reenact, enact, and update the aesthetic, political, and social impact of Black cultural movements in new and very different contexts."[68]

The globally familiar asks us to consider how the "loop links" of hip hop practice, as it is intensified through digital media production and circulation, generates vitality in a specific place and time and with particular young people: in Delhi in the second decade of the twenty-first century among young men who are otherwise imagined to be on the margins of change. Moreover, it pushes us to consider how hip hop's aesthetic of flow and rupture, as Arthur Jafa describes its practices of omnivorous bricolage, when made digital, amplifies offline practice of b-boying, rapping, or painting through an online representation *of* practice (a practice of practices, as it were).[69]

In so doing, the globally familiar suggests that hip hop's aesthetic of assemblage and improvisation is now eminently digital in the ways it is consumed, practiced, and produced. One could argue that videography and photography and perhaps even social media literacy are integral skills (maybe even hip hop elements in their own right) for an aspiring twenty-first-century hip hop artist.[70] As such, the globally familiar pushes us to consider the ways in which hip hop brings its musical, lyrical, visual, and kinesthetic modalities together into multimodal relations in ways that push against scholarly reductions of hip hop that pose its traveling traditions as solely musical and linguistic. As Delhi b-boy Sudhir once said to me: "It's not enough to learn a b-boy move from YouTube. One has to learn how to shoot it properly. Lots of cuts. Then, what music to put on? *Yeh bhi zaroori hai.* That is important too."

Sudhir's recognition that shooting and editing are important (too) marks the ways in which the young men in Delhi's hip hop scene imagined how their experimentations with hip hop, what Jeff Chang calls "the most far-reaching arts movements of the past three decades," created opportunities for social, economic, and political participation in ways that recursively shaped how these young men came to see and produce themselves and the city they call home.[71] Their interest in generating social and economic capital through their hip hop self-making projects opened the door for me to enter into their worlds as a collaborator and, with them, to imagine and theorize a digitally enabled shared anthropology.

An Ethnography of the Globally Familiar

It was February 2013. I waited with Jaspal Singh for Soni at the mouth of a South Delhi metro station. Singh is a sociolinguist from Germany with roots in Punjab, and Soni was, at the time, a nineteen-year-old Sikh b-boy and aspiring rapper from an economically depressed postpartition Punjabi enclave in West Delhi. As we waited, I found a sliver of shade on the edge of a parapet so Singh and I could sit and talk a bit before Soni arrived. Singh had connected with Soni at a hip hop concert featuring Snoop Lion (now, once again, Snoop Dogg) and various local hip hop acts a few weeks prior. Singh had asked him to come to South Delhi for an interview and a conversation about music production and generously invited me along for the meeting.

Singh and I had recently met after we found out we were both doing research projects on the emergent hip hop scene in Delhi. Singh had stumbled upon a conference abstract I had written about clandestine and improvisational hip hop dance sessions in South Delhi malls the year prior and contacted me to tell me he was going to be in Delhi in 2013 doing fieldwork.[72] Once we figured out we both would be in Delhi at the same time, we planned to connect. Soon after I arrived in Delhi in January 2013, we met over a reassuring meal of *dal chawal* (rice and lentils) and committed to supporting each other in our fieldwork endeavors.

While we sat waiting for Soni and took the commuter bustle in, Singh told me that he was planning to set up a recording studio in his new apartment, where he could invite dancers in Delhi's emergent hip hop scene who were interested in expanding their hip hop repertoires to record their raps and learn to produce beats. Studio time in Delhi, he reasoned, as anywhere else in the world, is expensive. Moreover, there were not many professional recording studios available in Delhi for young people to experiment with their hip hop–inflected musical ideas, even if they had the money to spend.

The idea of a providing DIY studio space, he believed, would not only give him the opportunity to develop relationships with young aspiring musicians in the Delhi scene and to capture the kinds of stylized articulations of self and world that they made available in their lyrics; it would also allow him to offer something back in return for the access that they provided him into their worlds. As we leaned against the parapet, I told Singh about the music video I had filmed for a crew of rappers from South Delhi the previous summer (in 2012) when I made my first foray into the scene. I described how, until the moment that this group had needed me to shoot this video, I had a difficult time getting in touch with them or having them take my interest in them seriously (once they found out I was not a journalist or a contemporary or legendary hip hop practitioner from afar). The digital single-lens reflex (DSLR) camera I brought with me to Delhi, I explained, facilitated access. Much like his music studio, the camera promised the exciting possibility for what our interlocutors perceived as a paraprofessional opportunity for self-production and circulation. Singh, after a momentary pause, said, "You should keep making music videos with the rappers and dancers we meet in Delhi."

Throughout my days in Delhi, I engaged with the young men I met as their cameraman, as their producer, as their personal photographer, and, eventually, as their collaborator. In so doing, I marked myself as another kind of familiar the global makes possible—the twenty-first-century male, Indian American anthropologist who arrives (largely because of the media representations of hip hop I saw from afar) and stands just offstage to document events and performances as they unfold.

During the two years I lived in Delhi, I took up any and all opportunities to create audiovisual content in conversation and, in certain instances, in explicit collaboration with young men in the scene. Throughout this book, I touch upon these digitally enabled shared ethnographic moments as instantiations of a hip hop–infused ethnography, or "hiphopography." For H. Samy Alim, James G. Spady, and Samir Meghelli, hiphopography is a way of conducting research that takes seriously hip hop practitioners' efforts to theorize and represent themselves in the world to become someone new. As such, hiphopography is an approach to research that attempts to displace the power differentials between experts and participants in typical social science endeavors by harnessing hip hop's aesthetic and epistemic sensibilities toward dialogue and improvisation such that all participants are imagined as experts.[73] Our coproduced knowledge was composed of the images, sounds, and videos that we made and, as importantly, the discussions we had about framing, producing, or locating them. These collaborative media artifacts could at once become the site for my (future) analysis as it traveled in social media as well as the vehicle that reaffirmed existing relations (through "likes" on Facebook) or created new ones for them.

Making together, while mutually beneficial, also generated moments of discomfort, uncertainty, and, at times, disagreement. These moments of difficult conversation centered around how best to represent the city and a subaltern Delhi masculinity through the aesthetics of hip hop as well as how far I would be willing to go to share my resources. These challenging moments drew attention to how my presence, as an older male Indian American from New York whom they perceived as closer to an authentic Black masculinity than them, could and should influence the ways in which they imagined an emergent Delhi hip hop scene. Moreover, my presence pushed them to think through and articulate what they valued as they actively shaped themselves as men coming of age in a city, as I described in the preface, that was grappling with its mediatized reputation as a place hostile to women and full of dangerous, itinerant, and unemployed men.

In the chapters that follow, I think through these instances of shared making as sites of possibility and friction to reflexively engage with what it means to do media ethnography in the digital moment and what sorts of surprising insights emerge when making together becomes an activity that, ultimately, is just as much about the cultivation of value as it is about the energetic immediacy of coproduction.[74] In this sense, the pages that follow offer a way to think through and engage with what Amit Rai has recently described as an affective ethnography in and of the media—one that traces the feelings of excitement, anxiety, and hopefulness linked to improvisational making with others against the backdrop of neoliberal valorizations of entrepreneurship and self-cultivation.[75]

The first two chapters foreground masculinity, its embodiments, and its relationalities in and through digital hip hop. In chapter 1, I discuss the ways in which cultural producers in the scene mobilize the globally familiar to forge friendship and enact heteronormative romance across difference in Delhi. I focus on Jay, an upper-caste Hindu Nepali living in a *jhopadpatti* (informal housing colony) in South Delhi, and discuss a music video we worked on together, ostensibly for the parents of his unrequited love, a young Christian woman originally from Mizoram (a state in the Northeast of India) who lived on the other side of the city and whom he met in a hip hop jam months prior. I argue for an attention to the ways Jay imagines his creative production and play through hip hop as a means to make, maintain, and deepen friendships across ethnic and class difference as well as bridge the religious difference and familial disapproval that separates him from his love interest. In so doing, I theorize how the globally familiar becomes central to constituting intimate relationships and emotive masculinities in the context of the globally ubiquitous social media logic of friend and the fracturing discourse of "love jihad" currently circulating in India while also revealing Jay and his crew's spatialized understandings of gender in the city.

In chapter 2, I discuss my travels with several b-boys and rappers as we sought out clothes, hats, sneakers, and other material signs in shopping malls, markets, and online spaces. I use our forays across the city to think through, as they remake their bodies in the visage of a normative hip hop masculinity, what sorts of relationships with urban space emerge through their search for the things they feel are essential to being and becoming hip hop. Along the way I theorize how *swag*—a globally circulating, gendered, and gendering popular term hip hop practitioners in Delhi deployed to understand the things they wanted (or, in some cases, rejected)—articulates with *fetish*, a term used to think through the magic of a thing's ability to congeal relations as well as its power to alienate. In so doing, I put the globally familiar into conversation with recent theorizations of style, citationality, and consumption to argue for a transnational gendered and racialized understanding of style and stylistic choices in relationship to the changing urbanity of Delhi.

The next two chapters foreground what I call digital hip hop and the kinds of exciting yet conflicted work and networking opportunities it generates for the young men I got to know in Delhi. Chapter 3 dives headlong into the relationship between the youth culture industry and the DIY digital hip hop production of my participants. I discuss how the globally familiar articulates what has been called immaterial labor in the twenty-first century. Specifically, I trace the ways in which Jay and others in the scene participate in the various gendered and racialized laboring opportunities that arise as a result of their online and offline hip hop creativity in Delhi's (and India's) emergent youth culture industry. I argue for an attention to the ways in which the kinds of cooperative, aspirational, and often free labor that my participants offer as artists and media producers reveal how capitalism continues to unfold in ways that create novel arrangements of gendered labor and aspiration.

In chapter 4, I discuss how digital hip hop creates a complicated political economy of recognition between visiting international hip hop actors as they seek out "authentic" Indian hip hop and young people in the scene as they mobilize their (media-influenced) understandings of class, race, masculinity, and urban spatiality to get the attention of these actors. Utilizing the example of the Indo-German Hip Hop Project, a soft diplomacy initiative sponsored by the German consulate and the Goethe Institut in 2011–12, I discuss the frictions that emerge between differently situated international actors as they all sought the same "authentic" male hip hop subjects from the same 'hoods, and the opportunities that arose for those young men who were able to effectively channel and perform a globally familiar spatialized subaltern subjectivity.

The final two chapters foreground hip hop place-making and an emergent racialized spatiality in Delhi. Chapter 5 focuses on the ways in which Sudhir and his crew's globally familiar representation of their urban village as a global 'hood is utilized by artists and activists to make their case for an alternate development model situated in a new urbanism discourse that calls for the scaling down of urban space. I discuss the consequences of how this move to champion urban villages as potential models for a future Delhi coincides with processes of urban change that have remade several urban villages in South Delhi as centers for nightlife and boutique consumerism.

In chapter 6, I explore how the category of race is summoned and deployed by the young men in my study to describe their experiences of exclusion in the city and their relationship to the neighborhoods they live in. I focus at first on a Somali refugee in the city, as he and his crew recount the anti-Black racism they face in Delhi through their raps. I use their testimonial to think through how other young MCs and dancers from diverse backgrounds mobilize race to describe their experiences of discrimination. In this reckoning, the globally familiar draws attention to how digital media circulations of hip hop, as a discourse that directly engages with discrimination based on essentialized notions of difference across the globe, produce a shared vocabulary and aesthetic by which to articulate and embody a sense of common difference among the diverse practitioners in the Delhi hip hop scene. I also discuss how potential solidarities across difference made possible through hip hop are fractured when certain actors are excluded from a Delhi hip hop scene as it seeks to understand itself in an Indian imaginary.

I conclude with an epilogue that describes where some of the young men, whom I first met in 2011 and who populate the pages ahead, are in their lives as I write the final draft of this book. Much of the anthropological writing on youth assumes its ontogenetic timeframe to be liminal, a period of time where an exploration of life leads to a blurring of social norms as young people learn to labor and come to terms with their ascribed social positions.[76] What does a return to their lives regularly over the course of several years, a return at least in part made possible by social media, tell us about the present and future for these creative young men, about Delhi, and about the global itself?

I also argue for an attention to how anthropologists can be tracked and summoned as familiars through the digital, long after we have returned home from the so-called field. I pose some thoughts about the ethical and political conundrums that arise as a result of this constant state of connection even as I discuss the opportunities that open up for us to think differently about how ethnography might be done in the digital age. The globally familiar, in this (final) instance, requires us to pay attention to how our intellectual work, as it circulates online, blurs as it comes into contact with our social media personae when we become searchable in online worlds. As it grounds us in the same everyday practices as our interlocutors, the globally familiar ultimately asks us to recognize ourselves as equally steeped in the enchantment and precarity that the digital produces.

I sat in Singh's *barsati* with Jay.[1] As Jay waited for his turn to record a rap in Singh's makeshift recording studio, he talked to me about love, hip hop, and music videos. As he talked, he carefully rolled up his sleeve and showed me a tattoo he recently etched into his arm with DIY equipment he put together following the instructions from a YouTube video. It was a stylized Christian cross somewhat shoddily etched into his skin. It was not his only tattoo. The cross sat next to several other amateur markings he had inscribed into his flesh: Hip hop in graffiti lettering. His crew's name. Others I could not discern.

"I have a girlfriend," he said, shyly smiling at me as I looked down at his tattoos, trying not to make a face that revealed my initial dislike of his indelible self-inscriptions. *What did he use for ink? I hope whatever he is doing is safe. Skin infections, hepatitis, and HIV are real dangers.* I tuned back in to hear Jay say, "She is from Mizoram and is Christian. Her family doesn't want me to date her. She lives about eighty kilometers away. I met her at a hip hop event last year. I have now converted to Christianity to be with her but still haven't convinced her parents that we should be together. You made a music video with Soni and Singh, right? Can you help me make a video? I want to make something for her parents, so they understand why we want to be together. I want to marry her." "*Bilkul.* Of course," I said. "I would be happy to help. When do you want to make this video?" "Soon. I have a couple of other video projects I want help with first. Then we can do this video, OK? My crew will help us." "Great," I replied. "I'll bring my camera."

Jay then returned to his writing book, where he jotted down his raps. His mouth formed his Hindi lyrics soundlessly as he practiced, waiting for his turn on the mic. In the background, I heard another MC rapping into the makeshift recording booth that Singh had set up in a bureau in the sitting room of his small flat. The booth consisted of found Styrofoam packing materials lining the inside of a bureau; a mic stand with a good-quality Rode mic, pop filter attached; and a relatively ancient mixer. There were three or four members of Jay's crew also present. They were just hanging out. They had no interest in recording raps. They were self-proclaimed b-boys. Later in the day, after the recording was done, they had an impromptu dance battle in the open space of the barsati. Jay joined in the collective dance space after recording his track. A few other b-boys who Jay and his crew met for the first time that day watched and took photos on their smart phones of the dancers. Then, some of them joined in. Singh, at one point, jumped into the circle of dancers and parodied some classic b-boy moves: A toprock. A simulated baby spin. Everyone laughed. A few of the guys patted Singh on the back as he jumped out of the circle, a big smile on his face.

In this chapter, I discuss the ways in which the young men I met in Delhi gravitated to digital hip hop practice because of the potential it offered to enact friendship and imagine romance across difference. The efficacy of these enactments relied, at least in part, on their desire to transform their male bodies to create recognition through a shared aesthetic. The power of the globally familiar, revealed in the mise-en-scène of Singh's studio, literally remakes Jay's flesh through needle and ink techniques learned on YouTube. Jay's body, now visibly etched, becomes a vehicle of masculine hip hop performativity and Jay, in turn, is ostensibly transformed into a global male urban subject, capable of making friends and finding lovers among those like him who also seek and reproduce a hip hop–inflected aesthetic. His marked body also becomes a permanent record of the kinds of hip hop–inspired intimacies and relations he has created in the city he lives in. Tattooing his crew's name on his skin, for instance, creates a permanent indexical sign that marks a spatialized and temporal relationship to his practitioner friends. The cross, in turn, is not only a marker signifying his willingness to convert for love but a symbol he associates with Tupac Shakur.

The globally familiar also asserts itself in Jay's desire to produce a music video, ostensibly for his love interest and her parents. The magical thinking that this video will open up the otherwise impossible possibility of marriage across religious and ethnic difference is testament to his faith in the transformative capacities of digital hip hop. It also speaks of the kind of fractured masculinity Jay grapples with as he at once seeks to produce himself as global while he still recognizes marriage and the normative courting ritual of seeking approval of his love interest's parents as a necessary step to ratify his relationship. His desire to produce a music video to express his partially requited love is, one could argue, similar to Laura Ahearn's Nepali interlocutors' interest in learning to write love letters in English.[2] By learning to communicate his desires through video, Jay can enact a kind of modern globality that hinges on a popular cultural audiovisual literacy and digital proficiency. In doing so, Jay is able to not only express his romantic love but demonstrate his capacity to embody a techno-futuristic male subjectivity capable of agentic transgression.

The intimate act of writing letters with pen and paper, of course, is quite different from making and sharing videos. Writing letters is an intimate correspondence between writer and reader. A music video that will inevitably circulate on social media, however, creates an open form of address. While particular audiences might be imagined in the act of creative making, the form and its potential for travel pushes one quickly into the realization that it might reach others. The video, Jay might imagine, will circulate on Facebook and garner likes. The likes, taken in aggregate, will work to solidify his relationship with existing friends. It might also find unexpected audiences and become the opening to make new relations in online and offline worlds.[3]

These new relations might also become lovers with the potentiality of becoming kin. They might even be kin that are already, as Daniel Miller points out, subsumed under the totalizing social media category of friend.[4] Moreover, these videos might create, in their circulations, the possibility for the young men to earn money. For the young men I made videos with during the early years of an emergent Delhi and Indian hip hop scene, these latent potentialities for unforeseen relationship, fame, and economic possibility were not (yet) at the forefront of their desire. It was a simpler time. Videos, like the one I made with Jay and will describe in the pages ahead, had a more innocent purpose—to create a public record of affect and intimacy while making something with friends.[5]

Indeed, music videos, unlike letters or poems or any sort of expressive text (or, for that matter, other intimate and immediate digital self-productions such as selfies or tweets), cannot be made (at least not easily) by one person. They require the labor, technical skills, and vision of many. If an aspiring rapper in the digital age cannot hire a technical crew to make a video for him, then the labor for this sort of endeavor has to come from those he can call upon as friends. The globally familiar, in this reckoning, fosters what Nicolas Bourriaud calls a "friendship culture," a technology not only of momentary enchantment but one that holds the capacity to forge new relationships and intensify existing ones through making together.[6] In this sense, the creative articulations and embodiments of friendship, love, and romance of Jay and his peers not only offer an entry point into how young men in Delhi navigate the possibility and impossibility of relations across difference. They also give us a sense of how idealized performances of gender are fashioned and fractured in the process of making and maintaining relations through DIY audiovisual production and the kinds of sustaining hip hop activities that make audiovisual production possible in the first place.

Once we recognize that terms such as friendship and love and their related passions are situated in making (and playing) together, it becomes evident that they are impossible to disentangle from reciprocal exchanges, in this case artistic products such as music videos (meant for digital circulation and consumption), the equipment it takes to produce them, or the labor it takes to make them.[7] Friendship through sustained (hip hop) practice confirms that the globally familiar is not simply bound in online social media spaces and the circulation of content but shapes the sweaty, everyday labor of co-creation. Co-creation makes visible an emergent masculinity tied to particular spaces and places in Delhi. The thing that is co-created—in this case, a music video—also reveals the gendering of the exchange and the relations that produce it. In this sense, the acts of making together and the circulation of the video chart a map of the city produced through affinities, desires, and the grit of masculinized hard play. This map reveals the gendered normativities, anxieties, and possibilities of love and friendship in contemporary Delhi. This map also locates me (and Singh) as relevant actors, perhaps even friends.

My role in the production of Jay's music video also offers an opportunity to reflect on ethnography as a practice of doing together, to engage carefully with the kinds of uncertain relationships that I developed with Jay and his peers through the exchange of time, bodily exertion (just try carrying a camera bag and tripod to shoot on location in the heat of summer in Delhi), aesthetic vision, and material things. Certainly, through doing together, Jay and I forged a shifting relationship that assumed future exchange. Yet there was always a bit of tenuousness, I believe on both our parts, about the risks of exchange and the weight of obligation. These dangers are reminders that sanguine activities that are generative of relationship, whether online or offline, always hold the gift of doubt and the potential for failure. We might consider, then, that the globally familiar, as a technology that forges friendship and aestheticizes romance, is also a conceptual device that simultaneously may offer a critique of their emergence.

Friendship in Delhi

Jay lives in a predominantly Hindu and ethnically Garhwali *jhopadpatti* (informal community) close to Humayunpur, one of the urban villages I spent time in while in South Delhi.[8] He lives with his father in a small two-room concrete house with a tin roof, typical of a jhopadpatti in the area. He and his father moved to Delhi a decade prior from Garhwal, although Jay claims the neighboring nation of Nepal as his original home. His father is a caste Brahmin and a caretaker for a small shrine dedicated to Siva as well as an informal leader in their small migrant community.[9] Jay and his dad's marginal economic status when read against his upper-caste status is a reminder that caste and class status do not necessarily coincide with each other in the subcontinent, and that rural-urban migration has the potential to intensify the disjuncture between the two.[10] Jay and his high-caste Garhwali peers' experiences of (what they gloss as) racialized discrimination is also a reminder that caste and class coincide with global assemblages of difference and produce gendered urban subjectivities that are at once particular and shared (I discuss race as a category of salience for the young men I met in Delhi in chapter 6).

The informal settlement that Jay calls home and the urban villages near it have become the homes of recent migrants who have arrived in the city in the last ten years. Recent migration to Delhi is an intensification of an explosion of migration that began soon after India's economic liberalization in the 1990s, which set adrift an estimated three hundred million rural inhabitants seeking refuge and economic possibility in India's growing megacities and emergent regional urban centers.[11] Delhi, along with other first- and second-tier urban centers across India, has absorbed these migrants, some of whom are seasonal workers who come to the city for a short time, leaving their families behind in their villages. Others arrive with their entire family, seeking a new life in the city. According to recent estimates, Delhi, as a result of the swell of migrants and the spatial remapping of the city to include farmland in Haryana and Uttar Pradesh, has nearly doubled in population since 1993.[12]

The newer waves of migrants who have made Delhi their home in the last decade have come from various locations in India that previously had little representation in the city. For instance, there has been an influx of people from the Northeast of India, fleeing political unrest in their region as well as seeking economic opportunity in the capital city of India. Migrants from Manipur, Mizoram, Sikkim, Assam, Arunachal Pradesh, Tripura, and Nagaland have all made their homes in pockets scattered around the city, often choosing to live close to long-settled and recently arrived Nepali and Garhwali migrants. These newer regional in-migrants join communities from other parts of the region that have constituted Delhi since partition. The violent birth of the nation produced waves of political migrants from Punjab who arrived in Delhi and were settled in various parts of the city.[13] From the 1950s onward, economic migrants from all over India joined post-partition newcomers to the city. Jobs—the Nehruvian promise of laboring opportunities in the big city—and the possibility to step out of what Appadurai allegorically refers to as "the glacial pace of habitus for the quickening beat of modernity," urged migrants from villages into urban centers.[14]

All these newcomers, naturally, have sought the help of kin, caste, ethnic, and religious community members to ease their way into new livelihoods. For instance, taking a page from my own familial history, my uncle and his wife and their small children moved to Delhi from Madras in the 1950s. They rented and eventually purchased a house in a Tamil Hindu neighborhood in South Delhi, a colony that was created as a result of the Land Acquisition Act of 1948 that carved out areas for development in South and West Delhi to accommodate new arrivals. Over time they tapped into the Tamil (Brahmin) community through the South Indian temple built soon after their arrival.

Many of the colonies that developed in South and West Delhi in the postindependence period became known for their tightly knit religious, ethnic, and caste-centric communities. The urban geography that emerged in this twentieth-century historical moment endures in the present day. There is still an association between specific Delhi urban enclaves and particular ethnic, linguistic, and religious groups. Parts of West Delhi, for example Punjabi Bagh, are associated with postpartition migrants from Punjab. In South Delhi, Chittaranjan Park is associated with Bengalis and R. K. Puram is associated with upper-caste Tamils.

In the last two decades, newcomers have complicated Delhi's urban terrain, insofar as their illegible diversity offers a stark juxtaposition to the ordered demarcations of spatialized class, ethnic, and caste difference that has been intensified through real estate–led development projects.[15] For example, in Humayunpur and Khirki, two urban villages I spent time in and write about more extensively in subsequent chapters, there were Nepalis and Biharis who had come during the building boom of the early twenty-first century as seasonal workers and stayed on to live among Jat farmers who claim having lived in these villages since at least the colonial period and Muslims who trace their inhabitations in the village to the partition era. Alongside them were newer arrivals from Afghanistan and Somalia. Some were temporary residents living in the villages while they got treatment in the private hospitals that have cropped up in the area. Others were refugees. They were joined by Nigerian, Ghanaian, Cameroonian, and Congolese students, all seeking inexpensive housing in the heart of South Delhi. This diversity creates the potential for friction between groups even as it holds the possibility for relations between them.

When I first met Jay, he was an avid b-boy and part of a crew of dancers from Humayunpur. He had met several members of his crew in school and together they had developed a relationship with hip hop's music, dance, and styles while spending time in internet parlors tucked into the folds of the urban village. As they began to practice their dance moves in the neighborhood, their crew grew. While Jay's crew was predominantly Garhwali, there were a few b-boys who claimed the Northeast, Punjab, and Bengal as their places of origin and came from different religious, caste, and class backgrounds. Their spatial proximity with one another in the urban village and its surrounds, coupled with their shared interest in hip hop, created the possibility for friendships that surpassed difference, no small feat in Delhi, where there is the constant reminder on the streets and in the media that any analogue of Otherness harbors the potentiality of violence. Their friendship, in practice, often centered on the small screen of the smart phone.

Filippo Osella and Caroline Osella, in an article on friendship and flirting, argue that male sociality across difference in Kerala is the result of South Asian cinema culture.[16] "Gangs" of college-aged young men in the small town they spent time in were able to connect with each other by going to the movies and taking part in the spectacle of the cinema, a pastime that continues to captivate young people across India. However, as I argued in the introduction, my time in Delhi suggested that the advent of the small screen of the smart phone has become a new and more immediate way to gather young men together in public spaces. As I walked through the streets of Delhi, it was a common occurrence to see four or five young men sharing a screen. In the evenings, the screen flickered and the boys' faces could be seen in the cracks between them, partially illuminated by the glare of the screen.

For Jay and the other hip hop practitioners I got to know in Delhi, watching each other's small screens preceded practice, and practice often would culminate with a small-screen viewing session. Often, the young men I got to know in Delhi's hip hop scene watched hip hop–related content: b-boy battles in France. A new music video from the United States. A dance video they had shot in the city of themselves performing in a park, in the mall, or in their friend's sitting room. On occasion, I ran into them watching a broader range of content, such as a K-pop (Korean pop) love song, or a short news video discussing corruption in India. They also posted memes on Facebook that they shared with each other on the street. These memes often had to do with male-female or male-male relationships. Sometimes they were quotes from famous hip hop stars of the past. Picture, for instance, a group of boys looking at a Facebook post of an image of Tupac Shakur with large white lettering over his face saying, "With you and me its all g. We've never been enemies because you've been such a good friend to me."[17] Laughing, they would collectively translate this quote into Hindi.

As Jay and his crew developed their hip hop–ratified friendships, they eventually created a dance collective that could represent their neighborhood in the emerging hip hop scene in the city. Each of them had Jay tattoo the name of this collective on their arms. This collective or crew met daily to practice their dance moves or to write graffiti (as some of the crew gravitated toward spray can art). Friendship across difference, as their activities suggest, emerges when there is the possibility of a shared endeavor. Hip hop thus emerges as a Nietzschean realization of friendship as a shared thirst for a higher ideal.[18] Hip hop's long-standing five-element discourse of practice, one that I heard repeated often in Delhi's scene, includes the pursuit of knowledge (the fifth element of hip hop) through the practice of hip hop's four creative elements: dance, MCing, DJing, and graffiti. In the twenty-first century it also includes the digital as a key element to produce knowledge (and relations). Jay's crew, as with many of the crews I met in Delhi, gravitated toward this mutually constitutive understanding of digital hip hop as knowledge through friendship, and friendship as the shared pursuit of knowledge through practice. For these young men, it was obvious that friendship and knowledge through practice could only develop when there was a healthy competition among friends.

When I first arrived in Delhi in 2011, it was clear that b-boying or hip hop dance was the practice that young men from the jhopadpattis and urban villages of Delhi took up as their primary engagement with hip hop. Hip hop dance—because it requires very little equipment, just some music and a willingness to push one's body to the limit—seemed an obvious choice over the more expensive practices of graffiti writing (which needs spray cans) or

DJing (which needs turntables and other equipment). Young men can easily tune into b-boy sessions from anywhere in the world on YouTube to pick up moves or simply to be inspired that what they did connected them to a world of practice. MCing or rapping began to pick up steam as a practice form during my time in Delhi. Rapping, too, at least initially, only requires one's voice, poetic willingness, and a desire to share as a prerequisite for practice. Rap, in polished or in rough freestyle forms, is also well represented on the internet with mainstream and underground hip hop music from all over the world available for consumption to anyone who is looking for it. Just type in *rap* or *freestyle* and a place-name into your YouTube search bar. You will be surprised at what you find.

Delhi hip hop heads took more slowly to the poetics of hip hop, however, as they felt rapping required a different kind of commitment than dance: a commitment to articulate in English, even if through mimicry, one's individual experience of the world through allegory, metaphor, and description. Over time, MCs in Delhi began to realize that Hindi, Punjabi, Bengali, and Tamil were legitimate and, in fact, necessary hip hop languages if they were going to connect to subcontinental audiences. However, it took time for them to come to this realization, in part because MCing or rapping also (eventually) required basic recording and production equipment and someone willing to learn how to operate it. Just as I was leaving Delhi in late 2014, a number of DIY home recording and video editing studios had popped up across the city, corresponding to a rapid increase in the number of would-be rappers. This boom was mirrored in Mumbai and, in subsequent years, in several cities across India. Rich and poor kids were all gravitating to hip hop music, partly in response to the burgeoning independent music and youth culture industry (see chapter 3), the growing number of international hip hop artists who were showing interest in the Indian hip hop scene (see chapter 4), and, finally, because of the enormous success of the first gully rappers from Mumbai and Delhi who rapped in vernacular Hindi.[19] Singh's recording studio and my music video work, in hindsight, was a pivotal step in pushing some of the MCs we met together in Delhi, like Jay for instance, to think about recording their own raps, making music videos, and, as we shall see later in this chapter, being at the forefront of creating DIY home studios of their own.

As hip hop music emerged as a socially viable and potentially lucrative practice, hip hop's dance forms continued to thrive in Delhi and Mumbai and spread to smaller towns and cities across India. B-boying and poppin' and lockin' required a commitment to movement, to cultivating the body in relation to other moving bodies. These bodily practices created a moving place for the young dancers I got to know: what Loïc Wacquant has called a place of "protected sociability" where male friendship is cultivated and relationships are made durable.[20] In the early years, mall courtyards, train stations, and public parks were the city spaces they claimed to enact this sort of protected sociability. In later years, colleges and community centers became sites for competition, often with international judges conferring large prizes to the winners of various types of prizes. Even as b-boying developed so that there were regular competitions across the city and, eventually, across the country, the spatial commons of Delhi continued to provide space for practice and play.

I spent many an hour watching crews of b-boys from several parts of the city playfully banter as they practiced moves in various locations across the city. As they danced, they assessed each other's prowess in relationship to their own abilities, sharpening each other by calling into question each other's skills. Their desire to dance together and to improvise produced other shared endeavors. They built dance floors out of discarded cardboard boxes, using electric tape they purchased for forty rupees a roll in a local shop to fashion a rectangular flat stage. They pursued opportunities to get paid for their dancing (I discuss this pursuit in detail in chapter 3). They went shopping together in gray markets of Delhi, where they purchased knockoff designer jeans, printed T-shirts, snapback hats, and sneakers (I discuss consumption in chapter 2). Friendship in the globally familiar thus emerges as a practice-generating practice. Relationships between the young men in the scene were perpetuated through activity and the aspiration this activity generates toward future shared endeavors. These activities, as Elizabeth Hallam and Tim Ingold argue, are at their very core improvisational, insofar as they produce life.[21]

Their shared endeavors were filled with playful banter and friendly competition. Friedrich Nietzsche, discussing his idealized notions of homosocial friendship, writes, "Let us be enemies too, my friends! Divinely we want to strive against each other."[22] These sorts of playfully fraught male relationships offer a window into how hip hop–involved youth imagine and play out their evolving understandings of male subjectivity. On the one hand, their approach to being friends with other males is constructed in familiar terms. The jokes, the banter, and the friendly competition were all reminiscent of the ways in which I experienced coming-of-age as a teenager in New York in the 1990s—always an air of aggression, an edge, a tension, coupled with a sense of youthful permanence: we will always be in this together. This is for life. What also struck me as familiar was their tough aggressive posturing, the mimicry of hip hop's hypermasculinist tropes as these young men walked around with a sense of bravado, as they performed a hard, brittle exterior.[23]

As I passed time with these young men, they revealed other modes by which to express and understand their gendered selves. For instance, young men in the scene from various backgrounds (with the exception of Nigerian and Somali men I met while in the scene) were entirely comfortable holding hands in public spaces or leaning against each other casually when in repose. From posing hard to lying on your male friend's lap, this localization of a hypermasculinized hip hop male subjectivity opened up a window into the ways in which gender and friendship are reimagined along other cultural coordinates that do not simply reproduce what has been consumed.

This sort of queering of received gendered norms from the United States was also evident in the social media interactions that young men from various South Asian backgrounds had with one another. Often, for instance, Jay's crew members would post emotional, written rants on Facebook about lost love or unrequited emotions next to photos of themselves cloaked in hip hop's hypermasculine posturing. Their male friends would respond in the comments section with heart emoticons and empathetic responses in Hindi/English. In each of these readings, hip hop produces a common category—male masculinity—that enables friendship across other modes of difference. Within this category of cis-male, memetic reflections of aggression and confidence comingle with softer intimacies that produce the possibility of same-sex physicality and sympathetic public displays of commiseration, something unfamiliar in the binaried masculinities of Euro-Western worlds.

As Jay's crew began to compete in local competitions, a couple of b-boys from other parts of the city joined their crew. Here the relatively new Delhi metro system and its capacity to bring together young people who live scattered across the city emerges as another vital infrastructure for forging friendship across difference and distance. The metro system now connects central Delhi to all its historical edges to the south, west, east, and north of Delhi as well as to Noida, Ghaziabad, Gurgaon, and Dwarka, the developing urban peripheries of Delhi that have spurred the need for a new name to capture the scale of the city as it reaches across states: the National Capital Region (NCR). The metro has facilitated practical efficiencies, such as enabling the flow of labor from one part of the city to the other. It has also resulted in the efflorescence of social relationships across the city. For the young men I got to know in South and West Delhi, the metro facilitated access to b-boy jams or battles in Gurgaon. It enabled young people to

form dance crews that included members who were not from the immediate neighborhood. The metro also created the opportunity for traveling b-boys to meet girls from parts of town distant from their own. In other words, the metro, with its ultraclean cars and stations, along with social media, became the infrastructural undergirding for friendship and even courtship to take place across the vast expanses of the city.

Once a young man from elsewhere in the city joined a crew in one of the South or West Delhi neighborhoods I spent time in, they too were subject to friendly enmity, the kind of masculine banter that only those close to each other can have without deleterious consequences. Often the banter combined jokes about racial, ethnic, and linguistic difference, an all-too-common form of socializing in India among close friends and kin, with jokes about someone's inability to perform particular (dance) moves. Of course, friendly enmity sometimes became more serious. During my time in Delhi, fractures and fissures between individuals and groups occurred, and crews ejected members or broke up altogether. Sometimes these fractures centered on hurt feelings that arose as a result of misunderstood actions or words. As hip hop became serious play with material consequences, the disagreements increasingly became centered on financial disputes regarding the money that crews earned as a collective and the irreconcilable differences that arose around how to share this money and who had the rights to it. In either case, the instrumentality and affect of friendship were entangled, revealing how self-interest and emotional investment are always in lockstep with one another.

While members of the b-boy crews I spent time with created friendships through shared practice, they also had another set of young people that they called friends. Often these friends were from their ethnic, religious, or linguistic community. These young men sometimes tagged along with their b-boy friends to hang out with the hip hop crew and watch them practice. More often, though, they passed time in their own youth-centered worlds, and the young men who participated in the hip hop scene had to reach out to them on their own. There were several instances when I accompanied one of the b-boys, graffiti writers, and MCs to socialize with young people who were not involved with hip hop but either lived in the neighborhood or shared an affiliation of some sort, whether religious, ethnic, or linguistic. These moments of homosocial conviviality recall Rahul Roy's 1997 film, *When Four Friends Meet*, where four young men from the northwestern Delhi enclave of Jehangirpuri meet with each other and the filmmaker to chat about their aspirations, desires, and fears.[24] While the young men I got to know in South and West Delhi were far more worldly in what they could reference in their conversations than Roy's interlocutors as they drew from a global repertoire of popular cultural references they picked up on the internet, their conversations hovered around similar and stereotypically gendered topics of interest.

Food, cigarettes, things they desired, the girls they longed to talk to, and occasionally news events made up the primary conversation topics in the spaces where "timepass" seemed the main collective endeavor.[25] The conversations about girls, at least when I was present, were never lewd; there was no bravado or telling tales regarding "eve-teasing" encounters. This was in contradistinction to the focus of discussion in *When Four Friends Meet*, where narratives of desire and longing quickly fell into accounts of sexual harassment in ways similar to those the Osellas observed in Kerala. Among the young men I spent time with, female objectification, as I soon discuss in more detail with regard to Jay's music video, was located in the realm of the unrequited, distanced, almost deific figure of woman: someone who transmuted into an ideal to strive for by changing oneself.

As some of the b-boys began to take up rapping as their primary hip hop engagement, their friends from their ethnic and spatial community became their primary referent for friendship in their raps and videos. In part this was a representational strategy that directly draws from hip hop's discourse on space and place, where city and neighborhood matter deeply. For those who traveled distances to participate in a b-boy scene, the opportunity to MC or rap allowed them to locate themselves in the city, to broadcast a sense of belonging that did not necessarily locate its center in global hip hop or a Delhi scene but in representations of experience in a specific neighborhood represented as *the* 'hood.[26]

For instance, in a music video Soni produced several years after I met him (which became his first hit and claim to national fame as one of Delhi's hottest MCs), he depicts getting attacked by a group of young men in his historically Punjabi Sikh migrant neighborhood in West Delhi as they attempt to steal his BMX bicycle.[27] He rides away from this group of young men, only to look back and see they are in hot pursuit. He runs into his house and his father initially defends him from the group waiting for him, throwing a brick from the balcony to chase them away. However, it is not until a group of bearded and turbaned Sikh men from the neighborhood arrive that he is able to finally chase away his assailants. These Sikh men in the video arrive to the scene silently. They do not say a word, but their mere presence forces the other group of young men to run. Throughout, Soni raps in Punjabi about his experiences of the dangerous, drug-infested

West Delhi neighborhood he grew up in and the redemptive potentialities of friendship. In this video, he reveals the ways being Punjabi, Sikh, and male in his neighborhood create an enduring solidarity that does not require a shared endeavor but relies on a shared history.

In several conversations over the last five years, Soni has talked to me about his family's experience of the 1984 attacks on the Sikh community and about how his ultimate project is a rap album entirely dedicated to retelling the story of partition. Soni explained, "I will call it 1947. It will be the most important work I do." Ultimately, Soni uses this particular music video to represent his reliance on kin, religious, and ethnic relationships within the context of his 'hood, even as his fame grows in the Delhi and Indian hip hop scenes and his relationships multiply. Friendship in the globally familiar is thus interjected into frameworks of belonging that precede it.

Jay, however, had a different outlook. In his estimation, his ethnic or even neighborhood affiliation was not primary. Instead, hip hop was a way to imagine a different future that included conversion to Christianity, a group of friends from various ethnic and religious backgrounds, and connections to hip hop practitioners from all over the world. As Jay moved away from b-boying toward MCing and music production and as he got older before my eyes, rather than moving toward a more bounded ethnic or religious identity, he continued to utilize hip hop to actively traverse boundaries. In part this was because of Jay's more recent arrival to Delhi, in comparison to Soni, whose family arrived in Delhi three generations prior from Lahore in what is now Pakistan. It is also due to the composition of his neighborhood, which, because it was filled with newcomers, did not have the same sedimented history in the city that, say, Soni had in the Punjabi enclave of West Delhi where he resided. Yet even though Jay saw himself as a hip hop border crosser and, over time, produced music videos that represented his interest in going beyond his inherited history, he related to me that the inevitability of everyday street violence in the South Delhi neighborhoods he traversed necessitated that he had a local crew he could call upon. He confided in me that if things really got bad on the street, he would turn to his male cousins and uncles in the neighborhood for support. Jay reminds us that despite his turn toward the horizons of *the* globally familiar, there is a recognition that his bodily safety, at the very least, requires tangible and enduring support locally.

As importantly, the video Jay asked me to produce with him also reveals the ways in which his understandings of intimate relationships reproduce locally circulating notions of difference related to gender. Consider that Jay imagined that the video he wanted to produce with me was, initially, for his girlfriend's parents. It was a way to convince them of the veracity of his commitment to their daughter and his newfound faith. In this sense, Jay, because he was reaching out to his girlfriend's parents, was reinforcing an understanding in the subcontinent that ultimately the family decides a young woman's future. In part, this move was a result of the disconnect between the intense emotion he harbored and the limited physical time he had with her. Jay, for the most part, developed his relationship with his love interest through social media. While they met at hip hop events from time to time, because they lived far from each other, phone conversations, text messages, Facebook messenger, and posts on Facebook were the only ways in which they could communicate regularly.

Jay's move to appeal to his girlfriend's parents was an attempt to break the dissonance that this open-ended communication produced, to link love and desire back to his girlfriend in a way that made sense to him in the South Asian context. The action required, then, was to directly hail her parents as those who had control of love and its possibilities. The video's content and stated audience thus reveals the kinds of uneven processes of change that globalization creates, where new conditions of possibility for expressing love and even maintaining love relations also reaffirm existing frameworks that regulate its expression.[28]

It is also important to reflect on the fact that Jay's representation of romance in light of the kinds of relationships between young men and young women in the Delhi scene reproduce a globally familiar understanding of gendered sociality in hip hop. Hip hop, in this reading, does not easily include young women in the collective space of shared endeavor. They are not, except in unusual circumstances, part of a world of practice. They cannot be friends on the same terms as their male counterparts. They are, rather, in the periphery and exist as subjects of desire and longing, as in this case, or as objects of derision (I discuss this in the next chapter) and misogynistic fantasy. As Marcyleina Morgan argues, hip hop has a history of positioning women on the periphery of practice.[29] The sort of reproduction of problematically exclusive gendered hip hop practice worlds in the Delhi scene reminds us of the ways in which the globally familiar is not necessarily a value judgment, something to aspire toward or push against, but a recognition of how globally networked media representations of gendered difference coarticulate with regional or local ones to produce unequal possibilities for making together.

Why Can't You Understand?

It was late April 2013. Jay picked me up in front of a landmark church close to his jhopadpatti with his cousin, Kama, a b-boy I met in Khirki and only recently found out was related to Jay.[30] I had not seen Kama or his Khirki-based crew in several weeks and we greeted each other with enthusiasm, exchanging a hip hop–styled "pound" and a half hug.[31] He laughed and said, "*Badaa bhai, kya kaise hain?* How are you, big brother?" I looked him up and down. His T-shirt, under a short vest, was tattered at the sleeves. He wore *chappals* on his feet and a pair of shorts even though the weather was getting chilly. We talked about the changing weather and I expressed concern that he could potentially get sick from the encroaching cold if he did not wear warmer clothes, quickly realizing I really did sound like an older sibling, a parent, or worse, an *uncle-ji*. He did not respond to my concern but instead abruptly changed the conversation, referring to me as "you" in the polite form rather than older brother, as before: "*Aap mera apne Facebook photo dekhne?* Have you [polite form] seen my Facebook photo?" We talked for a while about the images he wanted me to look at and whether he was going to be participating in any of the b-boy competitions that were coming up. Before leaving me with Jay, he reminded me to make sure I took a look at the pictures of his flare moves that one of his friends took of him in front of one of the many graffiti pieces scattered in the lanes and larger arteries around Delhi. After parting ways with Kama, we walked through the makeshift structures of the neighborhood where Jay lived and finally came upon Jay and his dad's house. In front of the house was a large statue of Siva with his *trisul*, or trident. Inside the first room was his dad, to whom I said hello, shyly (*namaste ji*), before Jay quickly ushered me into his room.

The mural was the first thing I saw when I entered Jay's room for the first time. In graffiti lettering, Jay had painstakingly written "Sonz of God." On the side of his graffiti piece, he had painted a picture of his girlfriend, replete with wings. As soon as I walked in, I also saw two young men I had met before sitting on the couch. One of the two young men was originally from Garhwal; the other identified himself as Northeastern. Neither were part of Jay's hip hop crew, but both were aspiring musicians from his neighborhood. They greeted me and, as I asked Jay about the mural—why Sonz of God?—they teased him in English about the portrait of his girlfriend: "Who paints an image of a girl? Take a picture. She looks just like you, except she has wings. Is she an angel? Will she fly away?" Then they laughed.

Jay ignored them and told me about Sonz of God. "I have been going with my friends"—he named several names, some of which I recognized as part

of his b-boy crew and others I did not recognize at all—"and giving food to poor people just near this place. I want to be a good person," he said with a smile on his face. "We think of ourselves as the Sonz of God." He then showed me the studio he had been slowly building, using found materials to create a soundproof space and slowly purchasing the necessary equipment to record tracks. He had a microphone with a pop filter and had used Styrofoam as soundproofing. I asked him where he got the equipment. "My father gave me some money. Also, I earned some money through b-boying." Why did your father give you money? "Because he wants me to be happy," he said cheerfully. "Also, I want to start a studio, so I can charge money for recording time."[32] Jay's father's approval and financial support of his hip hop studio can be read as a recognition of the entrepreneurial powers of the globally familiar and sits in distinction from the adult disapproval Jay might get on the street for his hip hop bravado. As Amit Rai argues, it is jugaad time in India.[33]

In the months prior to this encounter, I had made two music videos with Jay and one music video with Jay and a couple of his musical collaborators from Khirki. All the musical tracks were recorded elsewhere (either with Jaspal Singh or in West Delhi with Soni, who was the first b-boy-turned-MC to create a home studio in the Delhi scene). I shot the video footage for both videos with the support of Jay and his crew and did the editing for the final cut at my home. While we made those videos, Jay would come over by metro with his crew to my house on the other side of South Delhi. They would sit with me in my house for hours playing with my then three-year-old-son and smoking cigarettes on my balcony while we edited the video together and they learned the basics of editing. "Why Can't You Understand?" was Jay's first solo production. He produced the beat, wrote the lyrics, and wanted to shoot the video with me as a consultant.

As we sat on the plastic chairs in his room, he turned on the track. The beat was tinny, without much bass, and, surprisingly, all the lyrics were in English: until that point, all the raps he had written were in Hindi.

Tell me, tell me, what you want from me?
I'll do anything for her, because she is my destiny
Talk to your family, oh oh, baby please
Come back to me, oh oh, come back to me

I listened quietly. Jay's usually gritty voice and his usually philosophical and politically potent lyrics had given way to something raw and dissonant. In the chorus, it was clear he was appealing both to his girlfriend's family as well as to his girlfriend directly. He rapped in English to make a value claim, a claim to globality. He shifted his pronouns to make it clear that he was addressing the family of his girlfriend and his girlfriend simultaneously. The music, the tinny beat, and the synth keys playing over it sound like they were influenced by current K-pop rather than hip hop, whether past or present. The title of the track, coupled with the lyrics and their delivery, was an ode to the generational break he was experiencing as he attempted to build a relationship across various registers of distance. The song's lyrics seemed to accept that her parents would never understand their desire to be together even as they lamented it. The title, "Why Can't You Understand?," suggested that a lack of understanding is in itself a space for transformation. Within this representation of romance, Jay posited the idea that one had to go through ordeals, trials by fire, in order to come out on the other side as loved and recognized but not necessarily by the subject of one's desire.

Heteronormative romance in contemporary India, Ritty Lukose argues, is a flirtation that is not expected to extend beyond the temporary.[34] To court the idea of marriage outside the expectations and machinations of one's elders is to flirt with disaster. To love and be caught in love by one's kin at a young age is dangerous, even deadly. Jocelyn Chua, for instance, tells the story of Theresa, a sixteen-year-old Christian girl in urban Kerala whose parents find out about her love affair with a young Hindu Brahmin boy. Chua recounts a hospital visit with Theresa, who is recovering after a vicious beating from her parents.[35]

Contemporary stories of love across difference reflect older narratives in the subcontinent that speak of love that transcends difference but that, ultimately, produces serious injury or death when attempts are made to transmute romantic affects into reproductive durability. The Hir-Rajna, a poetic narrative written in eighteenth-century Punjab, for instance, tells of the lovers Hir and Rajna, who flee their village to realize their love, only to find death elsewhere. Farina Mir argues that the Hir-Rajna circulated in India at a moment when colonial power was in flux and offers an index of the kinds of uncertainty and anxiety that colonial rule generated with regard to tradition and the imminent possibility of social change.[36]

The same argument could be made in the contemporary moment about the kind of anxiety that urbanization, migration, and the growing youth population produce in India. The circulating myth of the "love jihad," where it is purported that Muslim men entice Hindu women into love marriages just to convert them, is just one example of how the fear of intimate relations across difference manifests in a period of uncertainty. Stories abound in the Indian news media about young couples running away from villages across

India to find safe havens in the city to realize their love. These stories often come into visibility only because the promise of love across difference is violently fractured when kin from the village track down the lovers and violently end the relationship. In news accounts, relatives who have committed violence against these fugitives of love are unrepentant. They justify their actions in the logics of caste, religious, or other forms of incommensurability.

In each case, these narratives often center on the ways in which urban life, and the kinds of globality it promises, threatens long-established social borders. The city is the place that might act as a safe haven for those fleeing reprimand. It is also the place where the potential for meeting someone who threatens the social order becomes possible. The road, the street, the mall, the urban college, or even the call center are all described as sites where men and women can meet with unforeseen outcomes.[37] This potentiality is amplified in the age of smart phones and social media, where contact and access can be surreptitious, persistent, and hard to track. The globally familiar, in this sense, produces the potential for a rupture of social norms in the spatial contexts of the city. It is constitutive of the possibility for Jay to meet his love interest at a hip hop event, the circuitry for them to stay in contact, and the possibility for Jay to attempt to make the temporary play of romance permanent through the socially reproductive act of marriage. This sort of rupture has been valorized in the Indian media to announce a generational drift away from prohibitive rules regarding intimacy across difference.[38]

Several surveys have been conducted by public and private organizations that state India's so-called millennials all respond favorably to intercaste, interethnic, and interreligious marriage. However, these hopeful accounts and survey-based research reports that proclaim the promise of the techno-urban to produce new freedoms are not the whole story. As the love jihad narrative plays out, online spaces also become locations to police those who have crossed boundaries. For instance, a recent article in the *Washington Post* on love jihad shows the ways in which right-wing Hindu groups use social media to track down couples who are from religious backgrounds and then publish their names on lists, calling on the faithful to punish them for their misdeeds.[39] This online policing, coupled with periodic physical attacks by right-wing conservatives on young urban dwellers engaging in what is labeled immoral activity (mixed-gender socialization, the celebration of the Western ritual of Valentine's Day, and so on), are testament to the enduring social order that persists despite and because of the new social possibilities brought about by the introduction of capital-intensive communications and media technologies.

After the track was finished, Jay asked me what I thought of it. I paused, unsure what to say, as I did not really like it. It did not have the gravity of the other music he had been making, in part because he was still learning the art of production but also because his lyrics felt too laden with hegemonic understandings of unrequited love. His voice, I felt, was unrecognizable as he petitioned his imagined in-laws. Also, his move to rap in English felt cathected, emotionally wired to what was expected rather than what was felt. "Yeah, it is good," I said diffidently, not wanting to impose my opinion. Jay then asked, "I want to shoot the video myself. Can you lend me the camera?" I hesitated. I was not sure I wanted to lend my DSLR camera because what would I do if, for any reason, the camera broke? *Who would pay for its repair? What would I use for my own projects? How would other young people I met in the scene feel if I gave my camera to Jay but had not lent it to them? Word would certainly spread that I was going beyond producing videos with people in the scene and giving out video equipment for them to produce their own videos.*

It took me a few moments (which felt like hours) to come up with a solution. "In a month I will be going back to the US," I said. "I will bring back a camera and sound equipment for you to use. But, beyond the video, I would like to think about a film project we can do together. Does that sound good?" "Yes," he said. "What kind of film project?" "What if we made a film about hip hop and money, or hip hop and friends in Delhi?" I replied. "Would that be good?" "Yes, but we will need lots of help from you." "OK, no problem," I said. "Also, when you go back to the US, can you buy me a professional tattoo gun? I will give you the money when you get back." I paused. *Will he give me the money when I get back?* "Sure, but I don't know anything about tattoo equipment," I replied. "I will send you a link that will tell you what to buy," he said.

This exchange with Jay and the conversation I had with Singh as related in the introduction, coupled with the impressionistic views I provided of our experience in the scene—Singh dancing in the b-boy cipha, my own discomfort when being asked questions I either had disappointing answers to or that caused me to question their or my own sincerity—open a discussion regarding ethnography in the globally familiar. What boundaries of relationality are encountered and blurred when ethnography meets hip hop and digital technology and their dual capacities to produce friends and extend networks? What sorts of tacit and explicit exchanges of labor, material gifts, and networks between ethnographer and interlocutor emerge out of an intersection between a deep engagement with the popular and ethnography, as each conspire to produce overlapping and, at times, conflicted representations of the world?

Jay's request for equipment and a tattoo gun, Singh's exhortation to make videos and his own endeavor to create a music studio—in addition to all the shared activities I have described thus far in this chapter, from b-boying to music production—reveal the ways in which mutual activity under the banner of hip hop produces social obligations and thus irreducible debts that placed me in complicated and ongoing relationships with those whom I sought to know and those I happened to get to know while in the pursuit of knowledge. In thinking through friendship and romance in the globally familiar, not as categories that can be taken for granted but as intersubjective relations that are constantly negotiated, it would be remiss of me to not discuss what these debts of relationality might mean for the practice of ethnography and the theory it has the potential to produce. It is especially pertinent given that the links of relationship and exchange I am studying are recursively wound up in my own representational endeavor.

As John Lester Jackson Jr. argues, the practice of ethnography has, since the writing culture critique in the 1980s, become "fiendishly self-reflexive" around issues that arise in being there and representing those whom we encounter.[40] These moves toward reflexivity, however, have arguably limited the practice of ethnography, so that we have either bounded our discipline in affectations of our own authenticity or we have ceded the ethnographic to bit parts in our philosophizing and theorizing projects. Jackson offers a way toward a sincere approach to ethnography that urges us to not only pay attention to but to push to the "front stage" those moments when laughter (and tears) arise in our ethnographic encounters and to recognize, as Annelise Riles argues, our interlocutors are already engaged in self-research and are potentially researching us as well.[41]

These moments of affective regard, certain doubt, and a recognition of mutual becoming, we may surmise, are instances of what Danilyn Rutherford calls "kinky empiricism." Here ties are created and "obligations that compel those who seek knowledge to put themselves on the line by making truth claims that they know will intervene within the settings and among the people they describe," are forged.[42] These truth claims are found in the moments we interact with those whom we seek to know, as well as in the ways in which we share with others what we have learned. They are also bound up in the shared endeavors we engage in with those whom we meet in the field.

These multiply located truths, of course, are always uncertain, receding, at the limits of our capacity to understand ourselves and those we meet in dialogue or through close attention to the moments, the days, the years, and the decades we continue to go back somewhere to learn about the messiness, hopefulness, and attendant struggles of being human. In this sense, Rutherford's call to a kinky empiricism and Jackson's appeal to ethnographic sincerity suggest a relationality, an entanglement, and a bounding up of obligation that neither a distanced reportage, a move to navel gaze, nor an effort to contextualize can quite capture. It places the unfinishedness of these relationships at the center of a disciplinary representational project that at times is as decidedly, even avowedly, prone to allegory as it is to description, as likely to mystify as it is to clarify. It also recognizes that the ethics of fieldwork are not found in easily scripted answers in institutional handbooks but are enacted in the moment when the ethical is understood in action (or inaction) and relationships are made, fractured, or taken in new directions based on what we do. In the final paragraphs of this chapter, I would like to try, through a discussion of explicit collaboration in relation to friendship, to extend Rutherford's theorization of the kinky and even the slinky recursivity of ethnography and Jackson's push for us to sincerely recognize ourselves in relationship to the ethnographic encounter.

My collaboration with the young men in Delhi's hip hop scene toward the production of music videos and eventually films, I think, offers a way into thinking about the sincerity, kinkiness, and relationality of ethnography as a kind of active ethical exercise located in the giving of material and immaterial gifts. They push us to recognize that the many instances of providing and receiving time, objects, and stories create momentum and debt that cannot simply be fulfilled through a fidelity of representation. These instances of sharing push us to think through what our interlocutors might expect of us as friends, and what doubts they and in turn we might harbor regarding a relationship built on limited time. The gift of doubt that emerges is not necessarily a fracture, a cause for a return to a vexation of the anthropological project, but a reminder of the ways in which doubt, action, and the ethics of research are entangled in productive and ongoing relationships.

Six weeks after my chat with Jay in his home, I returned to Delhi with a load of gifts in my bag. Several b-boys had requested authentic snapback caps from *Amrika* before I left. They went so far as to ask for specific team logos on their hats. Kama, for instance, wanted a Sacramento Kings cap, because he saw his favorite rapper wearing one in a video (I discuss style and shopping in the globally familiar in the next chapter). Soni asked me to bring him a piece of recording equipment and told me he would pay me back when I gave it to him. Of course, Jay's tattoo gun was in my bag. I had also bought two cameras, two mics, and two sound recording devices, to pass on to Jay's and Hanif's crews, a Somali and Afghan group of rappers introduced in the final chapter, on race and place in the globally familiar.

I saw Jay a few weeks after I returned. We met in our usual meeting place, in Green Park on the edges of Humayunpur and the posh enclaves that surrounded it. As we sat on a park bench, I handed him the tattoo gun and the camera and equipment. I explained how to use the camera and told him he was more than welcome to come to my house to edit the video if he liked. We talked for a bit and then he handed me the cash for the tattoo gun. It was short. "I only have this much for now," he said. "I can give you the rest another time." After spending some time on the bench watching a few American hip hop videos together on my smart phone in awkward silence, we parted ways.

Jay fell ill and so it was a few weeks before I saw him again. When we met at the park close to his house, he showed me a cut of the video he had made for "Why Can't You Understand?" I asked him where he had done the editing. He said he had bought a used computer a few weeks before and had edited it himself. He then pulled out his smart phone and brought us to the YouTube link he wanted to show me. The connection was slow so it took some time to load. While we were waiting, Jay pulled out two cigarettes he had bought from the *chaiwallah* (tea seller on the street) on the walk over to the park. He lit them both and handed one to me.

The video had two main sequences. The first was a midshot of Jay in the bucolic setting of one of the many parks in South Delhi. He stands on a bridge wearing purple-tinted aviator sunglasses as he sings and raps into the camera. His arms move up and down plaintively. The second sequence is in his room. Again, it is a midshot of Jay. Again, his arms move up and down plaintively. The Sonz of God mural and the image of his girlfriend he had painted on the wall peek out from behind as he sings the final verses of the song and the video ends. As I watched, I thought that the aesthetics of the video worked well with the lyrics, given his intended audience and the message he was trying to convey. The video offered up a view into Delhi that abstracted the city into a timeless space where romance has room to expand, to grow into possibility. The feel of the video, though, was more Bollywood than hip hop. Jay, in the video, had dressed up in a button-down white shirt and skinny black jeans. He had trimmed his already sparse goatee and combed his hair. I had never seen him dressed for romance before. I never saw him dress like that again. The video lived online for a few years, but when I looked for it in 2017 on Jay's YouTube channel, it had disappeared. It made sense that he erased the video from public record, as the clean-cut, plaintive image he portrayed in the video was a far cry from the street-savvy gully rapper image he has cultivated since.

Jay and I, in the year or so that I continued to reside in Delhi, would see each other regularly. The complicated set of debts between us—money owed, camera in possession, projects in the works, time and stories shared—propelled our relationship forward. Of course, eventually, I left Delhi, and Facebook is now the thread that keeps us connected (in the epilogue, I talk more about the digital and its capacity to extend the relationships one makes in the so-called field). Jay, like many of the young men I got to know in Delhi, always "likes" my posts. It is what friends do for friends on Facebook, after all. Every once in a while, I get a private message: "Bro, when are you coming back? We need to finish that film." This salutation is usually followed by some news from Delhi about friendships or romances that have broken and new ones that have emerged. Exchanges often end with the call for a gift: "Could you bring me a Chicago Bulls snapback the next time you come?"

We walked through the Delhi Land and Finance (DLF) Mall in Saket, just across the street from Khirki Village. The mall sits on a fifty-four-acre campus in the heart of South Delhi and consists of two conjoined shopping malls, an office space, and a four-star hotel. It opened in 2012 and is built on fields that were once grazing lands for the village.[1] Sudhir, a nineteen-year-old b-boy from Khirki, led us as we made our way through a layer of internal security between the two malls to head to one of the food courts and pick up a snack. "This food court is cheaper *bhaiya*," said Sudhir in English as we walked the distance between one mall and the other. His statement answered my unarticulated question, *Why are we walking to the other side of the mall to get food when there is a food court right here?* "You can buy us burgers or momos, OK?"

Along with Sudhir, I was with seven other b-boys from Khirki, and Sulu, a DJ and producer from South India who had lived for many years in the United States.[2] As we walked through the mall, we passed a man with a microphone promoting a cellular scheme. "Just one hundred rupees for free data. One hundred rupees for free data," he crowed loudly in English to the people walking by. No one walking by seemed in the slightest bit interested in his offer or aware of the contradiction his words expressed. Two other employees of the mobile carrier sat at a table looking glumly at the man with the mic as he continued speaking about the merits of the plan in an animated mixture of Hindi and English to disinterested shoppers.

Without hesitation, Sulu asked in English for the mic from the salesman. When he did not respond immediately, Sudhir loudly repeated the request in Hindi, "*Microphone kar do bhaiya*." The man reluctantly complied and handed Sulu the mic, the palm of his soft brown hands contrasting with Sulu's brittle, dark fingers as they simultaneously touched the microphone for a split second. Sulu began to beatbox into the mic and the b-boys began to dance in front of the marketing table. As they started dancing, some of them dramatically twisted their snapback hats to the side. The NFL, NBA, and MLB team symbols on the fronts of their caps took center stage for a moment, then receded into an amalgam of signs and supple, muscular movement. Bodies twisted and cavorted to the beat Sulu created with the clicks, pops, and vibrations of his mouth and throat that were amplified through the sonic circuit that the microphone and loudspeaker created. A crowd gathered. Some in the crowd pulled out their smart phones to capture the spectacle. After a few minutes, Sulu was satisfied at the event he engendered. He gestured to the man marketing the smart phone product to take back the microphone, but the man was now reluctant to take it back. His look suggested he would have liked us to stay for the remainder of his shift, so we could continue to gather crowds for him. We walked away laughing, back on our path to the food court. On our way we passed one of the sneaker shops in the mall. All the boys ran over to the Adidas display. "I want this," Sudhir said, pointing to a pair of classic Stan Smiths.[3] "But they are very expensive. *Lekin bahut mehenge.* I'll have to buy a copy in the market . . . *Shyed* [maybe] you can bring me back one from *Amrika*?"

The preceding scene offers a crowded snapshot of the many changes that have swept through Delhi in the last decade. The construction of large shopping malls that invite consumption (and the related destruction of grazing land and, thus, agrarian ways of life: what Karl Marx called accumulation by dispossession), the ubiquity of globally circulating brand symbols within the mall that generate desire, and the steady presence of the mobile phone that invites connectivity at a cheap, cheap price: all point to the shifting material, spatial, relational, and semiotic features of contemporary life in India's capital city. This chapter engages with the globally familiar in the thicket of these changes by taking as a starting point the clothing that young men involved in the Delhi scene desire to wear. What does the globally familiar materialize as desirable, consumable, and representative of a masculine hip hop subjectivity? How do these sartorial things shape gendered performances? What can we see of the city when these young men's desire for hip hop accouterments make visible circuits of spatial relationality that connect the 'hood to the mall and the market?

While Jay's tattoos indelibly marked his aspiration to transform his body through adornment to document his changing relationship in and with the city and to ratify his relationship with his friends, his potential love interests, and global hip hop, in this chapter, I focus on the transformative capacity of printed T-shirts with English catchphrases, brand-name sneakers, and snapback hats: the adjustable baseball or trucker's cap with a long front bill, a meshed or solid back, and, usually, an American sports team logo on the front. For the young men in my study, these were all sartorial accouterments that delineated distinction and provided the connective tissue to a form of American Black masculinity available in the circulating media forms they consumed on their (or their friends') smart phones. In this sense, snapback hats, T-shirts, and sneakers all comprised a familiar style that could materialize another place and way of being in the city they inhabited. Young people across the world, including in Delhi, utilize the term *swag* to describe a style that comprises some or all of these recognizable materialized signs.

Swag (short for swagger) is a gendered and racialized term originating in the United States that has circulated among young people across the world on social media. Swag delineates an urban way of being in the world linked to Black American masculinity and typified by a brash self-confidence, even as it is used to describe the very things that make this way of being in the world possible. I use swag in this chapter as an analytical concept to think through the relationship between particular things—like hats, sneakers, and T-shirts—and the gendered social and spatial relationships they produce in Delhi.

Swag can be glossed with the more familiar theoretical term in anthropology and European social theory: the fetish. It seems evident that fetishes—objects imbued with value such that they are transformed into exchangeable forms—accrue value precisely because they convey a gendered sense of power, even as they make invisible the gendering quality that comprises their value. These objects or things are what Marx would term "commodity fetishes," objects that obscure social relations and perpetuate unequal arrangements of labor, production, and consumption—but with a slight corrective. They are also commodity fetishes (or swag) because they quietly and unassumingly shape gendered ways of being across time and space.

On the one hand, as young working-class men in the Delhi hip hop scene quest for swag, they reify Marx's idea that capital produces an alienated relationship with the world by generating a need to gain possession of a gendered and gendering object without a sense of the political economy that consumption produces, nor a sense of how one is positioned within it. Certainly, given the economic status of these young men and their families, their fixation on "cool" sneakers, hats, and other accouterments as sites of masculine value could easily be described as a kind of false consciousness; a desire cultivated by capital that enmeshes these young men even more deeply into the unequal economic positions they current inhabit. An all-too-easy question emerges when thinking about the consumption practices of the urban poor: Why buy or dream of buying fancy sneakers when your family lives in a *chawl* (slum)?[4]

Sudhir's longing gaze on the Stan Smiths in the shop window in the mall falls squarely into this sort of Marxist analytical framework. His gaze suggests a fetishization of sneakers that will allow him to become an idealized global masculine subject and indexes a way of being in the world far removed from the material reality he occupies. Leaning on this analytical framework, we could even argue that Sudhir's regular trips to the DLF mall—built on grazing lands that once employed seasonal workers from eastern Uttar Pradesh like many of those in his extended family—to partake in global consumption betrays his and his kin's precarious economic and social position in the city as manual and service labor. Swag, in this sense, can only be imagined as an alienated and alienating set of materialized signs. These materialized signs, we could argue, implicate the market forces that make available these consumer items and the digital technologies that make them desirable as mechanisms of global capital that ensnare Sudhir and his peers in a system of perpetual inequality. As Jocelyn Chua explains, the public version of this discourse in India exceeds a Marxist reckoning of consumption and is explained as a moral failing brought on by globalization.[5] A moral indictment of consumption, of course, obscures the layered structures of inequality that produce immobility and desire in tandem and instead foreground the individual and their caste, class, ethnic, and racial background as the root cause of failure.

We can also see swag from a different angle—one that takes the perspective of Sudhir and his peers. For Sudhir and others in the Delhi hip hop scene, swag generates and maintains relations in ways that complicate the Marxian notion of a fetish as solely an "object" outside human intimacy. In this reading, swag is an integral component to creating a sense of masculinity that is distinct, to borrow from Raewyn Connell, from the hegemonic masculinity present in Sudhir's urban village or in Delhi, for that matter.[6] Rather than the flashy, tight clothes that reveal muscle and sinew worn by the children of Gujjar or Jat landowners who have benefited from the expropriation of the agrarian land in South Delhi or the subdued (but visibly branded) styles of upper-caste (and upper-class) youth, hip hop swag allows Sudhir and his crew to mark themselves as distinct.[7] By wearing loose jeans, T-shirts, snapbacks, and certain kicks, they become connected to what H. Samy Alim has called the global hip hop nation.[8] They are the material manifestations, the commodity chain extensions of the globally familiar, connecting hip hop contexts across distance as well as in the specific interactive social context of a Delhi hip hop scene. They connect these contexts not just through their sign value but by generating homosocial action and masculine experiences of collectivity.

In this sense, the hats, sneakers, and T-shirts the young men wore, desired, and sought out on their journeys across the city or in online worlds offer up a means to think through what Daniel Miller calls the "humility of things."[9] For Miller, building on Erving Goffman's work on "frames" of sociality, things order social relations and action in ways that are difficult to see and acknowledge by human actors within the frame. Taken in this sense, swag becomes what we could call humble actors that imbue masculinity in the subjects they adorn and worlds they inhabit, even as they remain obscured from sight, or divorced from an obviated theory of action, intention, or ideology. Hats, T-shirts, and sneakers, in this reading, cannot be seen merely as commodity fetishes but as biographical subjects, even agents, in the social worlds these young men produce in offline and online worlds.

Swag, when taken up as key (if humble) actors, reveals the third concern of this chapter: I am interested in the ways hip hop practitioners in Delhi imagine and relate to swag as things that are potent with (Black) masculine power from elsewhere, for those outside their practice worlds. Delhi hip hop kids I got to know deliberately wore swag to produce particular effects in the public spaces of the city. Snapback hats and sneakers, coupled with their skills as dancers, created a kind of fetishistic power for the young men I met in Delhi's hip hop scene—the power to, in Jacques Rancière's terms, produce a kind of dissensus, a tearing apart of the taken-for-granted social that relies on disrupting aesthetic norms.[10]

For instance, with a hat, sneakers, and the swag they imparted, Sudhir, taking Sulu's cue, could confidently ask for a microphone in the mall and proceed to dance in a public space that he otherwise might not have access to because of the way he is perceived as a child of migrant labor in the city of Delhi.[11] The globally familiar, in this sense, offers a way to analyze how gendered and gendering things become part of a process of social reinvention. In this reading, swag becomes a vital component for the young

men I met in Delhi to engage in creative resignification, a preliminary step necessary to produce oneself effectively in online and offline worlds, to not only hail those within an intended world of participation but to anticipate a broader set of social and economic possibilities that are unimaginable until they unfold.

Resistance and Cooperation

I met Harish one evening in late September 2013 as I walked down an alley in Khirki. He was on the way back from college, where he was pursuing a two-year degree in sociology.[12] He was wearing a button-down shirt and slacks. I almost did not recognize him and would have walked past him if he had not yelled, "Gabriel bhaiya!" to get my attention. He asked me where I was going, and before I could respond he invited me to the mall with him. He was meeting Sudhir and the rest of the crew later to practice dancing in the mall's clean tree-lined courtyard. I accepted his invitation. He asked me to come to his home with him first. He explained that he had to change his clothes before he could go to the mall, saying, "*Hip hop ka kapde pentha hu. I will put on my hip hop clothes.*"

I walked through the older part of Khirki with him to get to his house. His family's flat is on the edge of the twelfth-century *masjid* (mosque) that Khirki village is named after. The mosque sits in a state of disrepair. It is fenced in and watched by a *chowkidar* (security guard) hired by the Indian Archaeological Survey to guard the premises. The grounds around the historic masjid are littered with household refuse generated by families living in the encroaching and unauthorized buildings that surround it. I spent many an afternoon on the roof of the masjid with b-boys from the area, watching them smoke cigarettes and practice their moves. The chowkidar would wave them along when they walked into the compound, inviting them to use the space. The Islamic heritage site is, contrary to Anand Vivek Taneja's descriptions of some of South Delhi's Islamic monuments, alive; it is a vital space for young people in the village to play, practice, and simply hang out, even as its decay proceeds unabated.[13]

Harish and I walked up the steps of one of the recently built illegal cement buildings that encroach the space of the masjid and its grounds. It is where he lives in a two-room flat with his mother, father, and younger brother. His mom offered me tea as he went into the other room to quickly change his clothes. Harish returned soon after I started to sip the tea. He had changed into jeans, a light-blue T-shirt that had a Superman logo on the front, and a blue backward baseball cap with a New York Yankees NY on the front. I immediately recognized the hat as a knockoff. The NY was slightly crooked. The bill of the cap was a bit too long. Yet it still conveyed the power of the sign. Through the hat, New York appeared in Delhi or, put another way, the hat closed the distance across geographies and temporalities.[14]

Harish then put on the same sneakers he was wearing when I saw him coming back from school, a pair of Nikes that were also knockoffs but reasonably well made so that it was not evident. The Nikes, instead of bridging the distance between two particular spatiotemporal contexts—say, New York and Delhi—made this distance superfluous. By this I mean Nike sneakers conveyed a sense of dislocated and transcendent globality, a means to imagine belonging to a youthful ecumene without the anomie of difference serving as an immediate and jarring interruption.

Each of my quick interpretations regarding the hat or the sneakers, of course, rely on a reading of the brand logo—NY or the Nike swoosh—in addition to the material artifact itself, the sneaker and that snapback cap. This doubling (and at times disentangling) of the sign and the material thing has been a topic of interest for anthropologists as brands like Nike or, for that matter New York, circulate globally. As Brent Luvaas notes, the immaterial and material labor to produce these sorts of fashionable commodities occur at a great distance from one another.[15] A pair of Nike shoes might be designed in a studio in the United States but is manufactured in a factory in China, Indonesia, India, or Bangladesh. Even more poignantly, the value of the shoe exceeds the value of the material commodity itself because of the brand that is stamped on the side of the shoe. This, of course, renders the value of the immaterial labor that goes into the design of the shoe as greater than that of the worker's labor to make the shoe. Once in the form of a shoe, the labor to produce the sign and the material object is indistinguishable, whether the object is genuine or a knockoff.

Harish's sneakers and his hat are what James Siegel calls "genuine fakes," insofar as they do the work of indexing Nike and its globality, and New York and its global iconicity, even though they are not a "real" pair of Nikes or an official New York Yankees cap.[16] Genuine fakes call for an attention to disruption of global brands as trademarked private property. If, as Luvaas argues, "the strength of the Nike brand depends on its emotional resonance, the intimate sense of connection its customers feel within it and build around it," the brand's free circulation and its affective power open it up to piracy.[17]

Harish purchased his "genuine fake" Nikes and his New York snapback in a market that offers savvy shoppers factory seconds produced in India,

Bangladesh, or Nepal, as well as knockoffs that are more than likely produced in the very same factories. The "intimate sense of connection" that branded swag, whether real or fake, produces suggests that what we wear matters more because of the social imaginary and sense of belonging it intimates than the exchange or use value of the thing itself. In other words, clothes, as Emma Tarlo has written, matter precisely because they offer a way to signal group identification, hierarchical position, political affiliation, and a gendered, caste, and classed self-identification.[18]

Style—the possibility to choose one's clothing, to shape one's outward appearance—has historically been a possibility granted to the privileged. To trace style in a particular epoch among the privileged offers a means by which to understand cultural hegemony. As Gabriel La Tarde wrote at the turn of the nineteenth century, style or fashion follows the laws of imitation. Those without power, seeking to emulate those with power, mimetically take on their appearance.[19] Put another way, we cultivate ourselves in the image of those who have power. However, La Tarde insisted this mimetic gesture is not a mechanical reproduction of power that signals a kind of false consciousness but a complex and creative act of resistance. Michael Taussig, echoing this sentiment, argues for an attention to the ways our mimetic faculty operates as a complex technology to "copy, make models, explore difference, and become Other."[20]

Style (and dress), in the cultural studies tradition, has been theorized as a site to locate resistance as a material practice. In the 1970s, Dick Hebdige famously argued that style is the performance of "significant difference."[21] Writing in postwar Britain, Hebdige was interested in the ways a rigid class politics produced what he and others of his generation who were the progenitors of cultural studies termed "subcultures." The notion of a subculture was, as Victor Burgin argues, theorized among cultural studies scholars of that era as the congealed cultural practices of the working class that pushed against a top-down order of things.[22] Performances of significant difference, in Hebdige's estimation, were the creative moves the (White) working class made in terms of dress to magnify and make visible their classed difference in order to create a symbolic reversal. Hebdige and others working in the same vein agreed with what Walter Benjamin suggested fashion is intrinsically about: "an eternal quest for the new," a desire to break from tradition and custom, and the power relations they normalized, to realize previously unavailable social possibilities.[23]

Hebdige and some of his compatriots argued that the quest for visibility by subjects through a production of the "new" and the "resistant" were always subject to co-optation by capital.[24] Co-optation, in this formulation, occurred when styles originating within a particular class formation trickled "up" as a result of marketing efforts such that, if we take Hebdige's example of punk in the United Kingdom, ripped band T-shirts, safety pinned jeans, mohawks, and work boots became desirable to the middle class and the wealthy. Put in crude Marxist terms, co-optation took place when the capitalist base drew from the superstructure to reinscribe the materialist inequality that was being resisted in the first place.

In Hebdige's formulation, co-optation suggests a certain sense of originality and authenticity in the production of working-class cultural forms and, by the same logic, signaled an inauthenticity or fakeness for class Others who take up its styles. The notion of co-optation, in this sense, requires a discrete and original system of signification related to class from which borrowing and/or theft takes place. It also requires a materialization of signs from a particular system of signification into recognizable artifacts: relics that are fashioned out of the detritus of capital's production. These presumptive first assumptions of Euro-Western-focused cultural studies scholars, as Shane Greene has argued, always position subcultural formations in false opposition to hegemonic ways of being and reduce the aesthetics of the popular into a simple binary of either already always resistant or subject to co-optation.[25] The globally familiar asks for a more complex reading, one that takes twenty-first-century production, distribution, and consumption chains into consideration while foregrounding the ways in which context shapes the materialized meaning of signs.

Returning to the vignette with which I began this section, it is evident that Harish's transformation from one social type (working-class student) to another (b-boy) was made possible simply by changing clothes. Yet Harish, unlike the punk rockers of the 1970s whom Hebdige thought with to theorize subculture and style, did not make his own clothes or refashion existing clothes. Rather, he purchased clothes made in other parts of Asia by workers who, perhaps ironically, occupied labor positions similar to members of his family. Moreover, he did not differentiate between the real and the fake but centered his choice around the particular styles that indexed his relationship with digital hip hop as a practice, a way of life, and a set of relations.

Taking Harish's negotiation of swag as a starting point, hip hop style, as it is picked up in Delhi through social media circulation and face-to-face exchange, offers another way to think about performances of significant difference and processes of "co-optation." Rather than Hebdige's rigid notion of style as resistance, Harish's decision to dress as hip hop was about the potentiality of participation that it offered. While this potentiality is linked to a rejection (the dissensus I was suggesting earlier) of the figure of the migrant male laborer as a racialized economic and social type, it is also informed by Harish and his peers' desire to perform hip hop masculinity as a means to connect to those they otherwise would not have access to. In other words, Harish was not interested in performing his class position in opposition to the elite. Rather, dressing in hip hop styles and practicing hip hop's arts created the possibility for him to meet peers from different class, caste, and ethnic positions in the city.

What constitutes a hip hop clothing style emerged in the complex historical weave of postindustrial and racially segregated urban contexts in the United States. These contexts created, at least originally, a sense of style that at once rejected the previous generation's discourse on gendered fashionability even as it resisted the prevailing race and class order through stylistic innovation. Hip hop styles have shifted and changed over the last four decades. However, while hip hop's music, dance, and visual art continues to evolve in the localities where it is picked up, much of the innovative bricolage regarding what constitutes a hip hop clothing style has been replaced by a more conventional uniform that, at least for young men, comprises caps, sneakers, printed T-shirts, baggy jeans or shorts, and so on.

Across the world, these delimited signs of American Blackness are used by what Damani Partridge calls "unanticipated audiences" who find "power in aesthetics that never had them in mind."[26] These audiences, of course, are not necessarily practitioners of the hip hop arts. For instance, in Katherine Boo's creative nonfiction *Beyond the Beautiful Forevers*, about a slum in Mumbai, she describes a young man named Rahul. Rahul, because he had the benefit of landing a short-term job at a local hotel, is able to purchase a set of new clothes. As Boo narrates, "He came wearing an ensemble purchased from the profits of this stroke of fortune: cargo shorts that rode low on his hips, a shiny oval belt buckle of promising recyclable weight, a black cap pulled down to his eyes. Hip hop style, Rahul termed it."[27] Rahul, or at least Boo's depiction of him, exemplifies the spread of hip hop's style and the particular materialized forms it takes. For Rahul, there is no presumption that he is, or will be, a dancer, rapper, or graffiti artist. Hip hop style is simply a sign of urban hopefulness (also recall Devan, who appears in Ritty Lukose's book *Liberalization's Children*, and whom I discuss in the introduction).

In the recent nostalgic television series produced by Netflix that traces the birth of hip hop, *The Get Down* (2017), the wild variations and borrowings that comprised a hip hop fashion in the 1970s and early 1980s are well represented. Leather pants, big sunglasses, cowboy hats, and flashy suits, as the series shows, were equally as hip hop as T-shirts, jeans, and sneakers. In the years that followed, however, this broad range of style associated with a hip hop lifestyle narrowed. Sneakers, gold chains, baggy denim jeans, and snapback hats became firmly associated with hip hop's authentic Black street fashion. These stylistic markers were subsequently broadcast across the world, through the circuits built and maintained by the culture industry as well as through unanticipated sites of diffusion and circulation, as hip hop's street style.

The corporate domestication of hip hop fashion unfolded quite differently from that of punk rock. Rather than a one-directional process of co-optation associated with punk, where the culture industry appropriated the subculture's styles, in the early years of hip hop, rap artists directly engaged with the culture and fashion industry to promote and circulate hip hop styles and practices nationally (in the United States) and globally. We could read these artists' active participation in the cultural industry as ambivalent. For example, in 1986 the rap group Run-DMC, based in Queens, New York, signed a deal with Profile Records to release the album *Raising Hell*. The album included a track called "My Adidas," which was released as a single that year. In the track, Run-DMC promoted Adidas sneakers as an integral component of the group's wardrobe, and, by extension, Adidas sneakers as a "street style" staple became associated with hip hop so much so that Sudhir's longing gaze fell on a pair of classic Stan Smiths in a mall in urban India more than thirty years later.

Yet as Derek Ide argues, Run-DMC also rapped on the same album lyrics like "Calvin Klein ain't no friend of mine," rejecting a certain brand logic that did not seem to include Black people as part of its aesthetic, nor could be translated into an authentic street style.[28] The selectivity that Run-DMC evinced in choosing to align with Adidas and not with Calvin Klein, argues Ide, highlights a particular orientation to street style, to "swag," that conveys a classed (in addition to raced and gendered) sensibility linked to American urban Black culture. This move to place certain brands as legit over others through rap continued throughout the 1990s and the following decade. For instance, twenty years after "My Adidas," Jay-Z endorsed Evisu jeans over Diesel on his track "Show You How."[29]

There are two takeaways here in relation to Delhi hip hop. First, the ways in which signification related to a hip hop way of being locates itself in specific branded things, that is, Adidas sneakers, and additionally the way these branded things suggest an authentic, biographical relationship with "the street." Second, hip hop artists have ambivalently cooperated in linking particular brands to a hip hop way of life that is inextricably connected to the street in all its classed, gendered, and racialized connotations. This ambivalence regarding the culture industry and its promotion of particular lifestyles through brands is foundational to hip hop's discourse about itself as a technology of bricolage that celebrates the margins and critiques inequality even as it hustles to participate in capital, recalling Mbembe's words regarding the contradiction of Blackness.[30] I discuss this contradiction in the next chapter, on (immaterial) labor and the ways in which the economic opportunities in the city's burgeoning youth culture industry that arose for the exceptionally talented dancers, rappers, and visual artists I met in Delhi, while met with enthusiasm, were also seen as a loss, a relinquishing of the freedom that comes with collective creativity.

It is also important to note that Delhi-based hip hop practitioners' relationship to branded swag was shaped not only by hip hop but by the lack of fixity that branded items have in the age of "genuine fakes." As Luvaas notes, the indeterminacy of the branded sign in the contemporary moment allows for an easy embrace of the branded knockoff as the real because "the real" has lost substantive credibility.[31] Also relevant here is Sasha Newell's argument in his work on the *sapeurs*, or dandies, of Francophone West Africa. Newell suggests that if people have recognized modernity itself as a productive bluff, a performance that does not necessarily have substance, then whether one wears something real or fake, an original or a copy, is irrelevant.[32] What matters is the performance and the affect/effect it produces.

In Delhi, first and foremost, the snapback hat, printed T-shirt, and sneakers allow young men to signal and ratify their affiliation to global hip hop and membership to a Delhi-based community of practice. It is a first-order practice; one dresses oneself in hip hop's garb as one begins to practice its creative forms. In this sense, as Constantine Nakassis recently wrote, donning a pair of Adidas or a snapback hat with a team logo is more akin to a form of citation than a form of co-optation or appropriation. Citations, Nakassis argues, "re-present some other social form or discursive event in one's own voice but keep it in quotes, simultaneously reanimating and bracketing what is cited as not quite one's own."[33] Nakassis suggests that this sort of close yet distant relationship to a social form or discursive event elsewhere allows for a kind of play with signs that changes the meaning of what is being cited in ways that reflexively point back to the sign while creating new meaning. Nakassis's theorization of citation, what he calls "indexical co-presence," drawing from the rarified school of linguistic anthropology theory based in Charles Peirce's twentieth-century work, has a lot to do with the globally familiar.[34]

Harish's donning of a New York Yankees hat, Nike sneakers, and a Superman shirt can be read as a reflexive engagement with global hip hop and with American Blackness in Delhi. This reflexive engagement is, on an everyday level, about congealing a sense of global hip hop personhood in Delhi through the evocation of signs he has picked up through his consumption of circulating media. For Harish and his peers, it is also about performing masculinity differently in order to connect to other hip hop practitioners in the city and beyond. We could also surmise that Harish's hat, sneakers, and T-shirt allow him to deploy a stance of resistance associated with hip hop and, by turn, with American Blackness that allows him to reimagine and reconfigure his relationship with Delhi. Performing resistance, in this case, opens the possibility for relations across classed borders as well as signaling the promise of getting paid.

(Digital) hip hop, in this reading, becomes a technology for the appropriation of other popular cultural signs toward the production of swag. Indeed, as several scholars of hip hop have argued over the years, hip hop's power lies in its voracious capacity to incorporate various popular cultural symbols to reproduce itself.[35] Superman, Nike, and the New York Yankees, when simultaneously donned by Harish, transform into hip hop, even as Harish becomes hip hop by donning these signs. In turn, Superman, Nike, and the New York Yankees all signify Harish as a different sort of male urban subject than when he wore the college uniform in the working-class community he calls home.

Nakassis argues that if citations are not reflexively bracketed, that is, if style is borrowed and made one's own without quotation, it becomes "over style."[36] Over style, he argues, is not believable and is subject to rejection by one's peers. In the Delhi hip hop scene, style and over style related to sartorial choice was a regular topic of debate in online and offline worlds. The term *swag* became an index for these debates. Over the last couple of years, these debates around swag in relation to practice have intensified as hip hop has grown wildly popular among young people from various class, ethnic, and caste backgrounds across urban India. After I left Delhi, the young men whom I got to know well—Soni, Jay, Sunil, Sudhir, and Harish—who were just starting to rap and make YouTube videos or organize parties and underground dance jams, became widely known as pioneers in the scene and people who represented "real" Delhi hip hop.

These young men took on the mantle as the progenitors of the scene and felt a responsibility to police the boundaries of what hip hop is and who could belong to a hip hop community of practice in the city and in the country. After 2015, the matter of clothing choice in debates around hip hop authenticity in Delhi were always in relation to new-to-the-scene rappers, dancers, and graffiti artists who used social media to circulate their practice in the form of videos in the hopes of generating interest. Those who displayed swag (in their material choices and in their aggressive stance) without evincing a sense of what these progenitors felt hip hop was about—representing the city of Delhi, representing one's neighborhood, representing one's personal struggle, representing hip hop's historicity—were seen as performing over style.

For example, in an online debate in 2017, Jay posted on Facebook a question directed to his Delhi hip hop community: "What the fuck is swag?" Several comments responded to the query sincerely. One responder stated, "Stuff we all got." Another responder stated, "Bro, swag is our *tashan* [style]," formulating an inseparable and circular correlation between materialized signs and style. Yet another responder posted a new video by two Delhi rappers, Magical and Raxxo, called "Anusar Swag" (According to swag), stating, "Watch this video, you'll know about swag." In the video, the two rappers (whom I did not meet while living in Delhi and who were considered new MCs in the scene) rap about their misogynistic and materialistic stance on life in a shopping mall, decked out in printed shirts, sneakers, and sunglasses.[37]

The sneakers depicted in the video, rather than being newfangled and high tech like many of the branded sneakers now on the market, were, like the Stan Smiths that Sudhir desired, throwbacks that were originally released in the 1980s. Indeed, by and large, the swag that young people desired in the Delhi scene was designed during the early years of hip hop. As Jaspal Singh suggests in his writing on semiotic "wormholes" in the Delhi hip hop scene, there was a consistent harkening back to a 1990s American hip hop past through specific materialized and immaterial signs (say, a reference to the Bronx in relation to Delhi) to produce an Indian hip hop present and future.[38]

Other responders to Jay's sardonic query critiqued swag in subtle and not-so-subtle ways and, in doing so, pointed out how some people in the Delhi and Indian hip hop community were committing egregious acts of over style. One offender happened to be a young woman. One poster said, "*Swag wali topi* is swag ☺" (The person with swag's cap), referring to a rap video made by a female YouTube sensation, Dhinchak Pooja, about her snapback hat. The comment was a subtle critique of swag and all things associated with the term as over style. Indeed, in the Delhi hip hop community, Dhinchak Pooja (also from Delhi) was seen as someone using hip hop style and performance

simply (and crassly) to gain YouTube fame (she had more than 1.2 million hits on her video the last I checked).[39] The critique, in addition to pushing back against her claim to Instafame, suggested that Dhinchak Pooja, as a young upper-middle-class woman, had no business trying to represent hip hop in Delhi.[40]

Jay responded at the bottom of the thread to all the comments by arguing for street style, which he suggested was different from swag, and by explaining that swag "was founded by a new generation of kids." Swag, in other words, was over style because it was embraced by those who do not know what hip hop is and, in their quest to go viral, had simply jumped on the bandwagon. Jay, positioning himself as an elder in the scene and "in the know" about hip hop, argued that "street style" related to hip hop was authentic because it had history and did not rely on any particular items or markers of clothing—any swag—but emerged from "the street" and was a part of the lifestyle choices of the hip hop artist. In so doing, Jay made a case for understanding hip hop style and citationality as having more to do with what one does and who one is than what one wears.

As Jay's Facebook remark suggests, echoing what I heard from others in the Delhi scene, citation and membership evaluation hinged on one's capacity to innovate as a dancer, MC, or graffiti artist. There is no doubt that hip hop packages a class- and gender-inflected American Blackness as something to consume (and wear) but also offers itself as something to practice, perform, and perfect. Hip hop, as a result, becomes fashion in the broadest sense of the term, a means to remake oneself anew while partaking of, and even reveling in, consumption. We could call hip hop a technology of being (and becoming), what Maurice Merleau-Ponty would call a fundamental orientation to the world that does not differentiate consumption from creation.[41] As legendary hip hop pioneer DJ Kool Herc argues, "People talk about the four hip-hop elements: DJing, b-boying, MCing, and graffiti. I think that there are far more than those: the way you walk, the way you talk, the way you look, the way you communicate."[42] This way of being in the world requires certain material "fetishes" to substantiate and maintain itself. However, it is not solely based on material things. That is, certain material effects are linked to an orientation in the world based on practice, and certain (bodily, speech, and creative) practices are linked to specific material affects, but someone can surpass these links and generate new ones because of the power of their creative practice.

Over style, in this sense, occurred when there was a mismatch between clothing style and one's ability to dance, rap, write graffiti, or produce music.

Over style could also be pointed out when certain dance moves or lyrical styles were overdone or taken up as one's own rather than as a borrowing from someone else. Those who dressed in hip hop's garments and overstated their membership but were not perceived to have the artistic quality and/or a knowledge of hip hop's history to back it up were painted as pretenders, out for fame and money. The fact that these debates took place on Facebook offers a reminder of the ways social media creates opportunities for communities of practice to deliberate and define group membership through globally circulating concepts (like swag). These debates, while they were localized in Delhi, were inflected by similar debates going on elsewhere in virtual simultaneity. That these debates focused on the relationship between style (over style), creativity, and intention (to become famous, or to just do hip hop) reveals the import of swag among practitioners in the Delhi scene.

As importantly, Delhi practitioners of hip hop did not simply don their attire or perfect their moves for their peers, or even for a global community of practitioners. Their clothing choices and their hip hop practice, as I suggested at the beginning of this chapter, were also directed toward other publics. Now, to be sure, snapback hats and sneakers, while they might hold a particular meaning within a global hip hop community of practice because of their generalizability as hip hop markers of global Black masculinity, hold very little specific distinction for someone who apprehends their materialized signs in public space. That is, to borrow from Goffman again, there is no frame by which these signs can be apprehended, no system of meaning that allows for a particular reading of adornment.[43] For the uninitiated spectator, all that can be seen is "significant difference"; a young man who under other circumstances would wear the cheap synthetic button-down shirt and slacks available at any bazaar is suddenly dressed differently. However, while the spectator has no citational knowledge to ascertain where this particular style comes from, or what a Chicago Bulls snapback versus an LA Dodgers snapback might signify, there is a recognition that these styles are global, that they come from outside India and change the way that these young people look and act. This is in distinction to Delhi hip hop kids, who recognize caps not necessarily as spatial indexicals but as signifiers connected to particular rappers and their entourages.

Sudhir and Sulu's impromptu demonstration in the mall reveals this relationship between material signs and performances of difference in public space. The power that the snapback hat and sneakers conveyed to them in public space, especially when coupled with dance, rap, and graffiti, allowed them to project a sense of the global in ways that complicated a reading of their bodies as migrant labor in Delhi. In this formulation, the snapback and the sneakers function as necessary fetishes that intervene and break social norms found in the normalized everyday aesthetics of fashion in Delhi. These accouterments are necessary insofar as they offer the vital possibility for these young men to claim a different masculine subjectivity in the public spaces they frequent in Delhi. For certain exceptional talents I met in the scene, hats and the right sneakers, at least initially, also facilitated a hip hop performativity that I argue was crucial to mastering their chosen hip hop element while moving toward eventually transcending the stylistic conformity of the hip hop uniform. Where did they initially evoke the power of the gendered fetish? In the mall, of course.

The Mall

In both the media and in scholarship, the mall has symbolically come to stand for everything good and bad that has happened since India liberalized its economy in 1991.[44] On the one hand, the mall symbolically represents new possibilities for Indians to engage with the global marketplace, a means by which to participate as consumer citizens in the postliberalization urban boom economy. The symbolic value of the mall in India became painfully apparent to me in the intimate sphere of my domestic life in Delhi. My partner and I decided to host a birthday party at our house for our then three-year-old son and invited his entire preschool class for the celebration. When the twelve fancily dressed mothers in their high-heeled shoes, their children, and the children's *ayahs* (nannies) arrived, I was not quite sure where I fit in the gendered social space.

Milling about our apartment, I tried to start a conversation with one mother about the changes that have occurred since I last lived in Delhi in 2001, hoping to have some sort of dialogue around the social change that has rewrought the city in which she lives from her particular class and caste perspective. When I asked her what she thought of the changes that have happened in Delhi over the last ten years, one of the mothers sitting close by, overhearing our conversation, immediately interjected, "Oh, lots has changed. We now have really great shopping and shopping malls. Before we had to travel to Dubai to do our clothes shopping."

Her comment reflects the kinds of shifts in consumption that have occurred since economic liberalization took place in the early 1990s. As Lukose argues, once the discourse of postcolonial production patriotism linked to the independence movement fell away, elites like the young mother who came to my son's birthday party could look forward to unfettered consumption in India.[45] No longer would they have to travel abroad to purchase their brand-name commodities. No longer would diasporic families, like my own, have to stash Levi's jeans and other swag in our suitcases for our cousins, aunts, and uncles back home.

In this sense, the mall has become a symbol of middle-class ascendancy, a materialized reminder of the consumerist aspirations that liberalization has spatialized in the cities of India. It is precisely on these grounds that academics and left-leaning activists, artists, and concerned citizens have all decried the shopping mall boom in India, a boom that has led to the appropriation of what was previously grazing or farm land through public-private partnerships.[46] In all my conversations with activists and artists in Delhi, they unanimously agreed that the mall was a symbol and a lived space for the so-called new middle class, those who have become relatively wealthy since economic liberalization in the 1990s.

However, economic and environmental arguments against wasteful infrastructural projects notwithstanding, the symbolic resonance of the mall cannot solely be attached to a singular class position. In fact, the mall continues to capture the imagination of the many in India precisely because it exceeds its presumably intended audience. If we examine the mall more closely, we can see that the conflation of the mall as a space that symbolizes the ascendance of the new middle class in India and the mall as a lived reality of the middle class does not quite mesh.

The mall space, secured by multiple layers of security, could be called, drawing from Marc Augé, a veritable nonplace where the deluge of images, signs, and symbols disidentify subjectivities and displace history.[47] However, unlike the sister development of the mall, the multiplex cinema, the masses are not so easily kept out. While the multiplex charges phenomenally high prices for ticket admissions compared to the talkies of old, a phenomenon that Tejaswini Ganti argues dovetails with the changes in taste that have swept through Bollywood as it has sought to remake itself respectable and thereby appeal to a middle-class audience, the mall does not have an admission cost.[48] Its entertainment is free and open to the public.

Indeed, the lack of public space in the city coupled with an equally strong desire by youth from other class, caste, and immigrant positions to partake in the city's changing built environs make the mall a desirable destination. The mall, in this sense, could just as easily be called a contact zone as a nonplace; it provides a public space where contact and the reevaluation of social meaning become possible.[49] The possibility for contact, as Mary Louise Pratt rightly suggests in her theorization of the contact zone, however, is unevenly produced.[50] Contact, in the malls of urban India, is mediated through surveillance, in both the literal and the figurative sense. That is, the symbolic power of the mall, the signs that evince the very discourse of consumption as citizenship that produced the mall in the first place, disciplines those who enter into its spatial field.[51] The literal surveillance and disciplining, of course, is evidenced by the dozens of security guards and hundreds of cameras in the mall complex.

In the figurative sense, the surveillance is self-generated. Indeed, *White Tiger*, a novel by Aravind Adiga, shows something of the social changes being wrought in India's cities through the intensely personal first-person narrative of a farmer from a rural village who has recently migrated to Delhi. In Delhi he lands a job as a chauffeur with a nouveau riche family. The chauffeur, as he takes his employers to the mall regularly, struggles to convince himself that he is worthy of entry into its climate-controlled spaces. Over several chapters, he finally concludes that, if he just wears certain attire, no one will notice him at the security checkpoint as different, an outsider: "Next morning, as I drove Pinky Madam to the mall I felt a small parcel of cotton pressing against my shoe clad feet. She left, slamming the door; I waited for ten minutes. And then inside the car I changed. I went to the gateway of the mall in my new white T-shirt. But there, the moment I saw the guard, I turned around—went back to the Honda City."[52] Here, Adiga reveals the self-generated surveillance involved in the maintenance of class, caste, and ethnic boundaries in contemporary India. The driver could only approach the gate before he forced himself back to the car to reassess the situation. The takeaway then, both for Adiga's protagonist and for the young men I got to know in Delhi's hip hop scene, is that by realizing that surveillance is self-generated, one can break free of social constraints and claim public space freely. The strategy that can emerge with the realization that it is only self-held beliefs that limit one's possibilities would be to engage in tactics that rearticulate the externally visible to validate entry. And so it is the case with the chauffeur in Adiga's novel, who finally dons a shirt with a brand name emblazoned on its front and walks confidently through the security checkpoint to gain entry to the mall, a space he has coveted for several chapters in the book. One could say the same for Sudhir and his friends, who don particular clothing and engage in a series of corporal performances to legitimate their presence within the mall.

I made several trips to the mall with several different crews of b-boys in the two years I lived in Delhi. The mall, particularly in the summer, was a place of respite. Air-conditioning, the expansive spaces, and the ready audiences of shoppers for an impromptu performance made the mall a desirable destination. However, it was a destination that was also heavily policed. Security guards patrolled the long corridors of the mall, closed-circuit television (CCTV) cameras watched the food courts, and the borderlands between the mall and the street, or even between two adjoining malls, were heavily secured. All bags had to be checked and, on occasion, young men, particularly African nationals, were asked for IDs.

The food courts themselves operated on a noncash system that required the purchase of a card (for fifty rupees) that could be "topped up" with additional currency to spend in one of the many overpriced food stalls. The cost to consume prevented many of the young men from being able to access the food courts, unless they had someone like me with them. As a result, while the mall was a destination away from the neighborhood, a place to pass time and potentially to practice one's dance moves for a receptive audience, it was not a place for material consumption.

While Sudhir and others would gaze with desire at objects behind the glass panes of the shops in the malls, sometimes even going into the shop and touching the merchandise (with the slightly nervous shopkeepers intently watching), they would never buy anything in the mall. It was too expensive. The sneakers, hats, and T-shirts of the mall were fetishes that were trapped behind glass. Like the vitrines of the museum, the shop enclosures held these fetish objects at a distance. The enumerated distance between these young men and the things they desired pushed Harish, Sudhir, Jay, and others to find alternative ways to acquire them.

Yet while they could not purchase things in the mall, it was a still place where signs could be consumed. The posters of light-skinned Indian or White women and men dressed in haute couture fashion, the many items on display in the shop windows, the clothing styles of the young people who lived in the gated communities of Delhi that they saw in the malls, the glass and steel of the structure itself: all formed the sensory field of the shopping mall. This sensory field, which signaled exclusivity and privilege, was the impetus to seek alternate ways for self-representation as well as set the stage for aesthetic disruptions, like the quick performance with which I began this chapter. These aesthetic disruptions also allowed Sudhir and other young men from similar backgrounds to push against being reductively seen as the children of migrant labor. The visibility these performances produced created opportunities for them to claim the spotlight as young creatives, in step with a globalizing India. Indeed, the mall, with its placid audience, their smart phones at the ready to broadcast any novel experience they might en-

counter and consume, provided an ideal setting for hip hop practice, in a way that other public spaces in Delhi did not. The smart phones that their spontaneous audiences eagerly pointed signaled to the young men the possibility of being discovered and the hope of material and social benefits that came with being found. As Sudhir once said to me, "Who knows who we will meet in the mall? Who will see us?"[53]

The mall's management, too, sensed the value of these young peoples' performances. Early in my stay in Delhi, after traveling to the mall with Sudhir and his crew to watch them practice a few times, I wondered out loud, "Why don't you guys ever get harassed by the security officers?" Sudhir's friend Karthik told me that security guards had kicked them out on several occasions when they first started visiting the mall regularly to practice. But one day, he narrated, a curious thing happened. The head of security came down from his booth where he monitored several dozen CCTVs around the mall and said to the security personnel who were harassing the youth: "*Bandh karo. Mujhe aapne nutya ki pasand he. Dusrevaleko abhi pasand he.* Leave them alone. I like their dancing. Others like it too." The others, of course, referred to the patrons in the mall who gathered with their phones whenever Sudhir and his crew danced.

These sorts of performative disruptions and the potential for discovery they made possible required the necessary swag. To acquire swag—at least affordable swag—b-boys, MCs, and graffiti writers had to shop in the various markets across Delhi where they could find inexpensive hats, sneakers, T-shirts, and jeans.

In the Markets

The mission to seek swag was a regular occurrence. Our shopping ventures, themselves spatialized gendered performances that mapped the city through Facebook posts of selfie images and impromptu recordings of b-boy sessions in parks and plazas, took us to several pirate and seconds markets around town. These jaunts were not as much about buying things as about being together on an adventure, a way to pass time. Hats, sneakers, and T-shirts were almost an arbitrary reason to make a trip and yet provided the impetus for an exploration of the city. In some cases, however, these journeys were specific. When a particularly high-profile battle or a music video shoot was scheduled, the trip to Palika Bazaar in Rajiv Chowk, Sarojini Nagar Bazaar in South Delhi, or to the Northeastern-run boutiques of Arjun Nagar became an instrumental mission. The metro, in all cases, facilitated these quests to find the necessary accouterments while exploring the city.

I got a call from Soni early one morning in November 2013. I had just dropped off my son at preschool and was trying to finish writing up a few field notes when the phone rang. "Let's meet in Palika Bazaar," he said. "I want to buy a couple of things for the video shoot." We had made plans to shoot Soni's first music video later that week, a video to situate a rap he wrote about education in India and turning to a higher power to find the right path. It was a track he wrote with Singh, not long after we met that day in front of the metro station. Soni rapped in Punjabi/Hindi and Singh rapped in German, each of them taking alternate verses. We had decided to shoot the video in West Delhi, where Soni lives, and in Khirki, where Harish, Sudhir, and their friends live. Before shooting, however, Soni felt we needed to get ready and to prepare everything in advance. Soni wanted to buy a few different printed T-shirts, a new pair of skinny jeans, and a new snapback hat for the video. He explained that he needed multiple T-shirts so he could have costume changes during the course of the shoot. I got myself ready and took the train to meet him.

Palika Bazaar offers a striking contrast to the ostentatious malls of South Delhi. The bazaar, which opened in 1978, is a byzantine underground shopping center located under Lutyen's Connaught Place, which was renamed Rajiv Chowk in 1995 to commemorate the late Rajiv Gandhi as a part of a movement to decolonize place-names across India. The bazaar consists of a maze of underground tunnels containing clothing and electronic stalls that have several exits leading back to the center of the *chowk*, or circle. The bazaar's merchants sell original, seconds, and knockoff (pirated) merchandise and, in recent years, have increasingly begun to cater to youthful shoppers. Ravi Sundaram writes about Palika Bazaar in his book on Delhi, where he broadly describes the city's development as a "pirate modernity," exemplified by the disruption of the rational-ordered and top-down development project by informal and vernacularized production and growth.[54]

For Sundaram, Palika represents the globalized bazaar, "sophisticated networks connecting local, regional, and international markets."[55] Palika, like the other bazaars my interlocutors visited not only to purchase clothes but also to buy inexpensive recording equipment, produce mix CDs, and print posters, was a site where the uncertainty of what is real and what is fake is policed by the state. Regular raids were conducted at Palika and other bazaars in Delhi during my time in the city by antipiracy units that, as Sundaram vividly describes, have grown exhausted attempting to distinguish between the legitimate and the illegitimate. Palika, in this narrative, emerges not only as the site where blurred boundaries of contemporary market logics are policed and where counterfeiters make their living but as a place where one of my participants could buy the necessary swag to produce a music video destined for YouTube circulation.

I met Soni just outside the metro station and together we descended the stairs into Palika. Soni knew just where to go to buy the T-shirts and jeans he wanted. He bought two T-shirts, one bright yellow with a print design and the word *vegetarian* emblazoned on the front, the other black with the text *80 GB heart disk* in pink-and-white lettering. I asked Soni if he was vegetarian. "Of course not, I'm a *Dilliwallah*. I love butter chicken." We looked at snapback hats on offer at various stalls, but none of them were what he wanted. "I'll get one in Safdarjung when I go next. They have better ones there."[56] He then pointed to the snapback he had on his head. "*Muhje ye hat us dukan me milee. I met* [found] this hat there."

I went several times with different rappers and dancers to Palika Bazaar as well as to Sarojini Nagar, another bazaar in South Delhi, mainly to pick up printed T-shirts like the ones Soni purchased. Printed T-shirts, short-sleeved cotton pullovers with English writing or popular cultural images emblazoned on the front, although I did not realize it at the time, were a central feature in the rather conservative attire that most young people in the Delhi scene wore. I say conservative because they exemplified what I would describe as the hip hop uniform: hats, sneakers, and printed T-shirts. My description of Harish's transformation from school boy to hip hop practitioner earlier, for instance, reveals not only the transformative capacities of these adornments but their almost dull uniformity. While the change of clothes afforded him (and others) the license to approach the mall in a different state of mind, the clothes themselves reveal a rejection of creativity in favor of conformity. By adorning himself with a hip hop uniform, Harish produces a doubling of creative rupture and conformity. This doubling was something that struck others visiting the Delhi hip hop scene for the first time.

In 2015 I returned to Delhi to participate in an artist residency at Khoj International Arts. During my stay, I met artists and musicians from Delhi, Cape Town, Colombia, Bangalore, and Ghana. I told them about my ethnographic engagements with the Delhi hip hop scene and most of them, particularly the Delhi-based artists, were astonished that there was such a thing as a hip hop scene in the city. When I found out there was a b-boy battle in Gurgaon organized by some of the dancers I had met a few years prior, I invited these artists to come with me and see for themselves. We arrived at the venue in the pouring rain. Two hundred young b-boys and b-girls were waiting to enter. Tina Schouw, a singer from Cape Town and known in South

Africa for her antiapartheid protest music from the 1980s and 1990s, was immediately struck by the printed T-shirts and snapback hats all the young people wore. She began to photograph each b-boy and b-girl in their T-shirts and hats as they entered the venue. Moreover, Tina began to compose a song taking the slogans of each T-shirt as the material for her lyrics: "Only the strong. Believe that. Only the brave, follow the details. Obey."

As she took the photos, she sang the improvised lyrics, attracting more of the young people to her and her camera. Tina eventually composed and recorded the song as a collaborative project with Soni.[57] I mention this story because it has everything to do with the ubiquity of the snapback hat and T-shirt in Delhi's hip hop scene. Tina's creative research methodology tapped into the power of the materialized sign as a statement of intent and affect, a means to solidify a hip hop scene in Delhi. Tina's collaboration with Soni, and her engagement with the b-boys that day, also hints at the kind of networks of connection that the globally familiar produces for kids in the Delhi scene, networks that I explore in chapters 4 and 5 when I discuss the relationships these young men made with artists, musicians, and activists in and beyond Delhi.

Over the course of several years, the ubiquitous hip hop uniform I initially encountered in Delhi gave way to creative reinterpretations. The significant deviations to this formulaic mode of hip hop self-presentation were enacted by some of the more exceptional dancers and MCs in the scene, who in 2013 were just getting started with their musical escapades. Soni and Jay, while they initially started with the "uniform," began to push past these accouterments in favor of sartorial choices that were either more understated or more provocative. In some cases, young men marked their uniqueness within the scene by emulating other globally circulating popular culture styles. One example of this was the embrace of Japanese and Korean b-boy and K-pop dyed and gelled hairstyles, which b-boys in Delhi borrowed, in part, from Northeastern young people in the city.[58]

These hairstyle deviations, along with the kind of self-tattooing practices some in the scene took on (as described for Jay in the previous chapter), became markers for a particular "Delhi style" that seemed the domain of those recognized as the best in the scene. Importantly, self-inflicted tattoos and in-your-face hairstyles were the domain of either those young men whose families wholeheartedly endorsed their creative endeavors or the emerging habitus of young men who were alienated from their families and lived with their friends or alone. These more permanent bodily practices marked a commitment to a hip hop lifestyle and, in turn, produced another set of sociomaterial relationships (recall Jay asking me to bring him a tattoo gun).

Clothing choices not necessarily associated with hip hop or with global youth culture also began to appear in certain tastemakers' repertoires as part and parcel of their swag. For instance, Soni began to wear a turban rather than rock a snapback hat as he gained fame in the scene, choosing to mark his connection with the Sikh community as part of his hip hop persona. Sunil, a Garhwali b-boy I introduce in the next chapter, began to wear plaid button-down shirts with only the top button on and a white T-shirt underneath, borrowing from a Chicano cholo style from the West and Southwest of the United States, to mark his distinctive difference. In either case, becoming recognized for one's skills allowed one to, in turn, become a tastemaker, to establish the localized Delhi version of what hip hop looks like and what sorts of material effects are necessary to produce that look. In this formulation, to extend Nakassis's concept of the citation a bit further, style associated with a particular creative genre is often linked to a recognition of artistic substance by one's peers as well as by various publics. Social media emerged as one site, in addition to the several hip hop events around the city, by which to generate fame within a hip hop community of practice and, therefore, feel emboldened to improvise on one's personal style. Live events, whether hip hop specific or improvisational, like the mall performance with which I began this chapter, were also a means to capture the attention of various actors, not least those who work in urban India's burgeoning culture industry.

Swag and the Culture Industry

The culture industry, wrote Theodor Adorno in 1967, "fuses the old and familiar into a new quality."[59] To a large degree, the culture industry thrives on the tastemaker, the person or people who are able to take up the "old and familiar" and produce something new. It is no accident that I first began to conceptualize the globally familiar as an analytic framework for this book when I looked back at the field notes I had written from a meeting with a branding agent who was passing through Delhi after producing a hip hop and skateboard event in Bengaluru the month prior. As we sat together at my home, she described the relationship she helped produce between the brand she represented and the youthful "Indian" subject as a project where difference is mobilized as content toward the goal of attaching certain affects—fun, excitement, joy—to particular global brands that seek to tap into the youth market in India. In this context, the old and familiar (to borrow from Adorno) were the youth cultural practices (hip hop dance, skateboarding, BMX biking) that could spark the attention and interest of young people in

India. Her idea that difference was at the center of the project, that it produced a quality that engendered an affective momentum necessary to sell things, however, did not just hinge on that fact that "Indian" youth in India were participating in these activities. Rather, she pointedly suggested, young, low-caste, working-class, or ethnic youth skating, b-boying, and doing rap in relation to a global clothing brand would produce a particularly effective and affective image of participation. This, she argued, was what was familiar in relation to branding work she did in the United States and Europe—where the image of diverse working-class youth was valued by corporate clients.

I evoke branding agents and my conversations with them at this juncture as a bridge to the next chapter, where I discuss how the events that branding agents produce, in addition to urban India's burgeoning nightlife and the efflorescence of DIY underground hip hop events (like the one I took Tina Schouw to attend), offered "tastemakers" in the Delhi hip hop scene opportunities for paid (and unpaid) work that promised the possibility of fame and material rewards. Yet these opportunities to provide the immaterial labor necessary to link localized aesthetics of difference to particular brands, as we shall see in the chapter that follows, also pushed the young men who came across opportunities to participate in the burgeoning industry to articulate feelings of ambivalence about their participation in capital's expansion.

Traffic was bad and I ended up arriving half an hour later than I expected in front of the main gate that led to Humayunpur.[1] Sunil and Guru met me at the entrance to the urban village. On this day, instead of heading inside and through the windy *gallis* (alleys) that, much like the ones in Khirki, were beautified by several large intricate graffiti pieces and murals produced by local and international street artists, we made our way across the busy road and away from Humayunpur into Green Park. Green Park is an expansive leafy green outdoor space at the foot of the colony that connects to the Hauz Khas heritage area and the village that lies beyond it.[2] These young men used various nooks and crannies of this sprawling green public space to practice b-boying, to pass time with each other, and, sometimes, as Sunil told me, to just be alone and away from everyone.

The park's grounds were one of two places I met with these two young men and their extended crew regularly. The other was in Surabh's small apartment. Surabh was a member of their crew who earned enough money as a club promoter to rent a small barsati (rooftop room with terrace) in Humayunpur. The apartment served as a meeting place for the crew, a site of refuge and relational play. I spent many late afternoons in the early fall of 2013 in this rooftop apartment, alternately watching the young men practice their moves and chatting with the young men and women, friends, girlfriends, and fellow b-boys who were the casual audience of their sponta-neous performances. In moments where the action or conversation halted, I would peer over the rooftop edge to ponder the changing landscape of their urban village, where historic ruins periodically made their appearance nestled among the drab contemporary buildings and the newer upscale de-velopment projects on the perimeter of the settlement that seemed, in the evening light, to ominously edge closer.

On this particular afternoon, Niraj, another of the Nepali youth from the crew, came along with Sunil and Guru to meet me. I had not seen Niraj since I went with the crew to a late-night weekly party in South Delhi where they danced regularly on stage, although he and I frequently exchanged mes-sages on Facebook. As we sat on the bench, Niraj and I began to discuss our last meeting in front of the club venue. On that day, he and I had spent considerable time outside the main velvet-roped entrance with the promot-ers of this particular party, the Hip Hop Project. These promoters were all loosely affiliated with their crew and were all young men between the ages of eighteen and twenty-two from the Northeast (Mizoram, Sikkim, Assam, and Arunachal Pradesh).

Guru played a beat he had found on YouTube on Sunil's phone in the back-ground while practicing rhyming and beatboxing. Meanwhile, Niraj began to share with me what he believed to be and experienced as the economic pos-sibilities of his and his peers' engagement with hip hop. "There are two ways we can make money as b-boys," he said in a mix of Hindi and English.

B-boying, where we get paid to dance at events and shows around the city, or we go and compete at the b-boy battles, where there are spon-sors who offer prize money, or we work for the clubs as promoters. As party promoters we get paid for each night we promote. It works out to about ten to twelve thousand rupees a month to be a promoter if you promote three to four parties a week [roughly the same amount he would make if he worked at a retail shop for forty hours per week]. It's not enough money for the long term but it's good for now. I am going to stop doing the promotion though, because it means that every night you are out late and sleep all day. Also, the bouncers treat us with dis-respect sometimes. You saw how they acted with us that night. Mainly, there is no time for practicing b-boying. *Mushkil se.* It's difficult.

Niraj, like many of the practicing b-boys, MCs, DJs, and graffiti artists I met in Humayunpur and Khirki, eventually saw hip hop as a means not only to forge friendships in Delhi, develop translocal connections, or even to

claim the city and its spaces as their own but as a way to make a living in the burgeoning youth lifestyle industry in the city. As local entrepreneurs and international branding agencies, working as proxies for global multinationals, seek new ways to engage the more than six hundred million youth in India who are twenty-five and under, new work opportunities arise in the urban centers of India.[3] As demographic data reveals, India is the most youthful country in the world, with approximately two-thirds of the total population under the age of thirty-five.[4] For the young undereducated and unemployed men I got to know in a fast-expanding and youthful Delhi, new opportunities that are emerging as a result of an intensification of interest in developing the Indian youth market segment have meant that the hip hop skills they have cultivated have become sought after by various commercial interests.

As these young men engaged in Delhi's entertainment and marketing industries as club promoters, professional b-boys, or rappers (MCs) in the various events curated by corporate cultural industry executives and consultants brought in as branding agents, their engagements shed light on the kinds of laboring opportunities that become available as a globally circuited youth culture industry takes root in Delhi (and other cities in India). These laboring opportunities hinge on my participants' performances as global youth subjects, evidenced in their stylistic choices as well as in their ability to perform as hip hop dancers, graffiti writers, and musicians. They also hinge on their curation and maintenance of their social media personae. Audiovisual material produced in lifeworlds and circulated in digital realms, as I discuss in this chapter and in the epilogue, become central to the kinds of creative work that have become possible in twenty-first-century urban India.

As importantly, these online and creative industry laboring opportunities also point to the lack of perceived and actual opportunity that young men in urban centers like Delhi associate with formal educational trajectories. Echoing in some important ways what Craig Jeffrey found in Meerut among the young Jat men he spent time with, the diverse hip hop–involved youth I met in Delhi decided from a young age that education-based stability and attainment were foreclosed to them and that the only way forward was through developing one's skills and networks.[5] As Jay once said to me, "*Main school mein accha nehin tha.* I've never been good at school. *Mujhe music aur video banaana pasand hai.* I like making music and videos."

In this chapter, I think through the globally familiar as a gendered and racialized laboring opportunity that brings "tangible and intangible assets" to the urban economy.[6] In the previous chapter, I discussed the kinds of swag and fetishes the young men in my study sought to legitimize (and empower) themselves as hip hop subjects; in this chapter, I discuss the ways in which their creative endeavors, in turn, imbue commodities with value. Drawing from Tiziana Terranova's discussion of free labor, Brooke Erin Duffy's discussion of aspirational labor, and Michael Hardt, Antonio Negri, and Maurizio Lazzarato's theorizations of immaterial labor, I ask: How can we think through the labor tied to globally popular artistic forms that are emerging in twenty-first-century urban India as capital intensifies its push to engender mass consumption in markets that fall beyond the putative middle class, through mechanisms that create the conditions for the appropriation of local cultural difference as content?[7] What is the role of the digital in creating the opportunities and products of this labor? Finally, if hip hop holds some form of political consciousness in its practices, a means to sign one's sovereignty through its kinesthetic and musical practices, what sorts of disruptions to capital are embedded in the long hours of play, practice, and performance of the young men I got to know in Delhi?

In the literature on digitally enabled changes in the labor market, the sorts of opportunities that have emerged as work have been either valorized as empowering, liberating, and even revolutionary or described as a dismal sign of increasing precarity in the labor market as the logics of flexibility, creativity, and entrepreneurship place the onus on individuals to cultivate themselves to succeed in the marketplace. I argue for a more nuanced engagement with creative (digital) play as it morphs into labor in the twenty-first century, one that does not necessarily cede its potential to critique the regimes of indifference that capital creates, even as its creative enterprise is harnessed as content that stimulates consumption. In this instance, the globally familiar reveals itself as embroiled in capital and its movements, even as it reveals the potential for disrupting its sensibilities.

Undoubtedly, hip hop's discourse on the hustle, a term in Black American vernacular that describes how innovative social performance has the possibility to create new economic and social possibilities for those on the margins of capital, meshes all too well with neoliberal paradigms for success where self-cultivation and an entrepreneurial spirit are imagined as the key to success. As Lester Spence argues, this relationship between neoliberal capital and hip hop has created very real limits on the possibility for hip hop to encompass and represent a radical politics of Black refusal in the United States.[8] Hip hop, as many scholars who have traced its rise to global recognition have lamented, has become a billion-dollar industry in ways that refute Paul Gilroy's hopefulness that ground-up artistic African diasporic movements hold the key to individual and communal liberation.[9]

In Delhi, however, while my participants embraced the entrepreneurialism of hip hop as a way to create new laboring possibilities, many also expressed their relationship to hip hop as a political discourse that has the capacity to create new forms of community across difference through practice that disrupt capital's workings by offering alternative narratives of experience in the heart of Delhi's urban change, an experience that does not necessitate that "cash money" is the end game of the hustle. These articulations of political consciousness were often implicit, embedded in the narratives I heard from my participants as they discussed their socially salient engagements with hip hop's artistic forms or evidenced in the ways in which they chose to engage in particular acts of public performance to disturb normalized social roles.

For instance, in Niraj's talk of weighing the money he can make party promoting against the time it takes away from b-boy practice, and suggesting he would choose time over money, hip hop can be seen in distinction to the kinds of economic opportunities it yields for its practitioners in Delhi. Niraj's comment suggests that the practice of hip hop has value in and of itself for him and his friends, a value proposition that amounts to a kind of refusal to the logics of capital. Given this, I suggest that if we take a close look at the popular cultural self-fashioning of the youth in the Delhi hip hop scene, not only as sites where new formations of labor as play and play as entrepreneurship emerge but as sites where capital is subversively and, in some cases, actively disrupted, we begin to see how the youthful actors in Delhi's hip hop scene are positioned and position themselves as gendered and racialized laboring bodies that create multiple readings of the aesthetics they perform for potential capture.

Aspirational, Free, and Immaterial Labor

Sweat poured from their brows and plastered their T-shirts to their bodies as they took turns dancing on the rooftop space. I sat inside Surabh's small room with a group of young men who were not practicing but were watching the dancers. From my vantage point inside the room, the doorway to the flat framed their movements and the afternoon sun made them look like they were glowing as they inverted and tangled their bodies in midair. I was tempted to take out my camera but resisted the urge, instead focusing my attention on the cold noodles on the plate that was being passed around by the young men in the room who sat in a semicircle, on the banter around me, and on the warm camaraderie between friends that reminded me of my teenage years in New York City, when I would regularly pass the time sitting on rooftops on the Lower East Side of Manhattan.

We were just finishing up the meal they ordered from a small mom-and-pop Nepali restaurant close by. As we communally shared the plates of food they ordered, a smart phone was passed around with video footage of an NGO-sponsored event that a few members of the group had recently performed in. As each plate passed, each of us took a forkful of noodles, rice, or chicken and shoveled it into our mouth. There were a few cigarettes burning at one end of the room. On the mattress, about ten feet from the circle, one of the b-boys in the crew who had promoted an event the night before lay sleeping next to his girlfriend, both seemingly undisturbed by our noisy talk.

The crew purchased the food from the Nepali restaurant on credit. When the delivery boy, about the same age as these young men, appeared on the stairs approximately an hour earlier, they told him they would pay him later. It seemed he had no choice but to comply as he stood in front of the thirteen or so young men who were present and awake and, after a few moments of uncertain waiting, he hesitantly walked back down the stairs. I resisted running after him to give him the money for the food. My decision not to run after the delivery boy, in hindsight, could and perhaps should be read as a retreading of Clifford Geertz's decision *to* run in his canonical essay, "Deep Play: Notes on the Balinese Cockfight." By resisting the urge to run, I placed myself as part of the young circle of b-boys. By laughing at their jokes, mainly crude insults thrown at each other in intimate jest, and by taking drags of the cigarettes they passed around the circle, I reinforced this idea. Some of the young men cracked jokes in Hindi after the delivery boy left. "Why didn't you talk to him in Nepali?" Surabh asked Niraj. "He is your people, after all. He would have listened to you better than he did to us." Niraj told Surabh to fuck off. Another voice chimed in, "For a hundred rupees a day, he doesn't care if we pay the restaurant owners now or later." Everyone laughed, including me.

The long hours of practice, featuring these sorts of homosocial interactions punctuated with jokes and laugher that were often about ethnic difference, girls, or money, were typical days for Niraj, Surabh, and his crew. This embodied practice and masculine sociality, when seen in relationship to the b-boy and party promoter gigs that they ostensibly yielded, can be read as a form of labor. Moreover, when seen against the Nepali delivery boy's job, their play as labor can be seen as something of a disruption of the kinds of laboring opportunities (waiting tables, delivering food, perhaps working at a call center)

that, under most circumstances, are the only jobs available to these young men.[10] This disruption becomes particularly salient if we consider that their decision to pay the owners of the Nepali restaurant later was not based on their collective ability to gather the funds necessary to give money to the delivery boy in the moment but was rather a power play, a means to demonstrate the difference between themselves and their peer who delivered the food.

This disruption, where hip hop–inspired creativity enhanced by social media can earn one a living that does not necessitate taking on a service labor position, recalls the kinds of valorizations of digital age creative and cultural work that emerged in the early twenty-first century. In these accounts, the internet coupled with creative acumen allow for new work opportunities to emerge that are not necessarily tethered to previously existing labor arrangements and thereby liberate the worker from previously limited and limiting livelihood choices.

Certainly, as Niraj, Sunil, and Guru gain employment as club promoters or dancers, they break out of social roles ascribed to them in the new urban labor market. Unlike their parents, uncles, aunts, and even cousins, they are not employed as drivers, restaurant staff, or domestic help. Nor are they pushed to work in mall-based retail stores. Rather, their aspirations and new laboring opportunities are co-created within the popular youth cultural networks that materialize as a result of the surplus capital generated in Delhi over the last decade.

To imagine and theorize their artistic proclivities as labor is to recognize the role of the internet in creating new labor arrangements, as well as to push against the notion that the arts, however subversive they may seem, sit outside capital. It also calls for an appreciation for the embodied, materialized, gendered, and racialized nature of work. After all, who but these young classed and racialized male outsiders could take up hip hop dance as labor in the context of Delhi? Taking this analysis as a starting point, these scenes of creatively embodied movement on rooftops or in parks can be read as what Duffy, in her work on female fashion bloggers, calls aspirational labor. For Duffy, aspirational laborers "seek to mark themselves as creative producers who will one day be compensated for their craft—either directly or through employment in the culture industries."[11] This sort of cultivation of self as labor, as I intimated earlier, is at the heart of the neoliberal discourse that clings to global capital as it flows into developing world contexts. In this paradigm, the market requires human capital and human capital is composed not simply of workers with skills but of individuals who have the capacity to remake themselves and the world in creative (and familiar) ways.

The hustle of hip hop, since its early days, has echoed this idea of market-driven self-making. The notion of the hustle as freedom, nestled within the discourse of hip hop, intertwines financial success with notions of sovereignty. As Robin D. G. Kelley explains, the opportunity for young Black men to turn pleasure, play, and a sense of freedom into labor in the North American context has been premised on the relationship between global economic structures that shrink the labor market and expand poverty in US cities while simultaneously creating the aspirational possibilities for young Black men to inhabit the role of cultural workers who are viable on the market precisely because of the constrained social and economic conditions they represent.[12]

These conditions, of course, require that these cultural workers produce a savvy and creative rendering of self, neighborhood, city, and nation to achieve success in the now global hip hop industry, a rendering that cleaves to and, somewhat paradoxically, subversively disrupts stereotypes of Black urban life. As world-famous hip hop artist Jay-Z, who has sold Brooklyn, New York, and the United States as part and parcel of his own brand image, raps in Kanye West's track "Diamonds from Sierra Leone," "I am not just a business man, I am a business, man."[13] Kelley's analysis, in important ways, holds true for the young men in my study as they aspire toward social and economic success while they struggle with Delhi's rapidly changing landscape of unequal opportunity grounded in social difference.

Aspiration, of course, needs fuel to grow. For Sunil, Guru, and Niraj, the fuel comes not only from the affects of engagement that the rooftop and park sessions bring, as friends gather to endeavor together (see chapter 1), but from the legitimization that paid gigs in the emergent youth culture industry, however small in their recompense, provide. It also comes from the recognition that youthful peers provide in online networks, which in turn creates the opportunities for paid engagements in the youth industry to arise in the first place.

This relationship between recognition and aspiration becomes important as it points to the ways in which the products of labor, in this case their self-fashioning, is the site where the dialectic of future possibility meets the labor one performs to create a desirable self in the present tense. Niraj's job as a party promoter, where he earns approximately ten thousand rupees a month, reflects the kinds of dialectic value that emerges between aspiration and material effort. Niraj and his crew are able to access this kind of work precisely because of their status in online and offline worlds as seasoned practitioners in the scene, the cool kids who can dance and, in some cases, make music. Their practitioner status enables them to labor as party promoters, translating their status on Facebook as hip hop artists into tangible effects.

Club owners hire Niraj and his crew because they recognize that these young people's statuses as cultural producers allow them to influence their online and offline youth networks. Niraj and his crew, in turn, use the networks created through their productive play to fill nightclubs in South Delhi, reaffirming their position as tastemakers, "the innovators behind the trends."[14]

As they stand in front of the clubs handing out flyers or, in some cases, dance for additional pay in the clubs, they legitimize the scene as authentic. Moreover, as they carry out the responsibilities of their roles as party promoter or club dancer, they reveal the ways in which the new labor arrangements in Delhi's youth cultural scene cleave to emergent and enduring racialized, ethnic, gendered, caste, and classed divisions of labor. In this division of labor, Northeastern youth are positioned as party promoters, DJs, and dancers in Delhi's club scene. The bouncers, those who act as security guards, are predominantly Gujjar—an agrarian caste community that lives on the edges of the development that steadily moves southward. Meanwhile the owners of the clubs are elite upper-caste Delhiites, Non-Resident Indians (NRIS), or members of the Indian diaspora who have returned to make Delhi their home in the last decade. Those who attend the parties are groups of young people who represent the diversity of the city. They are composed of the wealthy upper-caste youth who live in the posh gated enclaves of the city, the working-class youth whose parents form the labor pool that drives Delhi's development, and the growing number of internationals who find their way to Delhi from Europe, sub-Saharan Africa, and the Middle East.

The club scene, as it emerges in specific locales of the city—in many cases urban villages that offer the legal loopholes that enable a process of localized gentrification to take root (see chapter 5 for a longer discussion)—also point to the labor and land relationships that new frameworks of aspiration brought about by an influx of capital have engendered. In this political economy, friction between ethnic, classed, and racialized groups unfolds, as Niraj suggests when talking about his interactions with the bouncers. This sort of friction takes place between Gujjar bouncers and Northeastern party promoters who share the space just outside the club venue for hours. It also emerges in verbal disputes and (sometimes) physical altercations between club owners and their staff as well as between state authorities and the new nightlife establishments.

On several nights that I was out with one of the crews I spent time with in Delhi's hip hop scene, I would see the potential for violence emerging as youth from differently situated caste, class, and racialized communities in the city made contact. From the menacing teasing that Niraj and his crew endured from the Gujjar bouncers on a nightly basis, to the fist fights that took place between Northeastern and West African men over perceived affronts, to the violent ejection of patrons on the order of the club owners, the aspirational labor of my participants fed into a youth cultural scene that was founded on various hierarchies reflecting the urban landscape of difference in Delhi. These ethnic, class, and racial hierarchies, similar to my account of the way my participants avoided paying the Nepali delivery boy, point to the way in which capital's rearrangements of economic and social life in Delhi create new forms of status and instability. The violence I witnessed when I went to the late-night parties and after-parties with my participants speaks to another way in which capital is disrupted by difference, even as it creates new frameworks for it to emerge. It also speaks to the ways in which masculinity is cultivated such that ethnic, caste, and class belonging (and difference) are reinforced.

The club scene was only one site where laboring opportunities and their concomitant risks arose for my participants. In the last several years, India's growing youth cultural industry has sought out and curated a homegrown set of images of young people engaging with globally available youth subcultures and, critically, their representations of sociality to engender demand, desire, and consumption. The strategies to accomplish this became clear only after I met two branding agents (whom I mention at the end of the previous chapter), each of whom worked for large multinational marketing and branding agencies who represented a portfolio of multinational corporations. I had several conversations with these branding agents about events they had produced in several cities across India and the marketing philosophy they adhered to, which was shaped in large part by their own personal relationships to youth subcultural worlds and the industry discourse since the late 1990s, which has focused on marketing lifestyles and ways of being in the world rather than specific products. They suggested that there is a strong interest among global brands to produce a sustainable youth market in South Asia and that the development of the youth market requires novel interventions that hinge on locating and cultivating localized youth cultural production of recognizable global youth practices.[15]

To locate youth cultural producers, branding agents took to mining their online and offline networks for possible connections. Similar to my entry and access into Delhi's hip hop scene, the two branding agents I met found an international hip hop practitioner who introduced them to local practitioners in Delhi, Mumbai, and Bengaluru (see chapter 4 for a longer discussion on international hip hop practitioners, whom I call hip hop emissaries, and my engagements with them as gatekeepers in the Delhi scene). To cultivate a youth market, these agents produced events that brought together youth from across the city and that featured hip hop artistic practices—b-boying, graffiti writing, DJing, and MCing—as well as skateboarding and BMX biking. These events' success, of course, relied on the active participation of local skilled practitioners of each of these forms as well as, in some cases, the involvement of international hip hop practitioners, who came to Delhi to experience and participate in its emergent hip hop scene, some of whom I introduce in the next chapter.

These events, the branding agents argued, provide them an opportunity to harvest the audiovisual content necessary to, in the future, promote the brands that had originally sponsored the events. The images and sounds they capture in the events, as a result, become what I call *affective commodities*. They are commodities, in the sense that the audiovisual material has exchange value; and they are affective, in that their value is derived from the capture of "excitement, passion, even a sense of community."[16]

Affect, which I discuss in the introduction in relation to the globally familiar, is a heuristic and theoretical device that has made its rounds in the social sciences and in social theory in the last decade as a way to mark the social force of emotion and the publicness of feeling. While some of the theorizations of affect have called for a prediscursive approach, a way to describe what Brian Massumi has called the intensities that shape action, I am more inclined to think of affect as always already enmeshed in signs.[17] By calling the audiovisual content that is generated an affective commodity, I argue for an attention to the ways in which the semiotic material embedded in a photograph or a video elicits public response. By pointing to the propensity for the audiovisual material to be commodified, the creative play of the young people involved that produces it can be read as free labor. For Terranova, free labor is an apt description for the kinds of blurring between work, leisure, and play that the digital age has created.[18] By "free," Terranova suggests that, by and large, the labor that produces internet-accessible affective commodities is under- or uncompensated.

The long days my participants spent practicing in the park, working on tracks in a makeshift studio, creating an online presence by putting up photos, videos, and so on, with the cognizance that these activities would, at some point in the future, create value for them in their lives, and that some of this value could be economic, demonstrates the kinds of uncompensated labor that are attached to the complex aspirations of people living in the digital age. However, another reading of "free" in relation to labor that I put forward is the capacity for creative work to produce an expression of freedom, a sense or feeling of sovereignty. Terranova urges us to engage with artistically rendered expressions of freedom found in digitally enabled subcultural worlds as always already enmeshed and in the service of capital. However, in my engagements with youth in Delhi's hip hop scene, as I have suggested already and will more explicitly discuss in the pages ahead, I found myself reluctant to subscribe to this sort of totalizing reading of artistic production and grew increasingly interested in the ways in which my participants implicitly and explicitly disrupted the horizons of capital's expansion.

However, before I push against Terranova's reading of art and its complicity with contemporary formations of capital, it is important to recognize the ways in which creative play, as it creates a feeling of embodied freedom for its producers and consumers, does indeed make for a strong case that artistic production and consumer capitalism are in alignment and work to forge unexpected laboring possibilities. Indeed, the sense of freedom that my participants embody in their creative play as work suggests yet another way of describing the labor that my participants engaged in, a labor that focuses on the intangible affects of their productive endeavors. Hardt, Negri, Lazzarato, and, later, the Italian autonomists have referred to this form of work as immaterial labor.[19] Clearly, my participants' labor was by no means solely immaterial. There is nothing immaterial about bodies in motion during long hours of b-boy practice or the interminable standing and waiting that comes with party promotion. However, as these bodies in motion are captured in image or recorded sound, they become products. These products are immaterial insofar as they are affects enmeshed in a series of signifiers that suggest the possibility of freedom from historically wrought limits.

For the young working-class migrants as well as for some of the more economically well-off youth I got to know during my time in Delhi, the opportunity to produce affective commodities that have recognizable exchange value became an important impetus to further develop their skills, expand their networks, and learn how to self-promote through images, text, and sound. After all, the logic goes, what could be better than feeling free and getting paid for selling this feeling in your creative works? For my participants, the internet, then, became not only a social conduit but the way in which the young people in the scene could acquire and further perfect marketable skills that hinged on their ability to perform a version of globality that pitches unfettered possibility in urban India. In some cases, my participants' audiovisual production and circulation of their practices became central to their acquisition of jobs in the culture industry.

For instance, several MCs and dancers told me that club promoters and owners looked at the number of likes they received on their YouTube channels or on their Facebook posts before they hired them for gigs. In this sense, my participants' engagement with hip hop and its forms of practice, as well as with their audiovisual production for social media circulation, can only be read as deeply in tune with the market. Their labor, therefore, can be seen as an instantiation of a twenty-first-century hustle, one that recognizes that the desire to produce a feeling that is marketable is at the center of the new economy. As I argued in the previous chapter, this suggests that, rather than the almost romantic notion of co-optation that Dick Hebdige argued for when writing about the ways in which corporations in Western metropoles made subcultural youth rebellions marketable, we should imagine these young people in Delhi as collaborators who are working in full cooperation with capital's needs.

The implication, of course, is that the immaterial labor they willingly provide creates traces that leave as its productive ends a feeling, a sense of "well-being, excitement, passion" for India's globally aligned youth culture industry.[20] This notion of labor, then, as it is premised on the production of affect, extends beyond curated events where audiovisual content is harvested. It reaches into the private and intimate domains of their lives, the spaces where they socialize, sleep, play, and eat. Indeed, as Lazzarato writes, if we widen the notion of labor to include affect as a viable product, we begin to see several modes of work, which include work inside the private domains of the home.[21] An attention to the private spaces of the home allows us to see labor as a historically gendered category in the way it is used to describe societally meaningful work. A move toward the affective and the relational as labor also allows us to see that what have been designated as leisure activities, creative hobbies, or creative expressions of struggle in the past can now pass as affective and immaterial labor in the digital age. When we connect these creative activities to audiovisual production and circulation on the net, we can begin to see the complex relationship between aspiration, affect, labor, and the digital.

To tie together these relationships more concretely, let us return to the branding agents and the events they produce. Branding agents use the budgets they receive from their high-profile clients to foster the growth and development of a place-specific and highly inclusive youth subcultural scene. They do this in Delhi, and other cities in India, by producing events. These events are a smorgasbord of youth cultural activities that include b-boying, skating, rapping, and graffiti writing. They are often billed as competitions and offer prize money to the winning individuals or groups. These events benefit the young people in Delhi who seriously engage with the practice of subcultural forms, as they offer them venues to practice and gain exposure without having to fight for a claim for space to practice or be seen. However, these events, while providing space, a stage, and even recompense for the competitors who win the sponsored competitions, also act as audiovisual incubators where aesthetically tantalizing scenes of youthful Indian urban cosmopolitanism arise for capture and future circulation.

This quickly becomes obvious when one mills around these events and runs into at least two or three semiprofessional photographers and videographers moving through and documenting the unfolding event. Videographers and photographers represent another job that has emerged as a result of the rise of the creative industries. The young people I met behind the camera for these events were recent graduates from public universities in Delhi that house video, photography, or journalism programs and train their students for media industry jobs.

Branding agents who sponsor these events hire professional and semi-professional photographers and videographers to capture this material for future use, to promote the brands they represent by establishing lasting indexicals—relationships between the image of young people in urban India who are consummate in their youthful crafts and the product(s) they wish to sell. This is done on a much smaller scale in the clubs, bars, and even retail establishments around Delhi that are emerging in key geographic areas for burgeoning youthful lifestyles, whose owners engage in similar strategies. That is, they host events that are vibrant, "cool," and inclusive and hire the youth at the center of the scene to act as promoters to attract crowds. Then they photograph or video their events to promote their club as a hub of the new youth cultural scene emerging in the city.

A close look at urban India's emergent culture industries suggests the further intensification of globally circuited cultural production that diversifies India's offerings of (popular) cultural products beyond, say, the Bollywood juggernaut. This process of diversification seeks to create new links between youth in India and abroad, particularly the diaspora. It also links young people in India under the logic of twenty-first-century "youth," across spatial, ethnic, caste, and gender difference. A central component of this process of market diversification that relies on the suturing of disparate geographies of difference is the production of audiovisual material gleaned from the events that branding agents curate. The events thus serve two purposes. They offer an experience of a universal and equalizing youth culture for all who attend, an experience that is subtly attached to sponsoring brands. The events also offer up the culled audiovisual material of performance for use in future advertising campaigns.

The commodity image, a concept originally developed by Wolfgang Fritz Haug, points to the importance of the "aesthetic in the conversion of use value to exchange value."[22] Arvind Rajagopal, in his essay on the commodity image in the postcolony, stresses that the image cannot be seen outside the commodity itself: "the commodity cannot remain merely economic, and the image only aesthetic."[23] Rather, the commodity and the image are co-constitutive, material and immaterial, inseparable, echoing the notion of indexicality that Jan Blommaert and Piia Varis suggest is inherent in contemporary marketing practices where subjectivity, materiality, and politics collide in the aesthetic.[24] For Mazzarella, in his close study of the Mumbai-based advertising industry in the early postliberalization period, this has meant that advertising in India has to bend its practices to produce commodity images that suture what he refers to as the global and the local, aesthetic renderings that translate globally circulating commodities into viable and marketable products for the local Indian market. The result, he argues, is a quixotic combination of nationalistic and global messaging that is embedded in advertising campaigns designed by the emerging Indian creative class for the Indian middle class.[25] What I would like to consider for a moment is who is currently at the center of the laboring process forging what I call affective commodities, which, unlike the concept of the commodity image, are not focused on the image forms of commodity objects per se but on using the audiovisual capture of youth lifestyle in action to ratify particular products.

While Mazzarella correctly recognizes that the appropriation of "local" images are central to the process of branding for a particular cultural milieu, his ethnographic work focuses on how the expert creative class manufactures value through its circulation of the commodity image, making invisible the immaterial labor that might undergird the production of the image, particularly in our digital present. Aron Arvidsson, in his work on global branding, argues that rather than seeing the creative class as the architects of taste, we must see them as administrators, as bureaucrats.[26] As Paulo Virno notes, the "real productive force becomes not so much the creative class of art directors and advertising executives, but the mostly unemployed mass intellectuality of the urban arts, music, design and fashion scenes."[27]

This assertion, of course, places the immaterial outcomes of the very material and embodied labor of young people at the forefront of capital's expansion, particularly in a country like India where the population is overwhelmingly youthful. The "opportunity" for participation as immaterial labor in this burgeoning youth cultural market becomes particularly important for ethnic and low-caste migrants as well as for international migrants who live in cities like Delhi, as their production of authentic urban cosmopolitan imagery becomes increasingly desirable for those who are charged with the management and extrapolation of mass intellectuality's laboring forms. They effectively (and affectively) produce images of India's cities as world class in their representations of emergent cosmopolitanisms, and, we might add, do so for very little economic remuneration.

If we pay attention to these empirical instances of immaterial labor produced by the largely unemployed and marginalized youth in Delhi's burgeoning culture industries, we can see that the concept of immaterial labor, rather than irreconcilably diminishing the salience of communicative practice, as anthropologists have suggested in their critiques of the concept, enshrines certain forms of these practices as valuable performance.[28] As a result, content, or what I call affective commodities, becomes something more than the images of a b-boy breakin' or an MC rappin' and rests, instead, on a broader range of content of the produced hip hop event: the signs of value that are made by the bodies of the young people who participate in and populate the space where the event takes place. The b-boys' bodies in repose on the side of the dance floor as they wait to perform. The casual homosociality that is on display and subject to capture during the event; the embraces, limbs overlapping onto each other. All of this becomes content, transmuted into viable affective commodities. That is, it is not simply the obvious performance—say the b-boys who are dancing on the stage—but all the images and narratives that are gathered within the particular time and space of the event that become valuable. Critically, this content's value for branding agencies and their corporate sponsors lies in the familiar everydayness of urban youthful life that it produces. Were the branding agents to stage these events in a professional studio or only capture footage and images of the event itself, as opposed to social engagements unfolding on the peripheries of the event, the embeddedness of global youth practice in the everyday would be lost.

For the young people in the scene who participated and were made central to these events, the attention of the camera and the recording crews reinforced their belief that they were already famous; that, because of their exceptionality, whatever kept them in the margins of Delhi's social worlds had been overcome; and that part of the reward was financial gain. Here one can begin to see Marx's classic conception of the commodity as fetish reemerge inside the workings of immaterial labor, when products of these youths' labor, their affective commodity, emerge divorced from the ontology of the body that creates its visual referent and the lifeworld that gives it context. By evoking Marx in this context, we can surmise that young people in Delhi's hip hop scene, as they learn the exchange value of particular performances that create desired affective commodities, work to perfect these performances in ways that obscure their relationship with the city as particular subjects. That is, laboring as hip hop artists allows them to create a distance from the issues around gender, caste, and class that impact them as youthful subjects growing up in the city of Delhi.[29]

Yet to leave it here would be too simple, as what I have suggested would lead us to conclude that global hip hop's appearance among nonelite youth in Delhi, and the ways in which it disciplines them into new forms of laboring practice linked to processes of subject formation, creates homogenous conditions of unfreedom—that to study Delhi is no different from, say, studying Berlin, insofar as capital is structuring the same degrees of possibility and impossibilities in both contexts. Of course, the simple reaction to this sort of argument would be to champion the putative agency that hip hop forms as it creates new opportunities for social, political, and economic engagement, but I think the more subtle task at hand is to show how global forms, as they travel, reveal a far more complex context for everyday life that is specific to time and place and that evokes particular historical struggles that are intertwined with the story of capital as it continues its adventures through time and space. Here I think Aihwa Ong's argument—that studies of globalization that focus on either impositional capitalist formations or the resistant (and politicized) subaltern miss important facets of how globally circulating discourses are producing distinct and historically situated notions of personhood, urbanity, and nation—becomes an important space to situate the concerns of this chapter and, indeed, of this book.[30]

While affective commodities traveling through particular circuits work to inculcate desires that are valuable to the market, the audiovisual material I have discussed is also put to work in several other capacities: to create relationships across borders and difference and to engender various relationships with the city. This, of course, suggests that the self-fashioning projects of young people and their effects can exceed and potentially disrupt the market's demand for a particular kind of immaterial laboring practice and the subjectivities that undergird it. Sometimes I observed these disruptions as explicitly political acts that unfolded during a corporate-sponsored event. More often, they were embedded in the everyday contexts I described earlier in this chapter. These instances of disruption, I argue, reinvest the globally familiar with political force. In what follows, I analyze an event that reveals the ways in which hip hop actors in the scene, even as they labor to make hip hop part of their economic future, hold the possibility of actively disrupting hip hop as labor. I use my analysis of this event as a springboard to offer some final thoughts on the globally familiar and its relationship to gender, caste, labor, play, and the politics of freedom in the digital age.

Corporate Hip Hop and the Disruption of the Affective Commodity

When I arrived at the South Delhi college campus in early March 2014, where a globally known sporting goods brand was sponsoring a b-boying, graffiti, and skateboarding event, there were crowds of young men and women, many of them students who attended the college, milling around the booths set up by the brand that displayed their latest footwear and clothing offerings. At the small stage in the center of the courtyard stood a few b-boys, many of whom I knew from Khirki and Humayunpur and others I had briefly met when I attended b-boying events, corporate sponsored or not, across the city. As they waited to compete in the tournament, some of these young men were practicing their moves. Most were leaning against the wall and looking outward, posing in their baggy jeans, graphic printed T-shirts, and their backward snapback hats as they waited for the event to begin. Over in another corner, a small quarter pipe had been set up and a European skater, tattooed with board in hand, was quietly talking to a few young Indian men, presumably college attendees, who had encircled and were raptly listening to him. Behind the product booths there stood a "graffiti wall," made out of cloth stretched over steel poles, where a few graffiti artists were quietly spraying large pieces side by side, ventilator masks strapped on, several cans of paint neatly stacked in plastic bins by their side. In the back of the main event there was a stage, where, prior to the b-boy competitions and the skating demonstration, there would be a talent show, showcasing performers who attended the college.

Throughout my initial walk through the event space, I ran into young men and women I knew, b-boys and b-girls, graffiti artists, a couple of DJs and MCs, as well as some young men and women who simply passed time with their friends in the scene. Niraj and several members of his crew were among the twenty-five or so young people I awkwardly exchanged hip hop–styled greetings with. This greeting consisted of a handshake followed by a hug, neither of which were as firm or emphatic as what I grew up with in New York or as the greetings I would receive when I went to Khirki to meet the East and West African students, shop owners, and refugees I knew (none of whom made it to these sorts of events). These awkward hugs with the young men and women were no doubt filmed by the official content collectors, who were busily milling around the crowd taking photos and talking with a few of the participants on the side.

Before long, the b-boy battle started. Several crews I knew from Khirki and Humayunpur competed against crews I had never seen before, hailing from the far corners of the city. Some of the crews came in T-shirt uniforms that announced their crew affiliation; however, most marked affiliation to their crews by simply wearing similar colors. The event was judged by three older b-boys from the Delhi scene who would rate the quality of the contestants and promote the winner to the next round of the competition. The judges, in contrast to the contestants, who would compete for prize money, were paid for their roles as arbiters of quality, another work opportunity that many young b-boys aspired to as they gained fame and notoriety as dancers. The winners on that day were a crew from East Delhi. Before the open mic commenced and rappers and poets in the scene were invited to the stage, the paid MC of the event, a hip hop personality who had some fame in the Delhi scene, gave a short lecture on what hip hop was to the crowd, made up largely of college student spectators of the event.

To begin his public pedagogy, he picked a young girl in the crowd and asked her name. She responded, "Deepti." "All right, Deepti, do you know what is real hip hop culture?" She answered, hesitantly, "I don't know; must be dance derived from some country." "OK," he repeats, "dance form from some country, do you think it's right?" There is a pause, a short silence. He continues, "OK, let me tell you what is hip hop culture, it's a five-elemental thing. It's a creative five-elemental thing." The recapitulation of the universal tenets of hip hop, a formulation that I heard repeated in almost every hip hop gathering in Delhi, corporate sponsored or not, set these events apart from the kinds of guerrilla performances I described in my chapter on illicit b-boying in the shopping mall across the street from Khirki. Because there was room for a narrative explication, the aesthetics of the performances were given some context. In these retellings of the five-element discourse, the hip hop doyens who took the charge to educate their audience on hip hop reflected a kind of universalist take on its discourse. This universalist approach stressed practice and discipline and was in keeping with the corporate context in which it was delivered. (I discuss the competing visions of hip hop—universalist on the one hand, historical and particular on the other—in the next chapter, on international hip hop practitioners in the Delhi scene, and their interest in participating in, and capitalizing on, the Delhi scene.) There was little room to narrate the historical or political significance of hip hop.

When the leader of the crew that won the competition—Dhruv, a young Dalit man in his twenties who was originally from a small village on the Uttar Pradesh and Bihar border—got the mic, he decided to rap in English. However, prior to sharing his poetry, he began with his own statement about hip hop, one that steered away from the abstract and apolitical five-element discourse on hip hop offered by the MC, in favor of a universalist, political one. "Yesterday I asked someone what is hip hop. He answered, 'a guy, a Black guy who is rapping is called hip hop.' Yo, hip hop is not that. Hip hop is worldwide. It's in him [*pointing to the MC*], it's in that DJ, it's in me, it's all in you [*pointing to the crowd*]. The difference is that we are, we're just attracted to the commercial stuff . . . but we don't understand what is hip hop. All right, I don't want any music [*pointing to the DJ*]." Here Dhruv took a moment to point out that real hip hop is universal—"It's in him, it's in that DJ, it's in me, it's all in you"—and cannot be found in commercial "stuff." Then he began his rhyme: "I am just going to say the truth and the fact. It's a rhyme. First of all, who all know sixteenth of December 2012? Raise up your hand if you know this date. If you know this date FUCKING [*loud voice*] raise your hands up." The crowd started to nervously shuffle when he raised his voice and cursed. From my vantage point, standing on a small wall with a better view of the scene, I could see the police start to slowly walk over to the crowd. The organizer of the event emerged from the merchandise booth. A crackle of nervous energy filled the air. Dhruv continued, "Anybody in the store knows? What is sixteenth December 2012? Nobody knows that. Right. Because we are all commercial fucking people. Because we listen to Honey Singh and after that, we forget what is happening. You know, we are posting our pics on Facebook, 'yo, how I'm looking?' Nah. Well, let me say something."[31]

Sixteenth of December 2012, a Sunday became doomsday for a young
    pretty woman
All went good until 9:30pm when she took a bus for her residence.
No paranoid mind along with her man.
It was the wrong bus and the wrong prayer.
Suddenly things changed and she was attacked.

Her man was hit by the rod. Damn.

She moved to save her man till then she was grabbed.

By six faithless wimps . . . when the incident hit the news channels,
India was left numb.

After the brutal gang rape the girl was [in a] coma

When people, when people, when people, when people will come out
now to protest for your fun.

Now you're behind the bars, let India decide what about your son?

But wait, there is one more bar about the Indian government scars.

Twenty-second of December India Gate, when people turned out to
protest for her scars.

Thousands of people gathered grieving for the incident, thousands of
police across the park.

India was quiet and calm, piece in the arms.

Youth was divine, no sentiments of crime.

All for the justice to change the system, to change the dime.

When the police got the order for another crime. *Lathi* charge and
gas proved the *goonda raj*.[32]

Sending a message to the government through my art.

She could be my sister.

She could be my new.

She could be my one. I'll burn you.

She wasn't for fun.

Snatch your soul for all that you've done. I want to kill you.

But that won't change the destiny of that girl. I want to kill you.

But that won't bring her stars and pearls . . . I cannot believe no
Anna, no Sonia they were on the streets.[33]

They were not on the streets, but that is fucking politics.

You guys agree? You guys agree! [*louder*]

You guys agree? You guys agree? You didn't listen, right.

It doesn't matter to me because we are like this.

In his forceful voice that evoked and (re)narrated the highly publicized
and politicized Delhi rape case, Dhruv immediately changed the tone of
the corporate-sponsored event by telling a political story *as* hip hop.[34] Prior
to his ascension on stage, what was a tame affair where hip hop's forms
were performed alongside a skating demonstration and a talent show, and
where hip hop was explained, abstractly, as knowledge, suddenly, through
Dhruv's intervention, became a political space. Capitalism and its violent

effects, evoked in his condemnatory introduction of himself and the crowd to whom he spoke as "commercial fucking people," are brought together in his poetry. Dhruv's voice and tone, while in English and pitched to a youthful, decidedly middle-class, college-going audience, quickly alerted the police, who were otherwise an innocuous presence in the event. They pushed toward the stage. While their lathis were previously at their sides, they were now in their hands. The crowd, right from the moment Dhruv began his introduction to the end of his first verse, nervously stood in anticipation. Some dispersed, moving away from the main stage and back toward the area where the talent show had taken place. The branding agent and organizer of the event anxiously paced in front of the merchandise tent. Dhruv, in his personal, poetic, and passionate narrativization of the rape—which had taken place many months before and had fallen out of circulation in the media—by condemning the young men who were responsible for the attack and the politicians who were not "on the streets" in the same breath, single-handedly brought politics into a corporate-sponsored hip hop event that was seemingly envisioned as apolitical and "merely" youth cultural. Moreover, in his public grappling with the Delhi rape case through the lens of hip hop, he revealed an acute awareness of his gendered position, an awareness that several of the young men in my study articulated in the months that followed the deep rupture that this event produced as it stirred, through the mediatized sensationalism that had followed, the collective anxieties of the city. These mediatized accounts of the rape case, as I suggested in the preface, had singled out young, underemployed men from low-caste positions who live on the fringes of the city.[35] Dhruv's articulation of the rape case in this context, where his play as labor was being rewarded in monetary recompense, was his way of resisting the pressure to reduce his hip hop practice to labor, by grappling with the current political issues of his time that focused on violence against women. It also demonstrated his reflexive resistance to his own vulnerable position as a young Dalit male in the face of the public backlash that followed the Delhi rape case, which cast the violent Other, the perpetrator of crimes against women, as the low-caste and underemployed male.

While the previous example reveals the ways in which the production of the affective commodity can be disrupted in situ, Dhruv's following verse perhaps even more powerfully punctuates the economic and social conditions of (im)possibility that young men like Dhruv struggle with, and the kinds of disruptions to labor and capital that emerge when their narratives are enunciated in hip hop's lyrical forms.

Being commercial is not my aim
Underground fame is what my game
What you looking up is brown kid's name
Working in call centers is not my shift
Created my words, life is a dick
I am not the one you're gonna look up at
in *Dance India*,[36] dance shit.
Underground battles I rocked my [*inaudible*]
Worked in McDonald's
Cleaned the dish
Served French burgers, teas and drinks
My reality is beyond what I spit
I'm a b-boy with a beautiful hist
What I think is what I hit, I'm an artist
You might think that you've struggled a lot
But you don't need the work because it's still slot

In this next verse, Dhruv tersely discussed the realities of work in relation to his passionate engagement with hip hop. Evoking call centers and shifts in McDonald's, Dhruv called attention to the kinds of working opportunities that are putatively available to him and to the other young men and women in similar economic and social positions who share his stage while also revealing the tensions between the fame and economic reward that are made possible in his practice of hip hop. By suggesting that underground fame is his aim and that producing commercial hip hop is not, Dhruv straddles the tense middle that emerges when there is a recognition that his engagements with hip hop produce laboring opportunities but that this is, perhaps, not what he is after. What becomes critical here are the ways in which Dhruv draws on hip hop's poetic forms to imbricate his personal experience with political critique and thus create an experienced aesthetic that is not free floating and easily taken up in the projects of others but is firmly embedded in his experience of the sensible. The distinction between hip hop's poetics and its dance or visual forms becomes important in this case because it suggests that for "free" labor to retain its capacity to enact a sense of sovereignty, to disrupt capital, it must retain the capacity to tell the stories of those it represents rather than inhere to others' narratives of value. For an aesthetically wrought politics to emerge within capital's workings, its forms cannot be so malleable.

In some ways, Dhruv's somewhat exceptional enactment of a more overt political subjectivity is a reminder that, for most of the young people I met in Delhi, hip hop offered an opportunity for self-fashioning that scrambled social norms in ways that were not about changing the system but about changing one's own opportunities within the system. This decidedly post-modernist attunement to the world demonstrates how, as David Graeber ironically notes, no one, certainly not the state that has abdicated its responsibility to its subjects, is responsible for social ills and adaption; that it is the individual's responsibility decidedly aligned my youthful interlocutors' hip hop play with neoliberal capital's workings.[37] This alignment, which I discuss as labor in this chapter, is central to understanding the globally familiar in the twenty-first century, as belonging and participation are inextricably linked to the capacity that subjects have to produce and circulate themselves, and the city they live in, as imminently desirable. Hip hop and its postmodern ethos of the hustle provided my diverse participants a powerful means to sign themselves as gendered subjects in ways that offered them access to youth cultural work in a city that is collectively striving to locate itself in the global ecumene. Yet Dhruv's poetry suggests that hip hop's postmodern discourse that valorizes the hustle, despite its obvious alignments with neoliberalism, still holds the possibility to provide the means to disrupt capital. Moreover, Dhruv's passionate delivery of his poetry offers us a glimpse of youthful aspiration in Delhi that longs for something different, even if its political force is as ephemeral as a singular performance.

Once Dhruv surrendered the mic, the mood slowly reverted back to the tame event it was prior to his ascension on the stage. The MC asked that everyone gather around the quarter pipe for a skating demonstration in half an hour, while many of the b-boys who competed in the event continued dancing on stage. Some called me over to take pictures of them. I passed the next half hour taking photos of members of the crews from Khirki and Humayunpur before I jumped into an auto and made my way through the thickening late afternoon South Delhi traffic.

Months later, I ran into Dhruv in front of a grassroots b-boy and poppin' and lockin' jam for dancers run by a young man in the scene. This jam, unlike the corporate event or the mall, was not open to the public, and there was a small fee to enter. None of the young men from the Khirki or Humayunpur crews came, which I suspect was because of a combination of the entrance fee, the lack of prize money, and the absence of cameras. It was also partly because of internal feuds or "beefs" between crews in the scene, where crews will not attend an event if a rival crew are the organizers. As we waited for the organizer to set up his accounting system, a beaten-up laptop where he recorded the emails of the entrants, the fees collected, and so on, Dhruv and I talked about b-boying, life, and the future.

As we dodged the motorcycles that constantly whizzed by us in the alley in front of the basement space where we would eventually make our way inside, Dhruv told me that he was getting nervous that he would not be able to compete for prize money for much longer in the competitions because his body was getting older.[38] Clenching his jaw as he spoke a mixture of Hindi and English, he began to talk about ways he could make his living in the future doing the thing he loved most: hip hop. Eventually he asked me for advice on how he should pursue these strategies without losing his first love—b-boying. He was unsure that day—not the figure he cut on stage months prior, when he brought the force of his personal experiences, imbricated in his artistic practice, to bear on Delhi's hip hop scene.

We discussed potential futures and work opportunities that would allow him to continue doing what he loved. I suggested that perhaps he should go into video or music production, as these industries would continue to grow in the city and country. Or perhaps he should teach dance, I limpidly offered, knowing that everything I suggested in the way of career pursuits required capital investment in the form of training, equipment, space, and so on. I told him about my work with a few b-boys and MCs in the city with video; how I had been working with them to make their own music videos; and how, as a result of our initial digital collaborations, we were now working on making narrative films. Perhaps, I said, not quite sure if I had the time, we could do something together in the future; maybe I could work with him so that he could learn video production. Throughout my, in retrospect, rather insipid talk, he simply clenched his jaw and listened.

Months later, I saw on his Facebook page, underneath a photo of several b-boys from the Delhi scene, young men and women from different ethnic communities, castes, and class positions, the following pithy line written by him: "I am happy with my life, haven't choose any career, I dance, I breathe, flowing with the life's groove."

One Sunday in 2014, I waited on the corner of the main road in front of Nehru Place, the veritable technology mecca of Delhi where white-market goods in established shops compete with gray-market stalls that line the edges of the central plaza in the interior courtyard.[1] I had lost my phone the day prior in an auto rickshaw so I had to rely on the word of Rahul that he would meet me that morning on a predesignated corner in the market. Rahul had immigrated to Switzerland as a child from Delhi. He had returned to the city a few years prior and gained some fame as an aerosol (graffiti) artist. He was approximately twenty-six when I met him and had been living in a house his parents owned close to Khirki that he had transformed into something of a youth hostel for European travelers. When I was first introduced to him at a small party on the roof of his house, he mentioned that he wanted to look for a good wall to do a new graffiti piece.[2] He said he was open to speaking with me about the history of hip hop in Delhi and my more pressing interest regarding hip hop's infiltration into Delhi's working-class migrant enclaves if I was willing to join him on his mission the next day.

After standing for more than a half hour on the corner waiting for him, I started to become a bit restless. The market was quiet on this particular Sunday morning. Most of the shops were shuttered and an uncharacteristic hush covered its normally cacophonous plazas. I was about to give up when a small, beat-up van came tearing around the corner with Rahul's head poking out of the window. I quickly jumped in and found myself engulfed in a hip hop soundtrack. Rahul nodded his head and mouthed the words of a German rapper on the track he was playing from a makeshift stereo system in his vehicle consisting of two portable speakers precariously sitting on the dashboard wired to a beat-up smart phone. I kept waiting for the speakers to lurch off the dashboard and onto the floor.

We first drove to find parking, listening to music as we careened through various small streets surrounding the market. Neither of us said a word. Once we parked, we headed to a coffee shop Rahul suggested on the top floor of a building inside Nehru Place. It ended up being one of the ubiquitous Café Coffee Day franchises found all over India.[3] As soon as we found a seat at one of the café's garish orange tables, he launched into a monologue about his life as an Indian growing up in Switzerland, his forays into hip hop in the city of Zurich, the history of hip hop in Delhi, and the current happenings in the Delhi hip hop scene. I had to scramble to turn on my voice recorder and interject the purpose of my research and, with due diligence, obtain his voluntary consent for participation. Neither the technological fumbling nor the ethical posturing on my part distracted Rahul as he related the history of hip hop in Delhi that, according to him, started in 1991 when a Delhi-based DJ first started playing hip hop in the small, elite clubs of South Delhi after going to the United States to pick up the necessary vinyl.[4]

He then began to tell me about the contemporary moment: the inclusion of a larger base of practitioners who hailed from the working-class urban villages of the city, the role of the internet in spreading hip hop throughout urban India, and the incredible promise that the Delhi scene had to put India on the global hip hop map (reiterating and reaffirming what I already knew). He finally grabbed my attention when he started to discuss the role that he, other members of the Indian diaspora, and several Europeans, most notably Germans, have had in developing the contemporary underground practice scene in Delhi, particularly around graffiti writing, b-boying, and turntablism.

To illustrate his point, he described his role in organizing the Indo-German Hip Hop Project, which was conceived of and implemented by German aerosol artists and turntablists in 2012 and has continued in various cities across India. The project draws on the resources of the Goethe Institut—a German cultural institution that according to its website is dedicated to presenting contemporary "German culture" in India—to work with up-and-coming graffiti artists and b-boys in India's underground hip hop scene.[5]

His monologue started out brightly with a lot of hopeful talk about hip hop's growth in Delhi specifically and in India more broadly; the necessary role that international practitioners have in cultivating hip hop in India; and the role that funding organizations, like the Goethe Institut, have in supporting their efforts. However, his words turned gloomy when he began to discuss how the projects under the banner of the Indo-German Hip Hop Project were interrupted by some of what he proclaimed was negativity brought on by other international hip hop practitioners involved in Delhi's scene.

There was a lot of hate and friction created in [Delhi's] graffiti scene [by those coming from outside, from the United States] and hip hop is based on peace, unity, fun. We, in Europe, go over a piece if we can do something better. It just shows your character. Then the [Delhi] kids started going over people's pieces because they saw the older guys [from the United States] doing it. The kids we were working with in Delhi. So, I immediately noticed that there was a negative influence from US-based teachers coming over. They came from the West and brought this with them. The whole hip hop scene was starting to get a negative influence. Not from Peter [a German aerosol artist], who was really bringing a positive influence. He got these kids down here from a crew in Berlin; they are neutral kids, they love everyone, they are really talented. So, around the time this project was happening, this girl from the US kept going over other people's pieces. So, finally, we were at the Begumpur hall of fame.[6] I was with this guy who is also from Germany, who does street art. And I saw this girl from the US tagging over everyone's piece. And one of the kids [from a Khirki-based crew], Multan, had tagged over a German guy's piece. So, I saw this and I couldn't control my anger. If she [the girl from the United States] is representing like this, this is not the right way to do this, going over people's pieces. . . . Then [the Indian American MC from the United States, who is the boyfriend of the girl going over everyone's pieces] said, "Man, you are from Europe, man. You don't know shit. We're from America, man, where hip hop started. This is where hip hop originated. You are from Europe. We do 'throw ups' over pieces and don't give a shit. So shut the fuck up, you don't know what graffiti is." I didn't say anything. I thought if I talk sense to a fool he might call you foolish. Then I heard Javan [an Indian American b-boy in the scene] was talking about me. He said, "You know Rahul, he's a rich dude. He's not really street enough." You know, it hurt my feelings. I was not born with a gold spoon in my mouth but I had to work for what I have. . . . I realized that [the Indian American MC's] actual agenda is to show this image of India to sell his album. That when I figured out, "Whoa, he wants to stand in front of a bunch of poor Indian kids to show that is what I am supporting. He is really good at enacting a political stance. He is more American than he is Indian."

This chapter concerns itself specifically with the ways in which returning Indian diasporic and European hip hop emissaries like Rahul, Javan, and Peter are positioned and position themselves as key contributors to the scene, and as vital links to a global hip hop nation. Picking up on the previous chapter's focus on labor and work opportunities in the globally familiar, I discuss how hip hop emissaries see the young men in Delhi's hip hop scene, seek to capitalize on their creative endeavors, and, in turn, offer these young men incentives—both material and symbolic—to align with them. I use the term *hip hop emissaries* to mark the almost religious zeal with which practitioners from abroad bring in their enthusiasm to help hip hop grow in India. I also use the term *hip hop emissaries* to signal the kinds of support, financial and otherwise, that some of these actors get from organizations, like the Goethe Institut and other more informal hip hop networks, to promote hip hop in India.[7]

As hip hop emissaries arrive with a proselytizing passion to India—drawn in by digitally circulating accounts of a nascent hip hop scene in Delhi, Mumbai, and other cities—they bring with them well-rehearsed and strongly felt ideas of what they believe hip hop and an idealized hip hop practitioner to be. Of course, emissaries also bring with them their skills, networks, and material resources. Indeed, as they aspired to represent themselves to others as key actors in an Indian and Delhi hip hop scene, they needed to demonstrate that they were capable practitioners: b-boys, turntablists, graffiti writers, and the like. They also had to explicitly offer something—knowledge, material things, their networks—to establish themselves as figures who could potentially leave their mark on the scene for posterity.

Yet it was their biographically situated ideologies they articulated while engaging with Delhi practitioners and other emissaries that allowed them to position themselves in relation to a Delhi hip hop scene as vital links to a globally dispersed hip hop nation.[8] The ideologies expressed by actors from abroad produced competing visions of what hip hop is and who can be "authentic" hip hop practitioners. For instance, Rahul's argument that hip hop is a positive force was a means to claim an ideological position about hip hop connected to Europe (and his experiences there as a graffiti writer) in order to substantiate his position in the Delhi hip hop scene. "Positive," in Rahul's estimation, was related to hip hop's ability to transcend difference, to act as a universal that connected urban Indian young people to the global. Equally, his claim that American hip hop heads were negative, political, and only concerned about money was a way to differentiate himself from a particular way of engaging with and imagining hip hop that he located in North America. How do ideologies, like the ones Rahul articulated that day in Nehru Place, describe and deploy globally familiar understandings of racialized, gendered, and classed difference? How do they discursively position and digitally render Delhi's hip hop practitioners as gendered and racialized subjects, and the spatial communities they live in as 'hoods, slums, and the like? How did Delhi hip hop practitioners respond to and rearticulate (or contradict) these situated ideologies?

In what follows, I pay close attention to two particular ideological stances that emissaries articulated in various interactional settings in Delhi. The first, expressed by (and about) Indian American emissaries, could be considered a decolonial hip hop. This ideological articulation stresses that hip hop authenticity is rooted in the lived experiences of social, economic, and political marginalization produced and legitimated in colonial encounters and perpetuated in current postcolonial national contexts. In this vision, only low-caste, religious, or ethnic Others living in the "slums" of urban India are the rightful heirs to hip hop. Moreover, this hip hop imaginary suggests that a hypermasculine and aggressive way of being in the world was a legitimate, even necessary, means to represent oneself as a subaltern hip hop practitioner. In this version, the rightful heirs to hip hop—those who have been in the margins—always have to hustle because it is all about getting what is rightfully theirs in terms of material recompense.

The second hip hop ideology, articulated by European and Indian European emissaries, could be described as a universalist position. This ideological stance stresses the democratic possibility of hip hop practices; hip hop can be rightfully taken up by anyone. In this take, hip hop is ecumenical: a way to bridge difference through shared practice. This hip hop ideology stressed a respectable and inclusive way of being in the world by privileging its undifferentiating practices. Money, in this ideological framework, is secondary to practice. Real hip hop is free and freely shared. Anyone can MC, write graffiti, or dance, and all are welcome. In a nutshell, they subscribe to what KRS-One of Boogie Down Productions once rapped: "I'm not superman, because anybody can, or should be able, to rock a turntable, grab da mic, plug it in, and begin."[9]

The key premise I work with in this chapter is that while digital media circulations offer Delhi hip hop practitioners various takes on hip hop's discourse on masculinity, urbanity, race, and money, face-to-face interactions with hip hop emissaries amplify and make visceral these understandings. In short, emissaries bring with them a crackling, tangible, in-the-flesh understanding of what hip hop is and can be in urban India, and what it means to be hip hop. Emissaries, in this sense, are the embodied familiars summoned through the creative online and offline play of Delhi hip hop heads. Delhi practitioners' interactions with emissaries spur the reproduction of particular understandings of gender, race, ethnicity, and class within the context of Delhi and through the lens of global hip hop.

An attention to these emissaries' hip hop ideological stances allows us to track and trace the way in which ideologies travel and are deployed, debated, and find form in specific relations as well as in digital representations. As importantly, an attention to these two hip hop ideologies across various interactions allows us to see how Delhi practitioners legitimate themselves with the various emissaries they encountered and within the ideological frameworks they espoused. Indeed, Delhi hip hop practitioners had to navigate these geographically and historically tethered ideologies as they reached out to emissaries and sought to pull them into their lives. The "right" hip hop emissary, no doubt, could act as an access point, a node in a larger network, by which to forge new relationships or acquire necessary skills, knowledge, and things. To attract the persistent attention of a chosen hip hop emissary, to be in relationship with one over time, required a particular kind of performance that relied not simply on the perfection of one's hip hop skills but on the ways in which those skills tied back to particular understandings of what it means to *be* hip hop.

For instance, Multan, in the story that Rahul told me, aggressively crossed out Peter's graffiti piece at the Begumpur hall of fame. One interpretation of his move to cross out the piece—certainly the interpretation Rahul was suggesting in his narration of events—is that Multan sought to establish a relationship with the Indian American graffiti writer and her boyfriend by demonstrating he had learned a particular masculine, aggressive, and unapologetic way of being hip hop that they would recognize and approve. Multan's move was risky. By potentially ingratiating himself with one set of emissaries (the Indian American couple), he was literally crossing out the possibility of developing a relationship with others (Peter and his German crew).

In this instance, the globally familiar is not only the semiotic move that Multan deploys to convey meaning but the ideology that Rahul points to that surrounds the gesture, an ideology that indexes what it means to "be real" as a hip hop practitioner. This ideology, shaped by media flows and transformed into serious play as a result of the interventions of hip hop emissaries, was made explicit in the Delhi hip hop scene when competing interests were brought together during moments like the one Rahul narrated about the events at the Begumpur hall of fame. The situation that Rahul described is precisely what Stuart Hall would call the "micro-political context of the popular."[10]

As Hall rightly argues, "what matters is not the intrinsic or historically fixed objects of culture but the state of play in cultural relations."[11] What Hall suggests, and what Rahul's testimony reveals, is that hip hop is not a fixed cultural object, nor is hip hop's "realness" an achievable state. Rather, what becomes clear is that in each of these actors' social performances, there emerge distinct historically situated ideologies that they deploy about themselves and hip hop as they seek to stamp their imprimatur on the nascent hip hop scene in India.[12] The micropolitical context is thus revealed in the ways hip hop is inhabited and articulated by emissaries and the young men they seek to influence in Delhi's scene. What is at stake is a legitimate claim to belonging within what actors in the scene collectively imagined as a global hip hop nation and a Delhi hip hop scene.

These ideological performances, however, were not just familiar because they relate to debates regarding authenticity within hip hop worlds in various geographies. They index complicated transnational relations concerning gender, race, class, urbanity, and, ultimately, the extraction of value across postcolonial geographies. In other words, these traveling ideologies index a global politics of difference that is "bigger than hip hop" and that shapes the spatial and social worlds of youth in various geographical locations, including Delhi.[13]

Ideologies, Authenticity, and the Politics of the Familiar

The very term *ideology*, as Marx remarks, suggests a disembodied abstraction, ideas that can never quite get pinned down and are not materialized in any sort of form. This type of musing in abstraction, he argues in his classic indictment of the young German philosophers of religion in his day, does not allow us to see the ways in which beliefs, ideas, and theories that circulate in narratives about the world dialectically emerge *from* social forms and the material practices on which they are founded. In Marx's words, "The production of ideas, of conceptions, of consciousness, is at first directly interwoven with the material activity and material intercourse of men, the language of real life."[14] That is, ideas and ideologies are always in perpetual translation, filtered through the substance of embodied experience and material activity.

In hip hop scholarship, the term *authenticity* has been used to describe the ideological positions that global practitioners take on with regard to what constitutes real hip hop and a real hip hop practitioner.[15] The term *authenticity* can be seen as a corollary to *ideology*, as both suggest a strong, shared belief about the way in which a world and a subject is (and should be) constituted. These concepts share a predilection for pointing to their own fissures and impossibilities. The debate that Rahul shared with me with regard to right practice around tagging and writing over other people's graffiti art is a good example of the kinds of ideological baggage that surround what constitutes "authentic" hip hop. For Rahul, "real" or authentic graffiti artists do not tag over other people's work if they cannot do something better. In Rahul's estimation, it was the quality of the work that is of utmost importance. This strong sentiment, of course, relies on a fixed conception of quality where "real" graffiti is evident and recognizable. For those Rahul was in debate with, however, "real" graffiti artists tag over the work of those they do not deem "real" enough to *be* hip hop. It was not the quality of the piece that was in question but whether the artist could be considered real. These competing understandings produce a contradiction around what qualifies as real hip hop: the art that is produced or the artist who produces it.[16]

As we sat and talked over coffee, Rahul recounted that he was told by Indian American practitioners that authentic hip hop emerges from a quintessentially American experience of class and race. The statement Rahul recounted centralizes the Black American struggle as hip hop, and hip hop as inextricably tethered to the geographically locatable struggles of the African diaspora in the Americas. Real hip hop is American and Black and is produced by those who can lay an ontological claim to both. A contradiction arises: How is the Indian American hip hop emissary arguing that he and others like him have a legitimate claim to the Black American experience and to hip hop?

The Indian American MC who deployed this tactic with Rahul, in his lyrics and in the popular press, argues for an origin story of hip hop that includes immigrant experiences in the United States to rectify this contradiction. In so doing, he underscores hip hop as a discourse that links the experience of non-White, formerly colonized people in the Americas. "Real" hip hop, in this sense, legitimizes and is legitimized by those who have similar experiences of racialized and classed marginalization in the United States (and

Canada). Hip hop thus becomes a practice of solidarity in North America and, by extension, anywhere colonialism has impacted life.

Indeed, several of the Indian American hip hop practitioners I met, most notably the Indian American b-boy Javan, dubbed themselves organizers of the political sort whose work was to create new forms of solidarity among those who have been oppressed by (Western) history. Their partially articulated notions of hip hop as a social movement, an idea that lives in Afrika Bambaataa's and the Zulu Nation's notions of hip hop as a liberatory epistemology or in KRS-One's notion of hip hop as moving knowledge, became the means to articulate the historical connections between contemporary postcolonial subjects' lifeworlds and the effects of colonialism.[17] Their ideological sensibilities hinged on a knowledge of hip hop as a socially conscious art form that is steeped in African diasporic history. Their understandings reiterate scholarship that has pointed out the (re)emergence of Blackness as a category that creates solidarities between new and old African and South Asian diasporas in the United Kingdom, Canada, and the United States, even as it also produces tensions between them.[18] Their version of hip hop historicity also points to hip hop scholarship that discusses the ways in which hip hop's musical, dance, and visual forms have created a shared vocabulary to make visible a globally shared experience of inequality as a result of colonization (I pick this conversation up in chapter 6 when I discuss the ways in which hip hop creates connections [and fractures] among Delhi's racialized and marginalized youth).[19]

What is more, Indian Americans returning as hip hop emissaries did not just articulate their hip hop legitimacy in India as part of their diasporic legacy but imagined their historical connection to India vis-à-vis hip hop. As one Indian American MC poignantly notes in an interview he conducted for an online news magazine, "The craziest part is that hip hop culture is what brought me to India. It wasn't Sikhism or Indian classical music. I was tired of looking for brown folk making hip hop in North America and I found them all in here."[20] Hip hop, for this MC, allowed for a contemporary connection across contexts between South Asia and South Asian diasporic subjects that did not rely on historical cultural markers of belonging such as religious affiliation, cultural practice, or geographical belonging but on the millennial term *Brown folk*, a social category that has come to prominence in transnational South Asian digital popular culture.[21]

The category *Brown*—indexed on Facebook, Twitter, Instagram, and YouTube circulations—is one that articulates popular cultural connections and shared experiences between South Asian diasporic youth and digitally connected young people growing up in urban South Asia. It is a term that cuts across religious, caste, linguistic, or national belonging. To some degree, it does the same work the term *Desi* does for a previous generation of diasporic and South Asian urban elite subjects but explicitly rejects the linguistic and regional politics that Desi suggests.[22] Brown or Brown folk can also be read as markers of identification that are in constant conversation with global circulations of Blackness and Whiteness and that are cognizant of post-9/11 processes of racialization as an effect of the global war on terror.

For the diasporic emissaries I encountered in Delhi, not all Brown folk could be hip hop. Indeed, for the Indian American hip hop practitioners in Delhi's scene, hip hop could not—except uneasily—include diasporic subjects who had grown up in privileged class positions, whether in India or abroad. For these self-appointed gatekeepers of hip hop in India, distinctions of class as it coarticulated with race (and sometimes caste) became the basis for authentic participation in a borderless hip hop nation. Rahul, for instance, describes how his hip hop authenticity is questioned by Indian American hip hop practitioners because he grew up in Europe and therefore does not know about "real" graffiti culture. Moreover, Rahul argues that Javan's accusation that he is a rich kid and therefore not a legitimate participant in an authentic Indian hip hop community highlights how class privilege also becomes a means to marginalize. Rahul's bittersweet testimonial of how Indian Americans attempted to marginalize his role in the scene suggests that not only Indian Europeans and Europeans were delegitimized as hip hop practitioners but young men in Delhi deemed wealthy or even well-to-do were as well. For Javan and his peers who came from the United States, young people in Delhi from working-class, low-caste, and ethnically marginal backgrounds were seen as the true representatives of hip hop in India.

This discourse of authenticity based on class, caste, and ethnicity was explicit and articulated by Indian American emissaries. They legitimized their status and the status of the young people from Delhi's urban villages and jhopadpattis who aligned with them by arguing for real hip hop as something that, as one Indian American put it, connected the slums of the United States with the slums of India.[23] Hip hop and its practices, they argued, came effortlessly to the youth in India's slums. In one Delhi-based Indian American's words, "Hip hop came naturally to them. It connects us people from the street, in South Africa, Korea, Palestine, the US and India."[24] In this metaphoric connection, the emissary visualized the street as the connecting force between marginalized people who are located in various national contexts. The street, in this sense, functions as an allegory to harken to a history of linkages between formerly colonized peoples. This history indexes shared processes of urbanization across contexts through the metonym of the street. For these Indian American emissaries, hip hop was positioned as the natural political vehicle for those from the streets across the world, heirs to the failed promises of modernity and urbanization.

By making these sorts of ideological assertions, diasporic actors from the United States necessarily positioned themselves as closer to the street than their European counterparts. By drawing on their biographies of immigration in US urban contexts and their intimate connection to Black diasporic cultural practice and production, they staked their claim to the Delhi hip hop scene. Moreover, by claiming "Indian" youth from the 'hood were the natural heirs to hip hop, they solidified their relations with the young men they met in Delhi. The irony is that as Indian American emissaries conferred legitimacy to a local scene by identifying themselves as legitimate emissaries representing real Blackness and arguing for particular subaltern subjects as the heirs to hip hop in India, they constructed a quintessentially nationalist Indian hip hop that relies on the image of the urban slum as a validation of its authenticity. One result of their move to valorize a class-based nationalism was that it left out those who lived in the very same "slum," who practiced hip hop's forms but could not claim Indianness: for example, the Somalis and Nigerians. They, as I discuss in chapter 6, were on the margins of Delhi's hip hop scene.

The Indian American hip hop emissaries in the scene also drew on their Indianness to further legitimize their position as the natural cultivators of a Delhi hip hop scene: those who could translate hip hop's ideals properly across contexts. Who else, they felt, but diasporic subjects well versed in "real" North American hip hop but also in-the-know in India could cultivate hip hop practice in Delhi? Their performances of Indianness could be subtle or overt. Their self-stylizations drew upon notions of hip hop as an Indigenous form to legitimize its presence among the Indian urban subaltern. Language and other semiotic code-switching usually marked the ways in which Indian Americans attempted to straddle their positions between worlds and create new ones through practice. This code-switching was most evident in the ways in which Indian American hip hop emissaries would engage with others from the "outside," whether from the United States or from Europe. In these instances, their performances of legitimate indigeneity overlapped with their performances of American urban cool. This became evident in their syncretic clothing styles—*kurta* shirts, shorts, flip flops, and snapback hats. It was also reflected in their speech. Indian American emissaries would take Black American English expressions and mix them with Delhi English and Hindi slang. In terms of music production, Indian American musicians expressed a distinct interest in sampling classical and popular music of the subcontinent. This move to create a hybrid sound was not something Delhi-based producers and MCs were interested in doing, unless they were collaborating with hip hop emissaries who had an interest in musical fusion.

In contradistinction, the Indo-European and European hip hop practitioners who engaged with the ground-up hip hop scene stressed the universality of hip hop, the ways in which the arrival of hip hop practices to India promoted, in Rahul's words, "peace, unity, and fun." They also focused on the street as a key trope in hip hop; however, they argued for the street as a meeting place where everyone could come together rather than as a space that signaled a classed authenticity. In an online article detailing the efforts of the Indo-German Hip Hop Project, for instance, one German turntablist describes hip hop as "art forms [that] are sometimes also referred to as 'street culture.' Street culture thrives in urban centers around the world and does not discriminate between rich and poor because the aim is self-expression and free access to art."[25]

For the European hip hop emissaries, the street did not naturally belong to the subaltern, to those *from* the street. Instead, the street functions as the commons, where deliberation across difference is made possible through public art. In this universalist construction of hip hop and valorization of art as an inherently democratic practice, histories of Black diasporic experience that gave birth to hip hop are not necessarily salient except as a narrative device to situate the origin story of hip hop. "Hip hop started in the Bronx" was an opening line I heard from many of the European hip hop practitioners who came over to engage with the scene as well from almost all the economically privileged Delhi-based organizers of hip hop events. What little of the history of hip hop that these actors perfunctorily performed focused on the discourse concerning the four elements of hip hop and their link to the abstract conception of knowledge echoed in some of the global hip hop literature, which celebrates the spread of hip hop as flow and valorizes the notion of the cipha: the virtual and real space where participation in a hip hop nation takes place. This universalizing version of the cipha suggests movement of cultural forms and engagement with hip hop practices as unmitigated by the vagaries of local or global power dynamics and thus erases the history of hip hop.[26]

This erasure was not problematic to European and European Indian diasporic emissaries, however, as they felt hip hop's importance lay in its craft:

accessible to all, disembodied, disconnected, and unburdened by history. For these actors, hip hop's forms should be available to anyone who wished to engage in its forms with persistence: a universal set of practices that is easily adaptable to local conditions but requires expert knowledge to advance itself properly. European hip hop emissaries, as such (and as Rahul attests), could be neutral (recall he used this term to describe the writers from Berlin) or outside the politics of ideology or the history of place. Yet, even as they were neutral, they also depicted themselves as essential, as they brought a knowledge of hip hop practice to the local contexts they visited.

European Indian and European graffiti writers, MCs, and DJs I met also expressed a certain kind of frontier logic with regard to urban India. For them, India's cities were places where the walls were not surveilled and were open for graffiti, where talented b-boys and MCs were everywhere but as yet "uncorrupted" by ideas of the marketplace, and where new ideas born in the public sphere could be made visible. The ideological hip hop that these practitioners extolled did not address the relationship between historical conditions that create inequality within the context of contemporary Delhi. Nor did they engage with hip hop's legacy of speaking to historic conditions of inequality. Rather, they focused on discussing the development of the nascent hip hop communities of practice in urban India and the practical ways they could be expanded and supported.

Some European DJs narrated the future of hip hop in developing Asia as a fertile ground for further establishing their own hip hop fame and for promoting "a culture of hip hop in the country which is democratic, inclusive and sustainable in the long run."[27] This ideological rhetoric, of course, is strikingly similar to the discourse that accompanies development projects in the Global South, where the local is positioned in need and waiting for Western assistance.

Indeed, several European hip hop emissaries as well as some of the self-described middle-class Delhi hip hop practitioners in the scene described hip hop in India as a subculture in its infancy because the most highly developed hip hop practice in the Indian context at the time, particularly in the Delhi and Mumbai scenes, was b-boying. B-boying, because it is a technology of the body as opposed to more seemingly complex engagements with hip hop through technological means, was seen as inferior. Within this assertion, there is an implicit echo of modernization theory and the taken-for-granted notion that development in postcolonial contexts, in whatever form, must follow the direction of development of the West. Moreover, in their assertion that b-boying, the dance form of hip hop, was but the first stage of development in a hip hop scene, there is a devaluation of the bodily, kinesthetic, and aesthetic ways of knowing that b-boying indexes, a kind of dismissal that relates directly to the critiques of decolonial theorists, who argue for a delinking from the program and project of modernity that consistently displaces the body, the sensory, and the social.[28]

Yet to postulate a clear split between the two camps of emissaries—one Indian American, the other Indian European and European—would be facile. After all, both camps were interested in promoting hip hop "culture" in India, and both had a vested financial and affective interest in fashioning an up-and-coming Indian hip hop scene. This led to several collaborations between Europeans, who were interested in promoting hip hop or simply in practicing their hip hop element of choice in India, and Indian Americans, who had stationed themselves more permanently in the scene. These collaborations, which came about as a result of the infusion of funding by projects like the Indo-German Hip Hop Project, were fertile grounds for staging clashes between the two ideologies of hip hop at play. They also created a few persistent links between the youth in the Delhi scene, the Indian American practitioners, and European practitioners. These connections were forged, even if uneasily, over the shared notion that hip hop and its do-it-yourself practice ethos could function as an antidote to the status quo in encouraging self-exploration, the articulation of one's city as a place, and the enunciation of one's experiences as a youthful subject coming of age in a globalized world.

These collaborative instances resulted in a confluence of rhetoric regarding the Indianness of the hip hop scene in Delhi. Whether the decolonial political hip hop of the Indian Americans or the more pluralistic hip hop of the European and European Indian hip hop practitioners, both required images of an authentic Indian hip hop scene to complete their narratives for those back home. This search for a quintessentially Indian hip hop scene led hip hop emissaries to the same locations, to interact with many of the same young people. I was among these emissaries seeking out the same young people. My journeys along the same routes and linked to the same roots (at least with regard to the other diasporic actors I met) reflect the ironies and opportunities of practicing anthropology in the twenty-first century, where mapping cultural change is no longer the sole domain of the ethnographer but is a crowded field of those who seek out cultural practice and use the very same networks to arrive in the same places.[29]

The young people who populated the Delhi hip hop scene did not so easily fall into the reductive nationalist or nativist category of "Indian" or of the sedentary figure of the "urban poor." Indeed, as I have described in previous chapters, many of the practitioners I met in Delhi were relatively recent arrivals from mountain villages of northern India, farmsteads in the Gangetic plains, Nepal and the northeastern parts of the country, Afghanistan, and several countries in East and West Africa. Moreover, there were many participants in the scene who were long-term Delhiites and whose grandparents were migrants (a point that they made regularly to indicate their legitimacy in the scene). What became apparent is that for hip hop emissaries— whether decolonial or universalist—this diversity had to be reduced to fit a much narrower definition of what composed Indian hip hop.

For the universalist European hip hop contingent, a visualization of Indian hip hop could include "Indians" of all economic positions as well as hip hop enthusiasts and practitioners from all over the world who happened to converge in Delhi or Mumbai. Indian cities, for them, became the space where hip hop was happening. The city functioned as a container rather than a place with particular histories or, critically, a place where migrant youth engaged with hip hop precisely because of their precarious positionality in the city. While the universalist framing they promoted revealed something of the kinds of partial cosmopolitanisms that are emerging in the Delhi (and Mumbai) scene, what it did not allow for was an appreciation of the differential power dynamics of travel that brought a diverse set of people together. Indeed, the universalist position, where hip hop is imagined as a freely circulating discourse that creates equality or democratic possibility, cannot be mindful of the power differentials between traveling actors. The result of this discursive formation was that the Nigerians, Somalis, Kenyans, and Afghanis who engaged with hip hop in Delhi, while they could be included within the scene as it unfolded, could not be included in its representation.

For the Indian American emissaries, class and nationality became the key criteria by which to seek out legitimate subjects in Delhi (and in other cities in India) that could represent the Indian hip hop scene. The moniker *Slumgods* emerges from this desire to create a localized, national, and global notion of hip hop. *Slumgods* is a term that was coined around 2011 by a visiting Indian American MC when he worked with b-boys in Dharavi, Mumbai. Some of the young men in both the Mumbai and Delhi scene credited Javan and this particular Indian American MC for creating the "most authentic" representation of hip hop in India because they challenged the prevailing mediatized image of poorer locales in India's megacities as they circulated in mainstream films like *Slumdog Millionaire*.[30]

While they were able to push against images of deprivation in places like Dharavi by promoting global hip hop solidarity and class consciousness through the term *Slumgods*, they perhaps unwittingly obscured the migratory journeys and complex subjectivities of the young people who live in these neighborhoods. Whether it was Northeasterners fleeing political instability or Nepalis seeking economic possibility, these hip hop narratives of journey were almost completely obscured in favor of a localizing tendency that isolated the urban experience of hip hop in the 'hoods and slums of urban India. In their imaginary, Nepalis and the Northeasterners are all equalized as authentic Indian b-boys, MCs, DJs, and so on because they all live in the Indian 'hood and are, as a result, made central to the Delhi hip hop scene. However, this move to equalize them effectively reduced them to being static bodies stuck in the 'hood.

Moreover, in the quest to locate an authentic Indian subaltern, the decolonial hip hop contingent *also* made invisible the Somali, Nigerian, and Afghan MCs, b-boys, and graffiti writers in Delhi, much like the universalist contingent. While the Indian American emissaries did talk to me about the racialization of migrant youth in Delhi and the friction between different ethnic and racialized groups in the scene, they voiced a particular brand of a nationalist, decolonial ideology that prevented this talk from becoming visible in public forums precisely because it disrupted the notion of hip hop as a common culture of difference rooted at the interstice of a borderless national and class imaginary.

What became clear in my time in Delhi was that the universalist message of the Indian Germans and other Europeans became the predominant discourse in the scene, in part because of the flexibility of their version of a hip hop discourse that is more inclusive but also because of the financial backing that it had to produce regular events. The Indian American hip hop emissaries, however, were not without influence. They created events of their own and used their own networks to offer the young people, particularly those from the 'hood, the chance to become visible in public cultural productions, including events, music videos, and even Bollywood films. The message Indian Americans brought with them had a less substantial impact on the larger hip hop scene in Delhi, in part because they focused on certain youth from the 'hood over others and in part because the message was at times rigid, and therefore more easily dismissed, challenged, or pragmatically put into a more pressing and immediate economic and social context by Delhi hip hop practitioners.

Yet even as Indian American emissaries were marginalized within the larger scene, they were able to exert a powerful influence on young people who fit the category of poor and Indian and shape their worldviews through the filter of hip hop. Contrastingly, the ideological message that the European emissaries put forth—the universality of hip hop practice—was most readily parroted by the economically privileged "Indian" youth who dominated the scene by the time I left Delhi in 2014 with some notable exceptions.[31]

The emergent competing and often overlapping spheres of influence played out in each hip hop element. For instance, the graffiti scene was predominantly influenced by writers from Europe, while the b-boy scene was heavily influenced by Javan and other Indian Americans. Interestingly, in online communities, there was a convergence of discourse regarding the realness of the b-boys in the scene, many of whom represented subaltern positions, as they were working-class migrants with some claiming lower-caste backgrounds. Note the following quote from an Indian hip hop youth forum on Facebook, posted in 2016: "b-boys in India have done more for the real hip hop culture than any other fake ass rappers or dj's. . . . I am proud to work with Indian b-boys and b-girls and I got mad love for them."

This sort of sentiment lent a particular kind of credence to the Indian Americans who worked closely with these b-boys, a credence that they used to further their goals of pioneering a particular vision for the scene. It also pushed back against the notion voiced by the European emissaries that hip hop's dance forms were somehow a precursor to more complex engagements with hip hop. The practice forms themselves, as a result, became the site for youth to reformulate the received ideologies of their mentors as well as the site for contestation when fissures in each ideological formulation came to the fore, as Rahul's testimony at the beginning of this chapter reveals.

Indeed, each of these ideological framings were picked up, recirculated, and often reformulated by the youth in Delhi's scene to make sense of their historical position within the world of hip hop, Delhi's hip hop scene, Delhi, India, and the globe. The youth in Delhi's hip hop scene whom I met, whether middle-class and long-term Delhiites or working-class and recent migrants, were pragmatic about the kinds of ideological discourse that the hip hop emissaries performed, picking and choosing what to take up in order to best forge relationships within the available hip hop networks. For the young people, any kind of connection with the larger hip hop universe, or for that matter the creative or artistic world, represented extrinsic possibility, an opportunity to learn from others, gain wider exposure, meet new people, and potentially get paid for their skills.

In short, young people in the Delhi scene were able to take ownership of their image that, in some cases, contradicted the kinds of ideological pushes that the traveling emissaries of hip hop were trying to make. However, in their own image-making projects they were also mindful of the hip hop emissaries' politics and used them to forge their own possibilities within the Delhi scene. While (certain) hip hop emissaries were held in a certain amount of reverence, particularly as male role models for the predominantly male participants in the hip hop scene, hip hop–engaged youth were also able to dispel the larger-than-life image of the emissaries by pursuing their own agendas.

Delhi's Hip Hop Kids Weigh In . . .

I sat with a young Indian graffiti writer, Bhim, in a Dunkin' Donuts in Connaught Place, the center of Lutyens' Delhi and a resurgent commercial hub of the city as a result of an intense marketing campaign in the early twenty-first century to make it a lifestyle shopping destination. The US-based chain store was buzzing with activity as the writer showed me his latest pieces he kept in a graffiti photo book in his backpack. His graffiti book, consisting of photographs of pieces he had done around the city and of rough sketches of pieces he would make in the future, reminded me of similar books my friends and I kept when we were growing up in New York in the 1990s. The graffiti book functioned as an archive of an ephemeral practice. Pieces could be painted over at any time so the book was a testament that one had put something up. Conversely, ideas could be etched into the book but never transferred onto the walls of the city. Yet the graffiti book was also a liability. Many a prolific graffiti artist I knew as a teenager was prosecuted for vandalism because of the evidence held in their books and stored in their backpacks.

I returned from the nostalgic reverie the graffiti book had induced in time to hear Bhim tell me about a street-art festival that was currently going on in Max Mueller Bhavan, sponsored by the Goethe Institut and the Indo-German Hip Hop Project. After providing details about the festival, he said that it would be boring. I asked why. He explained: "Because the White guys that come here ask for permission to do pieces and the government gives it to them. When we ask for permission, we never get it. I would rather do graffiti anyway; it's more interesting. You know the difference between the two, right? Street art is legal and graffiti is illegal artwork done in public places. We are organizing another event at the end of the month as a response to the street-art festival that is going to be a graffiti event. Only illegal pieces."

He went on to tell me about the strategy that he and a few other Delhi-based graffiti artists mobilize when they go out to bomb (illegally do graffiti), which was to take a (White) European along. In this telling, rather than

using the category White, Bhim uses the Hindi term *gora* (White or light skinned). He narrated that the gora would be given the cans to hold, so that if the police came, he would legitimize the work and protect them from arrest, extortion, or a beating. "Yes, having a gora along helps a lot," he said with a laugh. Bhim argued that aside from providing safety, European graffiti artists who came to India also provided a material connection to the necessary supplies that he needed to make work: markers, spray can tips, and so on. Bhim's narrative suggests a cognizance of the power White male bodies have to legitimize otherwise illicit activity in Delhi and a recognition that the networks that the Europeans provide create a critical link for up-and-coming graffiti artists, not only to make work but to circulate their work to a global hip hop public. His use of White and gora interchangeably also reveals the kinds of translations of difference unfolding in Delhi, where contemporary global racial categories meet colonially charged South Asian ones.

As he spoke to me in Dunkin' Donuts, this young man, who lived in the suburbs of Delhi and who was from a relatively well-off family, evinced a recognition for both the universalist and the decolonial projects of hip hop in Delhi. Bhim even cited Javan when he talked about the politics of race and the position of White men in the Delhi hip hop scene. However, he explained that he gravitated to the network of European emissaries because of the various levels of support they provided him with regard to his pursuit of graffiti. Bhim had engaged in graffiti since he was in middle school and, at the time I met him while he was finishing high school, he would go out regularly for bombing missions, unbeknownst to his family. He described to me how he would sneak out of his bedroom window to go out and paint once he knew his parents were asleep. The stories he shared with me offered a counterpoint to the narratives of working-class Nepali, Bihari, Uttar Pradeshi, and Northeastern youth who live in Khirki and Humayunpur. While Bhim was able to access various emissaries and use White male visitors from Europe toward his own ends, the young men who reside in the urban villages of Delhi, for the most part, looked directly to the Indian American emissaries for direction and, in return, were linked with opportunities for public performance.

Recall Rahul's earlier reference to a music video in which the Indian American MC included the boys from Khirki in a performance. In this video, the Khirki youth demonstrated a kind of aggressive performativity that none of the other youth I met in the hip hop scene in Delhi engaged in. In the video, Arun, the youngest member of the crew of mostly Garhwali youth from Khirki, draws his finger across his neck as he looks into the camera while the Indian American MC raps in English. There is a close-up of his gesture. This gesture, analogous to Multan's move to cross out a graffiti piece, reinforces a hypermasculine aggressiveness that circulates in global hip hop while underscoring the political message of the lyrics of the track that highlights what the rapper posits as "Indigenous" knowledge and its possibility to destabilize the status quo. Recall that Rahul argued, in the same conversation I had with him in the Café Coffee Day in Nehru Place, that the inclusion of Arun and his friends in the video was to bolster the image of the MC in the United States as a political and conscious rapper, that these "poor Indian kids" were simply bit actors in the MC's self-promotion.

The young men in the crews who interacted more frequently with the Indian Americans saw the situation quite differently. The Indian American MC, like Javan, had been engaged with these young people for several years and made a point of including them in all his activities whenever he came to Delhi. Moreover, much like the Europeans who brought equipment with them or sent materials via parcel post, he brought back necessary and in-demand technology for the aspiring rappers in the Khirki-based b-boy crew to produce their music. In one interaction I had with Sudhir, who had an ongoing relationship with the Indian American MC, this material connection was made evident. As we sat to discuss a video shoot for his latest track, he made it a point to bring a mic that the MC had brought for him from the United States to allay my fears that the vocals would be recorded poorly. He said, "*Isme mera bhai diya.* My brother gave me this."

Sudhir, like many of the young men I met in Khirki and Humayunpur, relied more heavily on the support structure that male mentors from abroad offered, in part because of their chaotic home lives and experiences of migration and dispersal. They gravitated to the Indian American MC when he was in Delhi, not just to have access to a larger hip hop world or because of material needs but because they genuinely felt they received important mentorship from an older and respected male figure. The affective affinity between this MC and the youth with whom he engaged in the 'hood was indicative of his approach to hip hop. It also offers a glimpse at how the youthful crew he spent time with developed an understanding through their interactions with him of what hip hop was all about from his North American perspective.

Indeed, and especially for this particular crew of b-boys who had grown up in and out of Khirki, hip hop directly equated with friendship, closeness, and a relational bond that translated quickly into kinship obligations, as I discussed in chapter 1. The construction of these kin-like relationships also involved obligations of exchange, as do all kin relationships, as so eloquently and emphatically argued by Marcel Mauss in the early twentieth century.[32] The images of Indian youth from the 'hood no doubt did bolster the hip hop reputations of the Indian American MC as well as other diasporic subjects who traveled across the stretch of ocean and land between the United States and India, as Rahul bitterly argued. In turn, these North American hip hop emissaries felt responsible for the young people they developed relationships with in India and brought them material gifts when they visited.

These reciprocal relations, however, were stretched when crew members connected to Indian American emissaries wished to broaden their engagement with European hip hop emissaries, or with those who were interested in their story who were not necessarily involved in the hip hop scene at all. This was particularly true in the case of Javan, the Indian American b-boy who was a central figure in the Delhi b-boying scene for a number of years. Javan had resided in India for more than a decade and imagined himself as the Khirki crew's representative, guardian, and protector. While he was particularly adept at connecting these young men to opportunities, if they sought out someone on their own—whether other hip hop artists, journalists, or artists—they were met with heavy censure. In my time in Delhi, this led to conflicts between Javan and some of the Khirki b-boys.

An incident that crystallizes this sort of tension was when a local art organization based in Khirki called Khoj International Arts put several b-boys in Khirki in touch with artist Nikolaj Bendix Skyum Larsen. The artist was looking to make a film on working-class youth and their engagements with hip hop for an upcoming show sponsored by Khoj and the Tate Modern Museum in London. The film's thematic thrust was the story of hip hop aspiration among young men from working-class communities in disparate social, cultural, and political contexts by putting a narrative they would develop among Khirki's b-boys in conversation with a narrative they shot with an MC from a working-class neighborhood in London (yet another example of the globally familiar as an imaginary and aesthetic).

Two of the leaders in the Khirki crew, Sudhir and his closest friend, Raghan, agreed to take part in this film and brought in the rest of the crew for dance sequences. When Javan found out about this, he was furious. "Why can't they come study rich people here?" he rhetorically asked as we walked through the streets of Khirki on a warm summer day in April 2013. He felt "White men from the outside" would not do justice to representing these young men. In another conversation about the situation, he asked the poignant question of why White people from Europe and the United States continue to come over to excavate the stories of the poor in India. In the weeks that followed, Javan grew increasingly agitated because the youth had continued their relationship with the artist and his assistant without letting Javan know about it.

One day, he ran into the artist and his assistant when they were with the crew in Khirki and let them know what he thought about their "colonialist" project and told them, at the very least, they should pay the youth for participating in the film. I heard about this confrontation first directly from Javan and then, many months later, from Sudhir. Sudhir said, recalling his decision to continue working with the artists, "I wanted to tell my story and I am old enough to make my own decisions. They gave me money for the film at the end, once everything was over, but it was really boring talking about my life. Documentaries are boring." Much later I heard from Aarthi, an arts activist based in Khirki who is introduced in the next chapter, that the artists did not share the final product with the young men and that they were very disappointed not to have a copy of the film. Moreover, I heard that the artists had paid the young men in front of a space that they had collectively rented to practice their b-boy moves. The landlord had seen the payment take place (or more likely had heard about the White men giving money to these young men from a neighbor) and kicked the young men out of the space as they owed him back rent but had claimed they were broke.

Ideological Clashes, Relational Breakdowns, and Ethical Dilemmas

In the months that followed this incident with the artists, Javan left Delhi and he and I did not have a chance to talk regularly. He had been planning on opening a hip hop community center in Khirki to provide a regular space for Khirki's b-boys to practice. I had promised to help him in any way that I could after our initial meeting, even if that meant fundraising through my networks of educators, academics, hip hop enthusiasts, and social justice workers in the United States who were interested in and intrigued by the idea of hip hop education in India and willing to support its development. However, once I had spent time with him in Delhi, I began to grow wary of the ways in which he wielded his ideologies. His interaction with the two artists was just one of several incidents I saw where his own affectively saturated ideology overdetermined the outcome. Before I left Delhi in 2011, I had gotten Javan a job with an environmental NGO in Delhi. When I returned to Delhi in 2012, I found out from him and those I asked to give him a job that the situation had gone sour. As we sat in his flat, Javan told me that they were a bunch of liberals and did not want to change anything. He said, "One day I just stopped going into work." His employers had told me when I asked what happened that he was impossible to work with. "He is so arrogant," they said. "He thinks the world works differently than it does."

With regard to the artists, I agreed with some of Javan's indictment of them because his critique bolstered some of my own conclusions regarding the ways in which realist documentary has reduced the postcolonial (and diasporic) subject to images of deprivation. However, I also felt that the youth in the crew, many of whom were now in their late teens, could and should make decisions regarding the rights to their image under their own collective council.[33] If there was room for Javan to intervene or provide guidance, the confrontation with Nikolaj Bendix Skyum Larsen on the street with the youth present diminished, if anything, his authority that his word held undergirded by his ontological position as a hip hop emissary from the United States provided him.

In the months we did not interact directly, I began to hear from others in the scene about Javan's reluctance to "work" with me and his hesitation to allow me access to the youth in Khirki who he imagined were under his charge because I was a "wealthy" Indian American and an anthropologist to boot. I started to hear from several sources in the scene that he had described me as a source of money for the center and nothing more. This talk, coupled with previous dealings I had heard about from others or had witnessed in my time with him, distanced me from him and, for a time, from the Khirki crew.

My relationship with Javan reached a head when he abruptly emailed a message asking me to give him a sum of money that he claimed I had promised him earlier in the year. Not quite knowing what to do and feeling vaguely uneasy at the ethically confounding position of being asked, even pressured, by someone I imagined as a key informant for a monetary gift, I offered a sum of money to establish his hip hop center in Khirki that was less than what he had demanded and insisted I had promised. I also mentioned in my response that I felt uncomfortable hearing through our now shared networks that he was talking about me. This comment precipitated a protracted email battle and, in the end, no money was exchanged and plenty of acrimony ensued.

In retrospect it seems clear the breakdown between Javan and me occurred in large part because of a mistranslation in our dialogic performances of what I have called diasporic sincerity in previous work.[34] While I have used the term *diasporic sincerity* to locate the politically salient moments that ensue when diasporic subjects return to their putative homelands and engage with those who have never physically left, in this case I use the term to describe the performativity that ensues when two diasporic bodies intersect in the "homeland" and feel compelled to perform to each other and assess each other's legitimacy. The issue of hip hop complicates this already fraught diasporic exchange within the context of the homeland and the kinds of ideologies that cleave to perceived ontologies, as I have described in the previous pages.

In Javan's estimation, it seemed my performances as an Indian American from New York who grew up with hip hop but was now a researcher—and worse, an anthropologist—could position me in one of two ways: as a savior or a sellout. As John Lester Jackson Jr. notes with regard to his work in Harlem in a moment where gentrification was rife and the representation of those who were facing displacement critical, this positional binary is something that anthropologists working in communities that can claim them as their own often have to contend with as they seek to gain access to what is seemingly their native place, with all the implicit biases that nativity conveys.[35] Yet Jackson argues that this nativist conception is far from the actuality. Class, race, gender, and other forms of cultural binding and exclusion mediate relationships to produce a challenging, and at times insurmountable, roadblock to what we imagine our research agendas to be and how we actualize our relationships in the field.

For Javan, I initially filled the savior slot as he perceived me to be an Indian American who had grown up in similar circumstance to him but who now had money. In retrospect it seemed obvious that he had come to the conclusion that I could infuse his decolonial vision of hip hop in India with necessary resources and he, in turn, could provide me access to his world of hip hop in Delhi: quid pro quo. At some point, however, I morphed into a sellout, a wealthy academic who promised money but was just there to extract what I needed for my own gain.

My "'beef'" with Javan caused me anxiety for one reason: I became worried about how it would impact my relationship with the young men I had met through Javan and other hip hop emissaries connected to Javan. The complications that the situation with Javan yielded, however, actually proved a positive turn. As a result of my fallout with him, I wound up meeting several crews of young men engaged in hip hop practice that would not have necessarily been on my radar. Moreover, as our falling out was made public across several Delhi hip hop networks, the friction served as a catalyst for various actors to voice their opinions on the ideologies of hip hop currently at play in Delhi, their particular positions regarding who and what can be a part of

Delhi's hip hop scene, and their relationship to various forms of difference, all of which are questions I have reflected upon in this chapter.

In the next chapter, I explore how members of a crew from Khirki became part of an activist-led project that sought to produce an alternative plan for development in the locality. The activists and artists involved in the project saw these young men's globally familiar self-stylizations as a powerful vehicle for producing a creative and global reimagining of the city from below that could convince planners and city officials and their local constituency of a new way forward in urban development. In turn, members of the Khirki crew participated because they were close to one of the activists involved; they saw the project as an opportunity to gain local fame as well as spread hip hop in their community; and last but not least, they felt attuned to the political thrust of the campaign. The relationships forged between hip hop practitioners and activists/artists in Khirki offer a way to think through how the globally familiar—while it produces new political subjectivities for Delhi's b-boys and aspiring MCs—also reveals Delhi's urban villages as sites of dispossession and deeply contested urban spatial politics.

It was November 2013. I sat close to Sudhir on a *charpoy* (bed) outside Singh's apartment. On the small patio roof deck, jeans and T-shirts hung on the clothesline in front of us, gently swaying in the breeze. The breeze, while strong enough to move the clothes back and forth on the line, was not powerful enough to mitigate the harsh heat of Delhi's midmorning sun in March. Singh was inside the apartment busily making us coffee.

Sudhir and I had met earlier in the day on the main thoroughfare in Khirki. We then called Singh to see if we could pay him a visit. Singh told us to come over and to buy milk and snacks along the way. Sudhir and I took a long, winding stroll through Khirki to get to Singh's new place in Malviya Nagar, where he had set up his recording studio to work with aspiring MCs in the Delhi hip hop scene. Sudhir did not really know the way. I was surprised because he grew up in Khirki and by my estimation should have known how to make his way through its *gallis* (alleys) effortlessly. When I teased him about not knowing the way, he explained that when he was seven, he moved away from Khirki back to his village in eastern Uttar Pradesh. Before he left, he said, much of Khirki was farm and grazing land. Then he explained, "*Panch sal vapais aya to aisa lagatha tha*. When I came back after five years it looked like this": an unplanned and byzantine landscape, with buildings cropping up and others, simultaneously, being demolished.

As we turned a bend on the way to Singh's flat, we ran into one of Sudhir's friends, a young man I estimated could not have been more than fifteen but who I found out later was the same age as Sudhir: nineteen. At first, I had no idea that they were friends. As this young man trailed behind us, he and Sudhir exchanged a few words here and there before Sudhir finally introduced me to him: "This is my friend. He is a vegetable seller and his family is also from eastern Uttar Pradesh." In our short walk with him to the edges of Khirki, I found out he had dropped out of school in the eighth standard to help his father man the family vegetable cart. He now worked seven days a week pushing a vegetable cart in Khirki. After we parted ways with this young man, Sudhir said wistfully to me in passing, "Hip hop will allow me to do something different in my life."

We finally arrived at Singh's flat. As we sat and waited for Singh to prepare coffee, Sudhir shared a verse he had recently written that he wanted help developing. Before he shared his verse, he turned ever so slightly so he was partially facing me. He then pulled out a worn notebook of rhymes written in carefully lettered Devanagari script. The flies circled over our heads as he began to rhyme in Hindi. In his poeticized story, Sudhir (or his make-believe protagonist) bought flowers for a girl. She took them from him but then told him to get out, to make his way to the streets of Khirki and find his way home. The last verse of the rhyme was in English: "so, now, I am the bloody fool."

Singh walked in from his flat with cups of coffee in time to hear the final bars of the rhyme. He immediately began to interpret the bars he heard, focusing on the final, English verse. Singh argued Sudhir was making a gesture toward the effects of colonialism by using the term *bloody fool*. There was some confusion as we tried to figure out first what Sudhir meant by bloody fool and then what precisely Singh was suggesting by evoking the colonial period in relation to the teenage intimacies Sudhir shared through his lyrics. Laughter at our collective confusion ensued. As the excitement died down, I told Sudhir to try to write the next verse from the girl's point of view: Why did she reject him? What does she want? He muttered a few words about her wanting a *badaa admi* (big man) but was generally a bit stumped about what to write next.[1] Then he changed the flow of conversation and asked in Hindi, "Do you want to hear my verse for Aap Ki Sadak [your road]?" I asked, "What is your road?"

He explained that he and several other members in his crew had been working with an activist group that was conducting a multipronged campaign with the goal of reimagining Khirki's physical space. Part of their plan was to petition local politicians and planning authorities to create walking and biking paths in Khirki to connect it to adjacent communities and the metro and to revitalize public green space in and around the village.[2] "Do you know the *mandir* [temple] on the edge of Khirki? In front of the mandir, right where the big school on the corner is? We stopped traffic at peak time and did a b-boy set. Then I got a chance to rhyme."

> My name is Sudhir and I like to keep my city clean
> I like to keep it nice and green
> Yo, listen now in Hindi
> *He es sach* [This is true]
> Listen now in Hindi
> *Kya amir ma ghamand* [What is the attitude of rich people?]
> *Garib me saram* [Poor people hesitate]
> *Dono bed bhau ka rakthe baram* [Both (poor and rich) go different ways]

He then pulled out his phone and brought up his Facebook page. He scrolled down until he found images of the event someone else had shot that he had reposted. Eighty-three likes sat under an image of him, mic in hand, while he stood on a street not too far away from Singh's apartment. Sudhir's lyrics addressed the attitudes of the wealthy and the poor as the reason why Khirki specifically, and Delhi more generally, faced environmental issues related to development. For Sudhir, it was the attitudes of the rich and the poor, rather than anything structural, that needed to shift. Sudhir's articulation of how social class shapes life in contemporary urban India reveals his reflexivity regarding his own positionality. It also reveals Javan's influence on him, as he and many members of his crew had been close to Javan for years, taking in the decolonial ideology he espoused. However, Sudhir had softened what he had learned about decolonial hip hop, translating its received political message into a method for trying to communicate and bridge attitudes that promote difference in the village where he lives. The photo he showed me on Facebook, of him on the street commanding the crowd's attention, offered a visceral image of reception and the potential for transformation.

The activists, architects, and artists who organized Aap Ki Sadak came to recognize the power of Sudhir's artistic experimentations with hip hop as a viable tool for their project. I found out later that the initial plan of the organizers of Aap Ki Sadak was to conduct a ground-up participatory research study, where local opinions regarding the traffic mayhem in and around their village would be documented on video and the general flow of pedestrian traffic in the colony would be mapped through survey instruments. To initiate their participatory research plan, they enlisted several young people to help cartographically envision this slice of Delhi's urban space. Sudhir and his crew were hired as part of this enlistment to conduct surveys in Khirki, to help create a map that illustrated the flow and movement of people in and around the village. In part, Sudhir and his crewmembers were hired because Aarthi, one of the key artists and activists involved with the project, had known them for years. They were also hired because of the aesthetic appeal their authentic class-inflected positionality brought to the project. Their positionality, for Aap Ki Sadak team members, implied they brought a unique embodied and experiential knowledge of the village. One Aap Ki Sadak member told me that young men in Khirki have the best sense regarding the circulation and movement of pedestrian traffic in relation to vehicular traffic and so would naturally be good at collecting the kind of data necessary to document Khirki's traffic flows.

There was, of course, an irony in this rationale. As I described in my opening vignette, Sudhir, like many of the young people I got to know in Khirki, at once "knew" and were perpetually puzzled by the shifting terrain of the village. Sudhir, as a migrant from eastern Uttar Pradesh, had moved in and out of Khirki over the previous decade. While he was gone, the village changed dramatically. There were flaws in the realist fantasy that Sudhir and his friends, because they were from the village, would have some sort of insider knowledge of its flows. What the Aap Ki Sadak members mistook for knowledge was their aura of class-based urban knowing as it was channeled through their hip hop self-presentation. Their confident masculine walk, their urban attire, their regular pedestrian movements around the city, and their seeming ability to interpret the otherwise opaque city revealed—at least to the Aap Ki Sadak collective—what Thomas Blom Hansen and Oscar Verkaaik have termed "urban charisma."[3]

The notion of urban charisma is laden with gendered and classed normativity. Hansen and Verkaaik, for instance, point to the fictionalized and filmic character of the *tapori* (vagabond/hustler) in their theorization of the male subject of the streets, who alone can "navigate and manage" the urban sprawl and bring to it some sense of intelligibility.[4] The figure of the tapori has been imagined in Bollywood cinema over the last few decades as a street-level hustler from a lower-class and lower-caste background and, in Ranjani Mazumdar's estimation, cinematic depictions of the city from their perspective offer a visceral, vernacular archive of the urban in India that exceeds social science accounts.[5] To some degree, the Aap Ki Sadak organizers used the same elite gendered and classed logic to imagine these young men as capable of rendering Khirki intelligible.

The Aap Ki Sadak organizers, however, soon saw another possibility for these young men to contribute to the project, as hip hop artists. They later added a community art component to the Aap Ki Sadak mission that staged public hip hop interventions in and around Khirki. These spontaneous hip hop events were used to raise awareness around the kinds of mobility, pollution, and public space dilemmas this pocket of Delhi faced, with the rise of traffic and the erosion of green space. The demonstrations used the young men's skills as b-boys, MCS, and graffiti artists not only to raise awareness and change attitudes about the environment more generally but specifically to call for support from the South Delhi Municipal Corporation (SDMC) to recognize walking and biking as legitimate modes of transport.

Aap Ki Sadak's move to incorporate Sudhir and his crew's hip hop practice into their campaign marks the ways in which the male subaltern figure who is already imagined as a purveyor of local knowledge can be transformed into an even more powerful symbol to represent a future Delhi: a figure that can creatively bridge the local and global. In this sense, Sudhir and his crew's involvement with Aap Ki Sadak—and my attention to it—allows us to see the ways in which research on the emerging digitally enabled subjectivities of young people can open up vistas into the city-making projects of others to show how the globally familiar is deployed in unanticipated ways to reimagine urban infrastructure and lifestyles. In other words, it is a reminder that, as Appadurai argues, research in "the arts, humanities, film, media, should not be separate from research on the economy, infrastructure, and planning."[6]

The Aap Ki Sadak team was cognizant of this powerful coming together of subject and city making. Aap Ki Sadak recognized that the identity (and value) of a place is determined by its relationship with other places.[7] Sudhir's and his friends' hip hop artistic practice affectively linked Khirki to urban spaces outside India. In these other urban places, presumably in Europe and North America, pedestrianism and street art are given value. By linking Khirki with global urban contexts through Sudhir and his crew's subaltern masculine embodiment of global pedestrianism, Aap Ki Sadak was able to produce a powerful counterclaim against another globally familiar version of urban development. This other globally familiar version of the twenty-first century, as I suggested in the introduction to this book, valorizes a car-centric vision of planning and development that has taken over Delhi in the last two decades and has resulted in the construction of roads, flyovers, highways, shopping malls, hospitals, and gated residential communities. However, a car-centric version of urban development was not the only globally traveling discourse change that had remade the city over the last two decades.

Over the last twenty years, other urban villages in South Delhi, mere kilometers away from Khirki, have undergone processes of change that have hinged on valorizing their walkability and unique urban landscape, which combines a precolonial heritage aesthetic with a cosmopolitan "street-art" feel. In their efforts to cast Khirki as a cosmopolitan, walkable, and artistically rich pocket of the city, Aap Ki Sadak (in collaboration with Sudhir and his crew) found itself inadvertently describing a future Khirki in ways that were similar to these other urban villages. How does the globally familiar, as it produces and circulates a cosmopolitan urban aesthetic, contest normative modes of urban development while simultaneously valorizing other potentially gentrifying forms of global urbanity?

Equally important to consider are the ways in which the class-based politics that Sudhir voiced and Aap Ki Sadak deployed to create a new vision for development elides other politics of difference occurring within Khirki. How do these other forms of difference work to ultimately complicate processes of the vernacular gentrification that Aap Ki Sadak advocated for in Khirki? Finally, if we consider that Sudhir and his friends have limited possibilities for work and education (much like the young vegetable seller who migrated from eastern Uttar Pradesh), how does their involvement with a project like Aap Ki Sadak position these young men for the future? What are the limits of these opportunities for economic and social mobility? How are these opportunities and their limits shaping Sudhir's hip hop aspirations for the future?

Urban Villages and the Globally Familiar

I ran into the artist and activist Aarthi several days after the studio session at Singh's house. Aarthi was at the center of the organizing and implementation efforts for the Aap Ki Sadak project. Javan, the American b-boy I described in the previous chapter, first introduced me to Aarthi in 2012. After Javan's introduction, I began to run into her regularly in Khirki and had several opportunities to chat with her over coffee or chai about her work and her outlook on the present and future of Delhi. Since 2004, Aarthi had undertaken several public and community arts projects in Khirki. Under the auspices of these projects, she had met Sudhir and his crew when they were adolescents. Over the course of many years, she developed close relationships with them and their families. She watched them develop their interest in hip hop through their online forays and helped them cultivate their hip hop skills, playing an integral part in connecting them to Javan. She also found ways to incorporate them into projects in which she was involved, particularly if there was paid work on offer. When I saw her, I took the opportunity to ask her about the event Sudhir described days prior, where he and his crew stopped traffic on the edge of Khirki and he had rapped his verse and danced.

Regarding the event, she said, "I was really surprised people in their cars weren't furious. They weren't honking their horns or screaming at us. They quietly listened and watched and some even clapped when it was over. I also, because of the demonstration, had a chance to talk with the school principal. The [private] school, you know, is the biggest culprit in creating traffic jams at the space where Khirki meets Malviya Nagar, because of all the buses and chauffeured cars that come to pick up the children at the end of the school day." Aarthi then discussed how the principal had expressed an interest in having his students learn hip hop dance and rap. He had seen his students' interest piqued when the crew from Khirki began their show. Aarthi had noted it as well. She said to me that at first the students from the school were just looking the boys from Khirki up and down and had no interest in mingling with them. After they performed, the students all started to talk to them in animated voices. When she suggested to the principal that Sudhir and the other young men in his crew could teach his students how to dance, she related to me that he grew uncomfortable and agitated. Apparently, he said to her that he could not let those "riff raff" in the building and quickly added, "The students' parents would be very upset." She laughingly told me that he then asked her, "Don't you have anyone else that could teach them?"

Aarthi's account reaffirms the narrative that Sudhir shared in his rhyme: that of a class-based politics of difference that animates social life in Delhi. This narrative is a familiar one, insofar as media and scholarly representations of Delhi highlight growing economic divides as the primary arbiter of social inequality. Aarthi's story of the intervention, the school, and the principal's reaction to Sudhir and his crew also gives us a sense of Khirki as a distinct, demarcated place in the city of Delhi. Khirki, one of several historical urban villages in South Delhi, is named after the twelfth-century mosque in the heart of the village that has now been encroached upon by residential housing.[8] Urban villages are distinct in the urban geography of Delhi in that they are villages that have remnants of historic architecture from the precolonial period that have been subsumed by the sprawl of the city but still hold a special *lal dora* (redline) distinction that designates them as outside the regulatory jurisdiction of the Delhi Development Authority (DDA).[9] This has meant that Khirki and other urban villages have had a development trajectory that is unique in comparison to the rest of the city, insofar as local authorities are able to undertake or broker building projects without the DDA's approval.

In the last decade, Khirki's farm and grazing land has been developed by local *zamindars* (landlords) into inexpensive housing for incoming migrants from near and far. The development of housing in what were Khirki's grazing areas, adjacent to the main village, has created a new area within the village called Khirki Extension. Migrants from across the region and more recently from Afghanistan, Nepal, Bangladesh, Iraq, and throughout sub-Saharan Africa live and work in the bustle of Khirki. The flow of migrants to Khirki, however, is not a new phenomenon. For several decades prior to the influx of international migrants, Khirki saw an influx of seasonal migrant labor from villages across the Gangetic Plain.

Several residents of Khirki I spoke to recall a time prior to the existence of the Delhi Land and Finance (DLF) Plaza across the busy road from Khirki, when the entire area was land for farm and grazing.[10] In those days, farm laborers from Bihar and eastern Uttar Pradesh would come to plant the fields or to harvest them and then return to their villages. When construction on the DLF Mall complex began, roughly in 2007, laborers flocked to the village, again from Bihar and Uttar Pradesh, for the construction jobs that emerged. Initially shantytowns built with scavenged materials were quickly erected to house these new laborers, and over time these shantytowns gave way to concrete apartment buildings. Many of the laborers became permanent residents of Khirki and some brought their families from their villages to join them.

Since the mall opened, increasing numbers of migrants have called Khirki home. This is partly because of opportunities for work in construction, manufacturing, and in the service industry in South Delhi. In addition to the influx of regional migrants moving to the city for laboring opportunities, transnational migrants also started moving to Khirki around this time. The West Africans, East Africans, and Afghanis I got to know in Khirki said they chose Khirki, in part, because of the limited opportunities for working-class members of these communities to find housing elsewhere, due to rampant racism, particularly toward Africans but also toward Afghani, Nepali, and Northeastern migrants who have recently moved to the city (I discuss race and racism in detail in chapter 6). Many transnational actors from the Gulf states, Afghanistan, and West Africa also move to Khirki temporarily, to avail themselves of the services of private hospitals in the area.

Waves of in-migration, in part because of the limited housing opportunities elsewhere, have created a volatile microhousing market in Khirki. The

most precarious migrants deal with highly inflated rents and the threat of constant dispersal. They find themselves clustered in one of the few places in the city where landlords and their agents will rent out flats to them, usually at higher prices and without a legal guarantee of habitation.

The Delhi Master Plan written in the 1960s by city planners imagined urban villages like Khirki as places where cottage industries, such as pottery making and craft textile production, could be shifted from other parts of the city undergoing massive change in order to produce work and preserve the artisanal heritage of the city.[11] Now, places like Khirki are sites of small industry. Several small-scale textile factories, subcontractors for export-intensive clothing manufacturers, for instance, sit just behind the main thoroughfare of Khirki. In addition, shop fronts run by members of the various migrant communities that now call the village home line the main thoroughfare. There is the open-air barbershop, where an old TV blares and small crowds of Bihari and Uttar Pradeshi laborers pass time smoking *beedis* (herbal cigarettes) between work and sleep. Just behind the barbershop is a "piece wall" created under the auspices of one of the many community art projects in Khirki, some sponsored by Khoj International Arts, which has been based in Khirki since 1997.[12]

In 2011 Khoj opened a beautiful new arts residency space, which sits on the main thoroughfare and is resplendently white washed. I took to calling it the *safed mahal* (white palace) with Sudhir and his crew, as a joke that indexed its somewhat garish hypervisibility in the village. In 2013 a movement arts and dance NGO called Gati opened just next to Khoj. Each of these organizations, especially when they hosted events, brought a middle- and upper-middle-class Delhi crowd into Khirki's gallis and unpaved main streets.

Further down the street from Khoj is a corner where West African men and women hang out and catch up with friends and business associates from within their transnational community. Just adjacent to this corner is a Nepali restaurant where workers consume inexpensive *thalis* (plates of food) before they return to their laboring jobs. Just southwest of Khirki lies Hauz Rani, another several-hundred-year-old urban village that today mostly houses Muslim families that arrived during partition, a sizable Afghani migrant population, and an increasingly visible Somali refugee community. In the Northwest, Malviya Nagar, a middle-class colony built soon after independence, looms with its large open-air bazaar and several gated residential enclaves. To the north lies the Satpula bridge and dam, an architectural hydraulic marvel of the Tughlaq dynasty, now left, like many of the ruins scattered across the city, to the adventurous and the dispossessed.

The MCs who live in Khirki told stories of the village and its adjacent spatial terrains in their poetry. They also marked their relationship to the village and its surrounds through their embodied performative practice of b-boying in the public spaces in and around Khirki as well as investing meaning to its spaces in street art they generated. Some of this street art was produced with the support of Khoj, which has sponsored various public arts projects over the last decade by commissioning artists like Aarthi to undertake creative and engaged public arts initiatives. Other murals and graffiti pieces were produced by hip hop artists from Khirki or by enterprising hip hop emissaries who have come to see Khirki as a hip hop destination in Delhi, thanks in no small part to Javan. For the young people of Khirki (and surely others, including myself), these street-art murals and graffiti pieces functioned as landmarks, even if temporary and somewhat ephemeral. They became a means to locate oneself in the tangle of gallis that make up the village.

Often the stories I heard in raps or in conversations with the MCs, dancers, and graffiti artists who lived in Khirki were linked to specific locations within greater Khirki, where incidents, both humorous and grave, took place in their lives. There were common links across stories about Khirki and its surrounds. Many of the practitioners, for instance, discussed how they were often chased out of the small colony parks on the peripheries of Khirki when they congregated in the park for too long. These small parks were maintained by Resident Welfare Associations (RWAs), consisting of the owners of the properties that surrounded the "public space" who took care of its upkeep.

The RWAs were not inclined to have nonresidents, particularly the children of migrant laborers, use the space, unless the use was brokered by someone that RWA members held in esteem.[13] When they turned up on their own, Khirki's b-boys and MCs were seen as a nuisance and promptly shooed away by RWA elders or hired chowkidars (guards), who kept a watchful eye on the parks. Artists associated with Khoj often brokered the creative use of these parks for events, some of which featured Khirki's b-boys. Even Singh and I (at the behest of Javan, when we were all still on speaking terms) brokered a deal to use a public/private park space for a hip hop jam. I had to give the man who took charge of the space a bottle of rum in return for its use for five hours.

Other raps that Khirki MCs wrote centered on the mall, which was a key spatial location where Delhi b-boys and MCs made sense of and engaged with the rapidly shifting social geography of Delhi. Sudhir and his crew rapped about the mall and parks but also highlighted specific locations in the village or in the city of Delhi as sites of experience that shaped their social perceptions. In Sudhir's rap about his love interest and the flowers he gives her, for instance, he mentioned Krishna Gate. The "gate" is an exit from the village that leads to the Malviya Nagar market and gets its name from a nearby Krishna Mandir. I found out later that the girl Sudhir rapped about lives in Malviya Nagar and comes from a middle-class, upper-caste family. This gate was a portal into the different social world that Malviya Nagar offered, and in his rap it was also a sign of spatialized class difference. The gate, in relation to the flowers and his interest in the young woman, at once marked difference as well as the potentiality and limits of overcoming it.

Sudhir's spatialized rap offers up a version of Khirki as a place where experiments in India's urban future are taking place, where borders are being crossed and new relations are being imagined and in some cases realized. These sorts of hip hop–enabled encodings of experience across social difference in and across Khirki are also what drew activists and artists, like those working with Aap Ki Sadak, to MCs and b-boys living in Khirki. Indeed, Sudhir and his friends' everyday creative practice that reimagined their lives in Khirki as part of a changing Delhi linked very well with Aap Ki Sadak's vision to promote the village as an already global place in the city because of its pedestrianism, its public art, and the digitally savvy young working-class men who inhabited it. These young men, one could argue, performed cosmopolitanism, to borrow from Craig Jeffrey and Colin McFarlane, who argue for an attention to the cosmopolitan as someone who actively and creatively transgresses localized distinctions.[14]

Aap Ki Sadak's initiative to valorize Khirki's walkability, its public art, and its youthful residents' performative cosmopolitanism quickly placed Khirki in a comparative frame with other urban villages of South Delhi. These other South Delhi urban villages, also connected to precolonial heritage sites built by Mughal rulers from the twelfth century onward, have been reimagined by a new breed of developers over the course of the last two decades. They have worked to rebrand these urban villages, also legally protected by the lal dora, for a different sort of development project that draws on a new urbanist discourse, which stresses walkability, accessible public space, and opportunities for consumption.[15]

The appropriation of historical villages for urban place-making projects that seek to re-create, in part, a hybridized urbanity that draws from European aesthetic sensibilities regarding urban heritage and postmodern urban design has accelerated considerably in the last five years. Two urban villages in particular, Hauz Khas Village and Shahpur Jat, have become sites for a kind of development project that relies on the historical context of the village to construct a quaint retro-modernity that builds on notions of European urban space that value the pedestrian.

In these villages, the prototype of the walker involves tame ambulatory possibilities, decidedly tilted toward the cultivation of tastes and the enabling of consumption rather than the celebratory narratives of everyday ambulation that Michel de Certeau posits or the explicitly political *derivés* of French situationists.[16] Indeed, the newly renovated boutiques, restaurants, bars, and music venues cater to the young or the self-described cosmopolitans of the city and to the increasingly visible international cadre of internationals working in Delhi, as they offer an alternative space to the mall to seek pleasure through consumption. This very particular and localizable process of urban change could be described using the term *gentrification*.

Lucie Bernroider argues for precisely this, suggesting that we think with the concept of gentrification when engaging with processes of change in Delhi's urban villages that are an outcome of a particular symbolic economy ushered in by politicians and developers in the first decade of the twenty-first century that has attempted to recast Delhi as a world-class city.[17] The aesthetics that arise out of this particular form of urban development valorize the potential for youthful consumption and production that make beautiful the seemingly inconsequential forms of local difference. Race, ethnicity, caste, and even class differences are seemingly banished when walkability, public art, and heritage architecture, as they come together in Delhi's urban villages, are lauded as the future of the city.

Gentrification might seem a strange concept to work with in the context of urban India. After all, gentrification is a term that has historically been used to describe urban "renewal" processes that have systematically displaced the racialized poor and working class in North America, the UK, and Europe, supplanting them with the new bourgeoisie. How do the changes in Delhi, particularly in the urban villages of South Delhi, articulate with this term? One answer, of course, is that there are many situated gentrifications happening linked to processes that, as urban geographer Neil Smith argues, hinge on the skyrocketing property values of first-tier cities across the globe and on the various concomitant discourses on lifestyle that are enmeshed in the fantasy of property ownership. This macroeconomic shift, as Smith has suggests, cannot be seen as totalizing because it creates not a singular process of gentrification linked to rising property values or a singular notion of cosmopolitan urban living but multiple micro-processes across and within various urban contexts across the world.[18]

These processes of urban change are underanticipated by official planners in a city like Delhi precisely because they are driven by an increasingly differentiated set of needs and desires of urban dwellers. Rather than being solely precipitated by functional, economic needs, such as proximity to the city center, a lower cost of entry into private-property ownership, and so on, they have also been predicated on the meanings attached to urban places. That is, disparate processes of gentrification in our late-capitalist moment are partly predicated on the value of particular urban spaces that are produced through the cache of meanings that circulate globally but are determined locally. The lamination of desire onto place, of course, has the potential to incite friction.

In 2014 the urban village of Hauz Khas became a flash point, as long-term residents decried the regular crowds of South Delhiites, tourists, and transnational laborers (IT professionals, models, and so on) who made their way into the village in the evenings to revel in its playground of social fantasy. Hauz Khas Village has been undergoing processes of urban change since the 1990s, when fashion designers started to open boutiques in its quaint medieval streets.[19] In the last five years, these processes of change have reached fever pitch. The village became known as the Soho of Delhi, as new bars, restaurants, and clubs opened up in the village's nooks and crannies. In a recent effort, an NGO in concert with some of the remaining older residents of Hauz Khas tried to shut down the village's many illegal restaurants and bars. They argued that the existing legal restrictions on commercial businesses in the village had been flaunted, creating a sanitation crisis that the village's infrastructure could not handle. Their effort to bring attention to the unregulated development that has transformed Hauz Khas resulted in a temporary closure of several bars and restaurants. The closure was overturned by municipal authorities soon thereafter. The bars were once again full on the weekends.

The political economy that has spawned the development of these urban villages poses a set of questions concerning the relationships between the local zamindars, whose claims to property extend prior to the constitution of the Indian state due to the village's lal dora designation, developers, and, in Hauz Khas Village's case, the Non-Resident Indians (NRIs) who are returning to India to create lifestyle businesses in partnership with locals. While a more fulsome take on the political economy of Hauz Khas is beyond the scope of this book, there are some important takeaways regarding its rampant change story. Aap Ki Sadak's project to promote walkability, public art, and green spaces in Khirki, and my interlocutors' digital hip hop engagements, echo and straddle the spatial features of the two villages, inextricably connecting their trajectories of transformation with each other. In the years I lived in Delhi, Hauz Khas became a haven for local and international graffiti writers as well as a place where Delhi's rappers, many of whom were just gaining fame as I left the city in 2014, got paid to perform.

In Hauz Khas there is a set of walls in the edge of the village where graffiti artists—whether international hip hop emissaries or Delhi-based writers—ply their craft. This "piece wall" is part of a larger constellation of legal street art that can be found throughout the urban village. The b-boys, graffiti artists, and rappers I got to know in Delhi would often travel to Hauz Khas to pass time. They would come from all over the city in the metro and then walk up the hill to the village, bypassing the ad hoc valet street parking manned by entrepreneurial young men with large sets of keys dangling from their belt. My early adventures in Hauz Khas were with different MCs, graffiti writers, and b-boys who wanted me to shoot video footage of them amid the village's remnants of Mughal-era architecture.

As I got to know several DJs in Delhi, I began to spend time with them in the bars of Hauz Khas. I would also go with MCs to open-mic nights hosted by clubs and restaurants in Hauz Khas. There they would patiently wait their turn, just so they could spend five minutes rapping to youthful audiences of college students that they otherwise would not have an opportunity to interact with. A few times, I went with Sudhir and members of his crew. As the night ended, and after they had their moment on the mic, I would pass them a hundred-rupee note for the late-night auto fare back to Khirki.

After I gave them money, I would walk toward an auto to make my way home and wonder while walking at how the kinds of developments that have reshaped Hauz Khas would affect Khirki. When I found out about Aap Ki Sadak from Sudhir, I began to think about how the activists, by advocating for something as seemingly benign as walkability, might usher in changes that alienated the needs of Khirki's diverse migrant communities. My mind lit upon the murals and graffiti of Khirki that marked for me a tensile link between its version of urban life and Hauz Khas Village's version, which had fully mutated into a walkable heritage village.

Methods and Meanderings

Aap Ki Sadak was first conceived of as a means to engage the accumulated knowledge of Khirki's residents and the relationships that Aarthi and her collaborators had developed with the youth of the community over several years toward a project that would produce a collective good for village

residents: walking paths, the reclamation of Satpula as a public park, and so on. This grassroots effort linked the expert knowledge of architects, planners, and artists with the local and global knowledge that Sudhir, his crew, and other youth recruits brought to the table. Sudhir and his crew mobilized their knowledge, first as researchers gathering data from Khirki's residents about their use of space and their movements through the area and second as hip hop artists, toward pushing for a different kind of understanding and consciousness around what the city is and could be.

Undoubtedly, Sudhir and his friends participated in the project because they saw the tangible benefits it could provide. Aside from getting paid, participation in the project generated new relationships for them with the artists, activists, architects, and planners associated with the project. It also opened up new relations with the residents of Khirki, Malviya Nagar, and Hauz Rani whom they met while conducting research or while performing on the streets of these three adjacent neighborhoods. By performing in public for a clearly stated cause, Sudhir and his crew gained great visibility and notoriety in the community where they lived and beyond, as news media picked up the story of Khirki's environmentalist hip hop practitioners. By circulating their performances and the media representations of their performances on social media, they could broadcast themselves as politically engaged hip hop artists to their existing networks of friends and family as well as represent their village as the future of the city and a globally recognizable 'hood. As importantly, their new relationships with Khirki as researchers and artist-activists allowed them to reflect on and refine their understandings of difference in relation to space in Delhi and, in doing so, to develop an ongoing activist stance.

For the research component of the project, Sudhir and his friends interviewed other young people in Khirki with the rationale (provided by Aarthi and other organizers affiliated with the project) that young people know more about the spaces of the villages than their elders do. Young people in Khirki, so the logic went, spend far more time in the gallis and the various nooks and crannies of space that act as the connective tissue and the borders between Khirki, Malviya Nagar, the mall, and Hauz Rani than their adult counterparts. While adults in Khirki have a routinized relationship to space, such that their walks are determined by functional activities—walking to work, walking to the shops, going to the post office—young people wandered, played, and explored the physical spaces of Khirki with abandon.

To some degree, the notion that the young men did have a better sense of the topography of the village was true. In Delhi, the scope of knowledge about one's lived environs was undoubtedly determined by age and gender. In the streets of Khirki, young boys and girls under the age of twelve played in the gallis close to where they lived. Nepali, Northeastern, Afghani, Uttar Pradeshi, Nepali, and Bihari youth were on the street, regularly playing any number of games with each other: football, a kite flying session, stick ball, and so on. These interactions were gender mixed and at times ethnically mixed too. However, as young people in the village got older, this changed.

Those above the age of twelve and on the street were mostly young men. Young men over the age of twelve would roam around Khirki in small groups, congealed by a sense of ethnic or racial belonging. Some still wore school uniforms hours after school had been let out. They stood on the corners of alleys with their friends or found small areas away from prying eyes to smoke. They also made their way to the many small billiard halls, gaming rooms, or internet parlors tucked into the recesses of Khirki. Sudhir and his boys, as well as Hanif and his crew, would constantly roam (*gumthe*) in and around Khirki and further afield.

Young men in their teenage years, as the Aap Ki Sadak staff understood quite well, were prone to a broader exploration of their built environment and had the capacity to articulate their relationship to place and space as they moved through the authorized and unauthorized tangles of the village. Yet as I suggested in the introduction to this chapter, it would be a stretch to suggest that they "knew" Khirki, given its constant state of flux. Equally important to acknowledge were the gendered limits of mobility in Khirki. These young men had the chance to wander and get to know the village and the city precisely because they were young men; young women did not have the same opportunities. In part, this was because of the normative gendered expectations reproduced inside the households of Khirki, which posited that young women needed to maintain purity and not expose themselves to potential critique.

It was also because of the growing fear of gendered violence in the city. These limits translated into not only a different experience of Khirki as a place but a very different set of opportunities to access new relationships or economic possibilities, or even consume globally circulating media forms. Aap Ki Sadak mobilized this gender-specific experience of Khirki by having Sudhir and his crew, a group of teenage boys, collect the necessary data for the project without, at least publicly, discussing the gendered bias of the study. Moreover, the Aap Ki Sadak crew also relied on the class-specific experience of Sudhir and his friends as a legitimating feature for this research.

On several walks I took with Sudhir and his crew during the months that Aap Ki Sadak was conducting its research and staging various public events, young people from the community approached them as local celebrities, asking whether they were going to do any more performances in the near future. For young people throughout the colony, their incontrovertibly "cool" hip hop aesthetic was affectively linked with Aap Ki Sadak's project to reimagine Delhi. Sudhir's appropriation of a political slogan that appeared at the turn of the millennium in Delhi in his rap lyric "I like to keep it 'clean and green'" makes visible this connection. In this rap, Sudhir cleverly combines a citation of a previous era of civic environmentalism with his critique of contemporary class politics. This connection, through the idiom of hip hop, offered the young people who heard it performed in Khirki the opportunity to reflect on how someone of their generation made sense of the politics of place in Delhi.

This had a tangible impact. In the year after the Aap Ki Sadak project commenced, several members of Sudhir's crew would go on to work closely with another NGO in Khirki that focused specifically on environmental issues. Sudhir taught a beginner's hip hop dance class that attracted a large group of young people in Khirki, mostly tribals from Bihar and Jharkhand who lived in the nearby Jagdamba Camp and had seen Sudhir and his crew perform the previous spring. I was encouraged to see that there was a sizable number of young women between the ages of nine and fourteen in the class, given the paucity of young working-class women in the larger Delhi hip hop scene.

During or after their walks to collect data from their peers, Sudhir and his crew took me to abandoned buildings in Khirki: the rickety domes of a five-hundred-year-old masjid (mosque), the tunnels of the Satpula dam, and several small parks. These explorations offered me insights into Khirki's topography and history. This experiential knowledge, especially when I combined it with the vast literature on the historical development of Delhi, was undoubtedly valuable to me as I sought to understand the context for Sudhir and his crew's digital forays and hip hop self-fashionings. Yet because of the rapidity with which Khirki is changing and the instability of its inhabitants, Sudhir's knowledge of Khirki as a space and place was at best partial. Getting lost was part of the relationship one had with a place like Khirki if one inhabited it through its many changes. My experience of getting lost alongside Sudhir taught me something about the journeys he had before he could call Khirki home as well as the kinds of aspirations for the future he linked to hip hop.

Aarthi and several others involved in the Aap Ki Sadak project had, like me, engaged with young people over the years as they produced community artwork with members of the many overlapping communities that make Khirki their home. They too wandered with Sudhir and his friends or set up alternate spaces in Khirki for interactions to take place. They too learned about these young men's passions, desires, fears, and struggles. For instance, around 2010, Aarthi built a temporary kiln on one of the small RWA-maintained village parks and obtained permission from the RWA to host pottery classes for the children of itinerant Bihari construction workers while their parents worked to build the DLF Mall located across the road. Aarthi was also involved with a diverse group of youth in a local government school where she conducted theater workshops. This prolonged immersion in Khirki and among its youth, for Aarthi and some of her colleagues and friends, created an image of Khirki as distinct, vibrant, and multicultural. These close interactions with the youth of the community coupled with their long engagement in the community also gave them a deep understanding of the kinds of social, economic, and political struggles that the residents went through in their daily lives.

Aap Ki Sadak's efforts to use some of its collective's deep understanding of the everyday urbanisms of Khirki to promote a car-free pedestrian future, however, was more complex than Aarthi's previous community arts engagements as a solo practitioner. Rather than engaging simply with the village's existing population under the remit of "community art," Aap Ki Sadak was mobilizing the experiences of Khirki residents, particularly the younger generation, to make an argument for future development. Ultimately, one could argue, its vision for the scaling down of urban space relied too heavily on a new urbanism paradigm of walkability that has been critiqued in the United States and Europe for its susceptibility to co-optation for projects of gentrification within inner-city contexts.[20]

This posed a potentially deleterious outcome for the current migrant residents of Khirki, as it made the village visible in ways that could make it desirable to those in the city who sought a neighborhood that provided a (centrally located, cheaper, and more hip) alternative to the gated colonies in which they lived. In the months I lingered around Khoj's newly opened café in the heart of Khirki, I met several young "professional" Delhiites who had made Khirki their home precisely because of the appeal of its cosmopolitanism and pedestrian-friendly lifestyle.[21] The presence of the arts organization in Khirki over the last ten years had greatly impacted the community's residents. The arts organization created a hub for a network of artists and art enthusiasts from across Delhi to congregate and thus put Khirki on the map. It also encouraged those who attended regular openings and events to

eventually move into the neighborhood. I could not help but think about my own experiences in New York and San Francisco during my twenties and early thirties and the role that artists, arts organizations, and those associated with creative pursuits have had in the gentrification of working-class Black and Latinx communities in those cities.

The real estate agents I had made acquaintance with on my various jaunts through the community corroborated this trend. They would tell me over a cup of chai in their office that they were seeing more and more of a "professional type" renter coming to their offices. They also reported a growing number of Africans coming to rent in Khirki. While Aap Ki Sadak itself certainly was not going to be the engine that created wholesale change in Khirki and radically alter the demographics of the neighborhood, its project casts a spotlight on the kinds of change currently underway in Khirki and in Delhi more broadly. The interest of these young artists and professionals in living in a more pedestrian- and public-transportation-focused Khirki indicated a different set of interests and desires than those imagined of the middle class in India: the gated community, the car, and the mall. These interests suggest that Aap Ki Sadak's efforts, as they connected with Sudhir and his friends' desires and creative hip hop engagements, are linked to a broader set of changes that are underway in cities across India.

Perhaps the most direct and immediate consequence of Aap Ki Sadak's project was its plan to revitalize the area around the ruins of the Satpula. Satpula, during my time in Delhi from 2012 to 2014, was claimed by urban villagers who grazed their livestock and horses, groups of young people who use the open space in front of the ruins of the dam to play cricket and football, and several Khirki-based hip hop crews who used the dam structure itself as a meeting place to practice MCing and b-boying and to catch up over cigarettes.

Aap Ki Sadak produced a final exhibition in a hall in Malviya Nagar, which offered the public a chance to look at the proposed changes for Khirki. The event had in attendance all of Delhi's notable architects and planners, local politicians, and residents of the area as well as Sudhir and his crew dressed in Aap Ki Sadak T-shirts. The exhibition displayed maps developed from the data gathered through the mobile surveys, and videos of interviews with residents and of b-boy and rap demonstrations. The exhibition also had a large-scale digital rendering of a reimagined Satpula. This rendering included a reclaimed lake area just in front of the dam; a walking bridge over the *nala* (canal) that ran on the borders of the dam, to ease the movement of pedestrian traffic between Khirki and an adjacent community; and a landscaping plan that would reclaim the areas on the banks of the nala. These plans at first seemed exciting to me. The young men I met in Khirki who used this space regularly, I imagined, would now ostensibly have a cleaner and safer place to practice. Then it dawned on me that, were these plans to go through, Satpula would be transformed into an authorized space, a space under surveillance that these young men would find it difficult to enter or to do anything deemed illegal.

Weeks after the event, I walked with Irfan, a member of the Somali crew, from Khirki toward Satpula dam. As we walked, he told me that Satpula would soon be off limits for them because there were plans to convert it to a heritage site with an entry fee. "Soon," he said as we climbed over the gate between the main road and the Satpula area, "this place will not be a place we can hang out anymore." I asked him if he knew about the Aap Ki Sadak project and he looked puzzled. He had not heard of it, nor had he heard of any of the hip hop events that had taken place under its banner.

When I asked him where he had found out about these plans for Satpula, he answered emphatically, "The whole village is talking about it. You watch, they will charge money to enter the site. And we won't be able to use it anymore." Irfan's understanding of the potential changes to Satpula that traveled to him through his networks in Khirki, coupled with his lack of knowledge about Aap Ki Sadak's project, brings up two important issues and questions with which I will conclude this chapter. First, how are African migrants and refugees, who at the time of this writing were growing in number in Khirki and contributed to creating a particular political economy in Khirki, positioned regarding gentrification in South Delhi's urban villages? Second, how are Sudhir and his friends, who participated in the Aap Ki Sadak project that partly ushered in some of the changes in the village, impacted?

Khirki has seen a marked increase in the presence of African nationals since 2007, along with Afghani and Iraqi refugees more recently. Over (yet another) cup of chai, one older real estate agent in the area told me that six years ago, just around the same time that the mall across the street was built, she started to get African nationals seeking flats in the neighborhood. Landlords, she said, were not willing to rent to them at first but warmed to the idea when the agent told them they could charge a bit more rent. The United Nations High Commissioner for Refugees (UNHCR) officials I spoke to, who serve the refugee populations in Delhi, have opened three offices in the area around Khirki to serve the growing numbers of African and Afghani nationals who have rightful claims to refugee status in the area. The influx of racial and ethnic outsiders not only created an economic opportunity for landowners and property middle men; it also generated a particular set of frictions, conflicts, and solidarities among internal and international migrants and longer-term residents. What becomes important with regard to this chapter's focus is that the presence of the African community limited the possibilities of the kinds of wholesale shifts and changes that have occurred in urban villages with a similar walking sensibility and public art presence. Landlords, real estate agents, and the police found renting to African nationals far too lucrative to shift their attention to building for and renting to professional Delhiites. In turn, the presence of African nationals and their supposed criminality (as per media accounts) made middle-class renters hesitant to move into Khirki.

As I followed Sudhir and his friends' involvement with Aap Ki Sadak, I found it curious that the activists involved with the project were not concerned with this demographic change in their plans for urban renewal. I found this particularly perplexing because I knew that Aarthi and several other artists and designers involved with the project were actively engaged with members of the African transnational community who made their homes in the village and advocated on their behalf for their safety and fair treatment by the local authorities. The absence of African nationals in the Aap Ki Sadak plan, I suspect, was not because Aap Ki Sadak organizers were unaware of the kinds of economic and political shifts produced by the presence of international migrants in Khirki. Rather, by avoiding a discussion that put the political economy of Khirki real estate front and center, Aap Ki Sadak carefully avoided directly addressing the seething political issues revolving around a more complicated terrain of difference connected to African migration to Delhi. Aap Ki Sadak members, rather than taking on the complex interweave of class, race, and gender that produced the urban geographies of Khirki and its surrounds, instead chose to focus their efforts on producing a symbolic field that challenged the class-based barriers to sustainable urban development. To make their claims and petition for policy change, they engaged Sudhir and his friends as representatives of the youthful urban poor, who articulated their globality through hip hop.

Moreover, because Aap Ki Sadak had to appeal to the city's politicians and planners to implement its vision as policy, it created a narrative of change that was decidedly within the national frame. Thus, it was no surprise that the youth who were chosen to represent Aap Ki Sadak were regional migrants from Bihar and eastern Uttar Pradesh who could speak Hindi and looked "Indian." While Sudhir and his crew's classed and gendered experience within Khirki purposefully became visible in the project, other experiences of Khirki, like Irfan's, could not fit into this frame and so were left out.

And what of Sudhir and his crew? How were they affected as a result of their participation in this project? Let us go back one more time to Sudhir's verse—a verse he raps in public space—which not only reveals how he imagines change in the city but gives us a fleeting sense of his and his family's struggles. He raps of the divide between the poor and the rich. He makes it a point to call attention to how the poor "hesitate" in getting involved in political issues and in so doing limit their ability to shape possible futures. This verse allows us to see how Sudhir positioned himself as a committed representative voice of the poor.

What is perhaps even more telling, however, was the verse that followed his Aap Ki Sadak rap on Singh's terrace and that he ultimately recorded in the studio. This verse was one that he did not perform in public for Aap Ki Sadak. In it, he discussed his discovery of hip hop, dropping out of school, his brief stint in his early teens as a parking attendant in nearby Saket, and his subsequent return to school. This verse revealed the ways in which he felt he was constrained by the racialized labor market in Delhi, which positions low-caste migrants like Sudhir into service or manual labor positions. It also revealed the ways in which he imagined hip hop and education will allow him access to other possible futures.

After rapping this next verse, Sudhir offered some context for the lyrics. He told me, "My mom is paralyzed from the waist down. I have three sisters. My father is useless." I asked, "Is he in Khirki?" Sudhir replied,

> Yes, he is. He is a welder. I don't talk to him, though. I don't see him. When I was in ninth standard, I got a job as a security guard in PVR, a shopping complex in Saket. I got it to help support the family, because my father doesn't give us any, he just drinks the money away. It was the night shift. So, every day I would go to school. Practice my hip hop in the afternoon. Then, go to work. But I would be so tired. I would start to fall asleep at work. Once, my boss found me asleep and beat me. Then, some BMW in the parking lot had its tires punctured. Three men came and beat me, saying it was my fault. They told me to never come back to PVR or they would kill me.[22] So now I work a part-time job somewhere else. I have to work to help my mummy. My sisters.

What he shared in his rap and his explanation afterward amplified what he told me between moments on the microphone as we stood on Singh's balcony and looked out at the Krishna temple and the gate that marked the entry into Khirki from Malviya Nagar. It was a narrative I had heard from several of the MCs and b-boys in Delhi: a hope that hip hop would provide him with a way out of the dilemma he faced, a way to improve his situation and that of his family in turn. This narrative worked to bridge the conceptions of masculinity they had learned through hip hop with the gendered expectations they had received as young men coming of age in Delhi. For Sudhir, this narrative also offered him an opportunity to critique his father, who did not fulfill his responsibilities as a family man and breadwinner, while simultaneously expressing his angst over whether he would be able to do so himself through hip hop.

This gendered conception of responsibility linked to their carefully cultivated hip hop masculinity was one they repeated in the film produced by Nikolaj Bendix Skyum Larsen on hip hop aspirations across national contexts.[23] In a poignant scene from the film, the younger brother of one of Sudhir's crewmembers, as he sits on a bed in his flat located very close to the thirteenth-century Khirki mosque, narrates how his brother and his friends would go to the mall every day to practice and perform their hip hop moves. This was in the hopes that they would get discovered by someone who would provide an opportunity for them to make money, to transform not only their future but the future of their family (recall chapter 2 and my discussion of the mall, imagined as a site of transformation).

Aap Ki Sadak certainly provided a platform to get paid as researchers while offering the opportunity to be seen on several different scales. This opportunity for paid representational work was one of many that I witnessed Sudhir and his friends engage with while I lived in Delhi and frequented Khirki. Not all of them panned out well or provided a sustained network of engagement. However, taken together, these paid engagements were a reminder that their desire to find new economic opportunities through hip hop, in order to provide for themselves and their families, was just as important to them as voicing a particular political position from below. Aap Ki Sadak provided them one such opportunity and the possibility and hope for others.

Change

Many months later, one evening in Khirki, I was leaving an African speakeasy with a few members of the Somali crew. After months roaming in and around Khirki, I was still often disoriented. On this evening, I hesitated and said I did not know my way back to the main road. Hanif, my first contact in the Somali crew, laughed at my witlessness as he and a couple of others from the crew directed me through the now dark alleys and busy main arteries of the colony thronged with pedestrians. We quickly ran into an impediment or series of impediments. Several streets were being paved in the village and, since heavy machinery could not make it into the cramped gallis, the paving was being done manually. I stood and watched as Amin, an older member of the crew, explained to me that this initiative to pave the streets was the result of the Aam Admi Party's recent victory in the Delhi elections. The bigger streets would now be easier to navigate for motorcycles and cars, he said. Also, they would not get muddy and almost impossible to walk through when the monsoon rains came. I wondered what the links were between the Aap Ki Sadak project and this new road improvement initiative rolled out by the Aam Admi Party politicians.

A few days later, I met with Aarthi and had an opportunity to ask her. She said they were not directly linked and, in fact, the road paving was an unfortunate development as it would allow cars to access parts of the village that were previously inaccessible. This ran contrary to Aap Ki Sadak's aim of reducing if not eliminating vehicular traffic in the village. I also asked her about the invisibility of Africans in the Aap Ki Sadak project proposal, prevaricating a response with my own projected reasons for why this exclusion might have been necessary. She paid no attention to my reasoning and interjected,

> The Aap Ki Sadak project started well before the issues surrounding the African community became so central. If we had made the project now, I am not sure how we would have addressed it, but certainly it would have been a central concern for us. I am currently working on advocating for the African community with the local police and I am getting the runaround from officials in the central office and in the local police booth regarding the violence against African students. This is an issue we are working on closely now. The good news is, however, that Aap Ki Sadak has been funded through the SDMC [South Delhi Municipal Corporation]. That means that some of our initiatives will be implemented in the months to come.

Months later, the following appeared in the *Hindustan Times*: "Road redesign to help unclog Malviya Nagar. South municipal corporation gets go-ahead from traffic planning body. If successful, idea to be replicated in other areas as well."[24]

This is the unknown story that I want to tell
Listen to it what, very well
I don't want this to stay the world
It happens daily in my 'hood
Some of them they did what they could
They kept it secret
I'm digging it, deepest
One's force suffers everyone
Why they say there is human rights
When every Black is struggling for their lives
Too many problems, hard to put in one column
And yet no one seems to solve them
I see what they don't see, they see what I don't see
We share what we all see
But yet I don't see no changes
All I see is hating faces
Many people from different races
And every Black struggling for their rights

In his verse, Hanif, a teenage Somali refugee who lives in the South Delhi urban village of Hauz Rani, raps about the issues the African community in Delhi faces.[1] He connects these issues to problems he feels Black people face around the world. He calls these issues human rights issues because, as a Somali refugee who has had close contact with the UNHCR for a number of years in Delhi, he learned quite a bit about human rights discourse and was able to opine what he thought about the limits of human rights by posing the rhetorical question, "Why they say there is human rights when every Black is struggling for their lives?"

Moreover, through his avid interest in hip hop, he is able to link his knowledge of human rights discourse, his experience of discrimination and racialized violence in Delhi, and his knowledge of global anti-Blackness to the Black American experience of settler colonialism and slavery. His lyric "but yet I don't see no changes, all I see is hating faces," for instance, is a remix of American rapper Tupac Shakur's posthumously released 1998 hit song "Changes," where he raps about the United States and its racialized history: "I see no changes all I see is racist faces / misplaced hate makes disgrace to races."[2]

What I am interested in exploring in this chapter, at least partially, are the ways in which Hanif and his Somali crew use (digital) hip hop to understand their experience of gender-specific anti-Blackness in Delhi, and the kinds of ethnographic insights that emerged when I began to spend time with them and hear about their everyday lives in the city. In a recent article on globalization and race, Kamari Clarke and Deborah Thomas argue that while the structural forms and experiential reality of anti-Blackness have been well documented in North America and Europe, little has been written about how racialized thinking affects Africans living on the continent of Africa or elsewhere.[3] In their explicit articulations of anti-Blackness in relation to male bodies in Delhi through hip hop, Hanif and his Somali friends in Delhi offer an opportunity to reflect on the ways in which racism is structured and experienced for African men in the postcolony of India. What sorts of globally familiar racial logics emerge in the representations of their experiences in Delhi? How is this shaped by their consumption of global hip hop, particularly American-produced rap music? How does their use of race as a category of description and identification give us an insight into their masculinities-in-the-making as they come of age in Delhi? How is Delhi's spatiality shaped by incipient forms of racial thinking linked to new patterns of in-migration?

Racism, as Leith Mullings reminds us, is a term that came into common usage in the post–World War II period in the United States. It is a term that links discrimination based on notions of biologized difference with, in Mullings's words, "structures of power that emerge through processes of accumulation and dispossession within local and transnational contexts."[4] My time with Hanif and his friends, as well as other African nationals I met in Delhi, certainly offered up instances of how anti-Blackness is manifesting in India in ways that remind us, as Paul Gilroy recently noted, of the shifting global order that reveals new manifestations of connection between postcolonial geographies and the import of Atlantic histories and cultures in framing difference in these sites of contact.[5] Indeed, digital hip hop offered these young men a means and a method to use race as a category of description and analysis by which to understand their localized experiences of discrimination on a global scale. When narrated through rap, these experiences became the grist to create new relationships with other hip hop heads in Delhi's margins.

Indeed, it was not only the African students, entrepreneurs, and refugees I met while searching for hip hop in Delhi who described the discrimination, exclusion, and violence they experienced in the city as racism. Northeastern (as well as Nepali, Bihari, and Dalit) youth I met in Delhi also described their experience of exclusion and dispossession in terms of race rather than, say, class, caste, or ethnicity.[6] To engage with race and racism as familiar categories of description and discrimination in Delhi's hip hop scene thus required that I had to extend my thinking beyond Hanif's experience of anti-Black discrimination in the city. This chapter, then, also engages with the ways racism is evoked (and experienced) by a broad array of young male practitioners in the city. What emerges is an account of the complicated politics of difference at play in Delhi and the ways in which the globally familiar of race—vis-à-vis media accounts of systemic discrimination and popular resistances to them elsewhere—becomes a site of solidarity and creative production in Delhi, even as it also becomes a locus of fracture and impossibility.

In the last several years, Duncan McDuie-Ra has made a case for engaging with race and racism as a salient categories of difference in metropolitan India based on the accounts of his interlocutors from the Northeast of India.[7] He argues that Northeasterners, a synthetic category used to describe a diverse group of people from the very limits of India's cultural and geographic imaginary, are singled out in Delhi (and other Indian urban centers) because they appear phenotypically East Asian. The Northeasterners he spent time with in Delhi, he argues, describe this process of discrimination as a historically induced and structurally embedded example of racism in the context of South Asia.

McDuie-Ra's attention to the Northeastern experience has been instructive. He offers a reckoning of how social (and economic) exclusions in Delhi, for instance, produce a turning away from a national identity toward identities that are constituted within a global racial order. For instance, he discusses how the Northeastern youth he spent time with looked east, toward Korea and Japan, for stylistic inspiration—similar to what I observed (and have discussed in previous chapters) among Northeastern and Nepali youth who gravitated to Korean hip hop, K-pop, and Japanese manga for fashion cues, even as they consumed American hip hop.

McDuie-Ra also argues for an attention to the kinds of laboring opportunities in the retail industry that Northeastern young people have access to because they are seen as modern and global in relation to their working-class counterparts from other backgrounds. He suggests that this perception of Northeastern youth has fueled a process whereby these youth take up performances of significant difference to highlight and make productive their Otherness in the labor market. His arguments coincide, again, with what I observed in Delhi's emerging youth culture industry, where labor is gendered and racialized and young Northeastern and Nepali men occupy a particular niche within the emergent popular cultural political economies of urban India (see chapter 3).

However, while McDuie-Ra's work offers insights into the increasing salience of race as a category of difference in urban India, his focus on Northeasterners' experiences of discrimination and adaptation to the racial hierarchies of the city obscures the important relationships Delhi's Others build with each other. How do these relationships across difference mutually constitute how experiences of discrimination come to be called racism? As importantly, McDuie-Ra's analysis of race and racism in Delhi misses the ways in which popular media flows—such as hip hop, of course, but also social media circulations that broadcast instances of racism in Delhi and elsewhere—shape how a diverse cross section of young people in Delhi learn to categorize their experiences *as* racism.

Digital media circulations of racism, more generally, offered Northeastern, African, Nepali, and lower-caste and Dalit-identifying young men in the hip hop scene a shared idiom and aesthetic practice by which to describe their experiences in relation to unfolding events across the world. In particular, news of racialized violence in the United States—particularly instances of violence toward young Black men—were consumed in Delhi through reposts of news items and memes of the incidents. These mediatized events became ways in which hip hop and the Black male experience in the United

States intersected to create a common aesthetic and affective ground. For instance, there were several occasions I witnessed where Northeastern, Somali, and Nigerian youth consumed media about the Trayvon Martin case in the months after the Black teenager was killed in his neighborhood in Florida by George Zimmerman.[8] Jay, introduced in chapter 1, asked me to bring him an "I am Trayvon" hoodie when I was planning on traveling back to the United States for a month or two in the spring of 2013.

For Jay, the hoodie at once stood for a relationship with hip hop as well as his connection with the struggles of young Black men in the United States. The deployment of such materialized symbols as the hoodie perhaps become more significant when we see them in music videos that depict experiences of discrimination *as* racism in the city. For instance, in the 2018 music video by Arunachali (Northeastern) rapper K4 Kekho titled "I Am an Indian," he begins by showing an exchange between himself and a normative male Delhiite (who represents the ignorant hypermasculine male of India) in a public bathroom.[9] K4 Kekho has just gone to the toilet (the video uses close-ups followed by medium shots to how he has to stand on his tiptoes to reach the top of the urinal because he is short). While washing hands, he has an exchange with a tall, bearded "Indian" man who immediately asks him in English, "Hey bro, where are you from?" K4 Kekho makes a face and then responds in Hindi, "I am from Arunachal Pradesh." The video proceeds with K4 Kekho schooling his interlocutor about the geography of northeastern India and describing the kinds of racialized discrimination Arunachalis face in Delhi when they come to study there (citing the 2014 attack on an Arunachali student in Lajpat Nagar that garnered national attention, an incident I will return to later in this chapter).

K4 Kekho rocks a hoodie through most of the video, rhyming in a mix of English and Hindi. My point in drawing attention to the hoodie is not to overplay its symbolic significance. I hope you do not fixate on the hoodie! Rather, I am interested in thinking with the hoodie as a material and symbolic link between the discrimination that artists like K4 Kekho describe as racist and North American histories of racial oppression. Of course, hip hop and rap, in particular, do the work of making these connections, but I find the materiality of the hoodie and its social significance in the post–Trayvon Martin moment particularly compelling to think with when approaching digitality and the global racial order (recall my discussion of sartorial things in chapter 2).

With that said, let us return to K4 Kekho's video and rap. His lyrics push us to think about the intersectional ways in which racism appears in the city,

offering a witty, careful critique of the kinds of discrimination Northeasterners experience by pointing to a vulgar hegemonic masculinity associated
with men in urban centers like Delhi.

> Chuha jesa challo varna koi hum log ko maar dega
> Esa dektai jese who log sach mein hum log ko khaa dega
> Vegetarian hone se bhi lagtai nonvegetarian hain
> Aakh par ke dekhtai jese hum log koi alien ha
> [Walk like a mouse or else they will kill us
> They look at us as if they will eat us
> Even vegetarians seem to be nonvegetarian
> They look at us as if we were aliens]

As K4 Kekho raps the lines about how even vegetarians seem to be nonveg-
etarian, we see a dark-skinned, moustache-wearing middle-aged man looking with carnal lust at a Northeastern girl as he savagely eats a carrot in a
restaurant. The video then cuts back to K4 Kekho rhyming in his hoodie in a
smoky room with the words *I am Indian* scrawled behind him. In his visuals
and lyrics, K4 Kekho subtly connects Delhi rape culture to a hypermasculine vegetarian Hindu male subject. In so doing, he wades into the politics
of food in relation to intersectional forms of difference—a politics that has
national visibility in the current moment, as cow vigilantism (and beef bans)
proceed unchecked and unabated and target male Muslims as well as men
from other minority groups.[10] While the impact of this sort of moral policing by the Hindu majority has been discussed with regard to Muslims and
Dalits across the country, it also affects Northeasterners, especially in a city
like Delhi. In Delhi, Northeasterners are often disparaged by both Hindus
and Muslims because they eat pork as well as beef. The rise of the right-wing
Hindu's moral policing of food and the rhetoric they use to cast vegetarian-
ism as an index of superiority and purity, K4 Kekho intimates, does not give
them moral high ground when it comes to sexual politics in the city.

In his audiovisual play, K4 Kekho is able to associate racism with a virulent form of masculine (Hindu) nationalism. He is also able to claim a very
different gendered subjectivity for himself and for Northeastern men—one
that eschews a virulent form of masculinity. Moreover, as K4 Kekho links
local experiences of discrimination and national exclusion through symbols
associated with the Black American experience (like the hoodie), a direct
link between structures of power in Delhi and in the United States mate-
rializes to connect these geographies. By telling his community's story of
discrimination in relationship to the national politics of difference in India

and linking it through materialized signs to struggle elsewhere, κ4 Kekho is also able to create new connections and solidarities with others who experience similar unequal conditions in Delhi. Yet in his claim to Indianness ("I Am Indian," after all, is the title of the track), κ4 Kehko also creates a logic of exclusion that reinforces the nation-state and its synthetic borders as the basis for inclusion.

As my quick analysis of κ4 Kekho's video shows, an attention to race and racism as a *global familiar* opens up the potential for me to provide an intersectional and comparative analysis of difference in Delhi—one that locates gender, nationalism, ethnicity, religion, and class in its youthful discursive and aesthetic digital formations. Hip hop, as I hope the previous chapters along with κ4 Kekho and Hanif's lyrics have shown, generates "social resonances between [US] Black expressive culture within its contextual political history and similar dynamics in other nations," in ways that enable young people in Delhi to open a digitally enabled dialogue with each other around common, unequal conditions.[11] However, while hip hop brought Delhi's racialized Others together, they also placed them at odds, as highlighted by κ4 Kekho's nationalist lyrics as well as what I described briefly in the previous chapter when discussing labor arrangements in Delhi's burgeoning youth cultural scene.

Certainly, opportunities for participation and exposure in Delhi's hip hop world were not equal. While Hanif and other African nationals I met in Delhi certainly participated in the kinds of hip hop friendship cultures of production (as described in chapter 1), as well as establishing spatial and social relations in and around Delhi in their pursuit of swag (chapter 2), they could not easily participate in hip hop–generated networking opportunities.

For instance, while some of the working-class and lower-caste men I have introduced in this book experienced discrimination based on their perceived class difference and migrant positionality in Delhi, they could access artists, activists, hip hop emissaries, and journalists looking for an authentic "Indian" hip hop artist. Hanif and other African nationals, however, could not access the same relations. Nor could they access the jobs in the burgeoning youth culture as those we met in the previous chapter could, or, like κ4 Kekho, make a claim to the nation and act as representatives of an Indian hip hop in doing so. This returns us to Hanif's description of anti-Blackness in Delhi and the limits of possibility, even within a hip hop world of sociality, for young African men in the city. The globally familiar, when seen as a reproduction of anti-Black sentiment that produces exclusions and frictions in Delhi, is a reminder of the ways in which a globalized colonial racial order sustains and reproduces itself, ironically within the African diasporic artistic practice of hip hop.

Hanif and the African Community of Khirki

I first met Hanif soon after one of the several episodic eruptions of violence against African students, entrepreneurs, and refugees living in South Delhi that took place while I lived in the city. MC Zanoor, an underground MC and somewhat of a star in Delhi's hip hop scene, first introduced me to Hanif and his friends. Zanoor had performed at an India/Africa event sponsored by the Indian Ministry of External Affairs.[12] During the event, he had met several East and West African youth who lived in the city. They immediately gravitated to him because in his lyrics he discusses his intimate relationship with Africa and India by way of his Sudanese father and Punjabi mother. They also gravitated to him because he was one of the very few recognized hip hop stars in Delhi who showed a deep interest in their experiences as Africans in Delhi's margins.

Zanoor offered these relative newcomers to India another way to think about being between worlds through his poetry. He also became, for Hanif at least, something of a mentor.[13] Hanif would send him raps on Facebook Messenger, either written or recorded, and Zanoor would give him feedback. Hanif and his crew, in turn, offered Zanoor an affective and immediate connection to Africa. Months after Zanoor met Hanif, he introduced me to him and his friends during one of his trips to Khirki. I eventually began to spend time with Hanif, Salim, and Amin, and several other of their diverse group of friends, many of whom avidly wrote raps and aspired to become MCs. I ended up spending the majority of my time with the Somalis in the crew, who shared with me what they did to pass time while they waited.

They were waiting for the UNHCR to find them a "third country" that would offer them permanent asylum. While Hanif and his Somali friends waited for an opportunity to leave India, they went to school, learned Hindi, made friends, and engaged with hip hop's musical forms.[14] Some of these young men had been waiting for more than a decade at the point when I met them. Hanif, for instance, had moved to India when he was seven. He lived in Hyderabad until he was eleven, then moved with his family to Delhi so that they could actively work with the central UNHCR office in the capital city and find a way to Europe or North America.

Somalis were just one of the many African national communities who made their home in the city. In the past decade, there has been an increase in migration from Africa to Asia. Statistical data indicates that tens of thousands of people from more than a dozen East and West African nations have traveled to China or India in the last five years to pursue higher education goals, establish entrepreneurial ventures, or seek asylum.[15]

This migratory flow from sub-Saharan Africa to India and China reflects the rising status of India and China in the global economy as well as the increasing difficulty for migrants from the Global South to enter Europe and North America. As Africans find themselves living in the urban centers of Asia, they encounter localized versions of global discourses on racial difference, where Blackness is positioned at the bottom of a racial order developed during colonial rule and refined in the postcolonial period.[16] As Hanif notes in his closing stanza, and as I intimately observed in my time in the city, Africans in Delhi experience a virulent anti-Black racism in a national context where caste, religion, class, and language have historically been the categories that structure difference.

One afternoon, as I sat with Hanif, Salim, and several other Somali and Afghani youth at the Satpula dam, alternately taking turns rapping and talking, Salim began to discuss the rumor spreading through the village that Africans were kidnapping and eating people.[17] "How can they call us cannibals? Say that that we eat people? I mean, maybe they found an organ somewhere in some Nigerian man's fridge who is doing organ trading but how then do they think we are cannibals? That we eat people? They are racist. This is what we have to deal with every day as Africans in Delhi, and even we are not all the same." Salim's passionate narration of the story's contours touches upon the discursive violence that occurs daily in Delhi against African nationals. These sorts of racialized and often gendered narratives of difference, where contact with the Other is expressed in terms of inhumanity, are set in the working-class context of Khirki and Hauz Rani, where a large number of Congolese, Nigerian, Somali, Ivorian, and Ugandan nationals lived during the time I was in Delhi. While I performed some degree of surprise as Salim recounted his story, I had heard offhand accounts of Africans engaging in cannibalism and organ trading from other residents of Khirki before I met Hanif and his crew.

The story of cannibalism related to Africans in contemporary Delhi offers an entry point into how colonial discourses that entangle cultural and biological difference prefigure and produce racial hierarchies in Delhi. To be termed a cannibal in the colonial period was an accusation reserved for those relegated to what Michel-Rolph Trouillot calls the "savage slot," the position reserved for those outside White modernity.[18] Cannibal, along with indolent, irrational, barbaric, and savage, formed the terminology that Viranjini Munasinghe calls the British "colonial idiom" that established Africans and Indians as racialized subjects in relation to one another and to their colonial masters.[19] The cannibal narrative that Salim placed in contemporary Delhi reveals how this history lives on in the present and shapes future relationships between southern geographies, as eastward migration grows and urban centers like Delhi become the destination of students, entrepreneurs, and refugees from western, eastern, and southern Africa.

This virulent discourse of difference had several consequences for African nationals living in Khirki. For instance, this discourse precipitated violent attacks against Africans by groups of self-styled vigilantes, working-class men who were also migrants to Delhi. These unpredictable eruptions of violence should be seen in direct relationship to the sorts of dehumanizing stories that circulated in Khirki. As Veena Das has argued, the circulation of rumors that perpetuate notions of radical Otherness often form the logic for brutal acts of physical aggression against those deemed to be outsiders.[20]

These episodes of violence should also be seen in direct relationship to the political economy that emerges as Africans move into urban villages in South Delhi like Khirki. Landlords in Khirki, for instance, rented flats to African students, refugees, and entrepreneurs and often charged them higher prices. Several African nationals shared with me their housing stories and woes, complaining of rapacious landlords and real estate agents who found ways to extract extra money from them on a monthly basis. For instance, Salim told me how his father would have monthly arguments with the landlord over the electricity bill. The landlord would present large electricity bills to Salim's father, far too exorbitant an amount given their daily usage. Finally, Salim's father hired a *katyabaaz* to investigate and found that the electric meter recording usage was linked to two flats, their own and a second flat.[21] I mention this story, in particular, because Hanif used this anecdote to write a freestyle rap during one of our many sessions at Satpula about power and its many different forms. I also mention this story because these sorts of dilemmas that placed housing at the forefront of social interaction were offered to me as evidence of anti-Black racism by the African men and women I met in Delhi.

Landlords also allowed African nationals to set up illegal kitchens and bars in residential flats in exchange for higher rents. These restaurants and flats were, according to several of the kitchen operators I talked with, protected by the local police in exchange for a monthly payoff. Local residents in Khirki and other urban villages I frequented where there was a growing

African population were deeply incensed at the rising rents and the advent of a culturally alien social life that they perceived was ushered in by African nationals when they moved into the village. The kitchens, as many of Khirki's older Bihari, Nepali, and Garhwali residents expressed to me, were places of indiscretion. In their eyes, these semipublic social spaces fostered social drinking and gave license to nonkin male/female relationships. They were, in a nutshell, perceived as a corrupting force in the community. In this case, notions of cultural difference with regard to male/female sociality, dress, and even food (Khirki residents complained to me about the smell of African food) melded together quite quickly with ideas of essential, biologized difference.

In the time I got to know Hanif and his Somali friends in Delhi, they described to me in detail the complicated politics of difference related to African bodies in Khirki. They also introduced me to the many illegal kitchen and bar operators as well as the African nationals who lived in Khirki and frequented these kitchens. In the spaces of the kitchens, I observed Hanif and his Somali friends interacting with Francophone West Africans, Nigerians, and Kenyans. Tales of racism on the streets of Delhi were an everyday topic of conversation, a way to bridge the linguistic, religious, and cultural differences among the diversity represented from the continent. English became the common language by which to narrate the everyday and exceptional racialized violence they experienced.

Hip hop and other popular African diasporic music—Naija pop, for instance—was another means to connect the African diasporic subjects who shared time and space as well as aspirations and challenges as they made their lives in India.[22] Hanif and his friends had several Nigerian friends with whom they developed relationships, in part, through hip hop. In the kitchen, they would discuss new music that had just come out, or they would talk about sharing the music they had produced. In a few effervescent conversations I witnessed in the African kitchens of Khirki, plans were hatched to record tracks together.

Yet even as there was an opportunity to commiserate about the travails and travesties of living in Delhi and to discuss the possibility of collaborating on creative endeavors steeped in the globalized African diasporic musicality of hip hop, there was also the possibility for the specter of anti-Blackness to arise between Africans from different parts of the continent. Recall that Salim suggested, when telling me about the fantastical story circulating about African cannibalism in Delhi, that Nigerians were involved in the organ trade. The idea that Nigerians were deeply involved in illegal activities was embedded in a local (and transnational) discourse about Nigerians as criminals in control of various internet-related scams, drug trafficking, and so on.[23] This discourse of criminality associated with Nigerians, as it became localized in Delhi, worked to encompass all Africans living in the city.

Delhiites would use the term *Nigerians* as a category of description by which to describe Africans and, in that vein, suggest that all Africans were criminals. Salim's specific, even if offhand reference to Nigerians and the organ trade is a reminder of the ways in which anti-Blackness can be subtly perpetuated among those in the African diaspora. Salim does the work of differentiating himself and other Somalis from Nigerians, even as his story regarding cannibalism is meant to create a common category that produces a sense of solidarity between himself and Nigerians by talking about their shared experiences of discrimination.

These sorts of casual comments, which placed the burden of anti-Blackness on some of the pan-African community of Khirki over others, sometimes manifested in more direct and immediate conflict. In one instance, the police came around to harass all the African nationals in the colony by asking them to show their visas, after people complained that a couple of men identified as Nigerians were fighting on the street in the early hours of the morning. As I sat with a Kenyan and Ivorian friend of mine in a kitchen soon after this incident, I heard people muttering to each other that some Nigerians were in fact the problem, and their countrymen in Khirki needed to rein them in. Some of the Nigerians in the kitchen took offense and a heated debate ensued regarding whether it was really Nigerians who were fighting in the first place and, if it was, whose responsibility it was to address the issue. Finally, one of the Nigerian men, Peter, who exported hair from India to Lagos, unequivocally said that it was not "Nigerians" who were the problem, but it was the Igbo people from the Southeast of Nigeria who were always causing issues, and that other Nigerians had nothing to do with it. Peter's move to further differentiate and shift the burden of responsibility to another tribal group reveals the pernicious ways in which structural forms of racism activate enduring ideas of localized difference in new social contexts.[24]

For Hanif, Salim, and the other Somali youth I got to know, African kitchens became venues where playful banter with Nigerians, Ivorians, and Cameroonians opened up the space for debate and potential conflict around who could legitimately stake masculine claims to Africa, Africanness, and Blackness. Nigerian men, for instance, would question the Africanness of Somalis by commenting on their build ("you're so skinny, not like an African man at all") or their proficiency in Hindi ("you're an Indian, not an African;

you speak Hindi!"). They also pointed out that the Somalis were accepted by Muslims in Delhi and that the Muslim residents of Hauz Rani went so far as to protect them from Hindu thugs in the neighborhood. "They call you guys 'Bilal' and keep you safe. We're just Christian cannibals to them," said Peter laughingly one day while we all sat in a kitchen in Khirki passing time. By referencing Bilal, Peter drew attention to the ways in which Somali men, in particular, were legitimized in Hauz Rani by their faith. Bilal Al-Habashi, one of the companions of the Prophet Muhammad, was African. Peter recognized that when the Muslim residents of Hauz Rani called Hanif and his crew Bilal, they were being recognized as part of a global Muslim *umma*.[25] Through these discursive moves, young West African men suggested not only that the Somalis were not as African as they were but that they did not face the same issues in terms of discrimination.

Salim, Hanif, and their crew learned to respond in ways that demanded respect. With English-speaking Nigerians, this meant mobilizing the bits of Pidgin they had learned to make counterclaims about their experiences as Black men in Delhi. Moreover, they utilized their knowledge of hip hop as a means to demonstrate their knowledge of the dominant registers of global Blackness and their aesthetic repertoires. It is telling that one young man in Hanif's crew was called Biggie by all the Nigerians in Khirki as a moniker of respect. "Biggie" was, of all the Somalis I met, the most proficient in Nigerian Pidgin. He was also quite literally larger than his Somali peers, but, most important, his style, knowledge of American hip hop, and ability to rap allowed those who knew him as Biggie to connect him to the internationally acclaimed late Biggie Smalls, a rapper from Brooklyn who was murdered in the late 1990s.

In addition to connecting me to African nationals in Khirki and elsewhere, Hanif and his friends introduced me to their Afghani, Nepali, and Northeastern friends. This set of friends, young men that Hanif and his crew met in Khirki and Hauz Rani or in other places in South Delhi through school, were all interested in hip hop music and in experimenting with production and the poetics of hip hop. The group interacted in Hindi and their social engagements consisted of meeting each other in different locations in the city to hang out, smoke, and make music. Often, these sessions would take place in Satpula. The relationships they forged with each other through the stories they shared about their respective experiences of racism in Delhi, as well as their more general "race talk," carried over into the realm of social media.

In several instances, Hanif was playfully called "Desi Nigga" by this diverse group of young men. It was a moniker he embraced. For Hanif, Desi

Nigga was an apt and appropriate descriptor of his indeterminate subjectivity: the in-betweenness that his decade in India had produced, an in-betweenness that placed him between global understandings of Blackness and Indianness. *Desi* is a globally circulating term that indexes a connection to India, which doesn't necessarily require national identification but rather requires a sense of belonging to the cultural worlds of South Asia.[26] While the term in South Asian diasporic circles has been perceived as a northern term that inextricably links place (*desh*) to a subjectivity that creates solidarity between Hindi-Urdu speaking people while excluding other linguistic communities, for Hanif's friends, Desi simply marked Hanif's deep cultural and linguistic connection to South Asia.

Nigga is a term that is the reappropriation of the plantation epithet *nigger* that emerged in the United States during slavery. *Nigger* carries all the weight of White supremacy and the structural devaluation of Black life in its enunciation. *Nigga*, on the other hand, as Marc Anthony Neale argues, indexes "concepts of blackness that are mobile, fluid, adaptable, postmodern, and urban and embodying various forms of social and rhetorical flow most evident in hip hop."[27] Hanif's embrace and use of *nigga*, no doubt, indexed a relationship with the Black American experience but decoupled the term from any geographic specificity. For Hanif, *nigga* was glossed in a way that suggests his self-understanding as a social and cultural hybrid, a mobile and fluid agent in his lifeworld. Yet his use of *nigga* as a self-descriptor also points to a deep recognition of his Otherness, an Otherness that is all too apparent for Hanif and his Somali crew as they understand the various Hindi-derived argots of Khirki and hear narratives of alterity applied to them by people who imagine that they could not possibly understand what is being said.

Hanif began to use the term *Desi Nigga* on social media posts. One of Hanif's selfie photographs, tucked between a post of a hip hop music video followed by a story on Somalia, revealed him in the back of a car with a New York Yankees cap with a caption that read "desi nigga." Hanif, by casting himself as a Desi Nigga in relation to the image of him looking into the camera with his red-and-black Yankees hat cocked to the side, resists the kinds of racialized exclusions that he faces as a Somali in Delhi by making his experiences of difference central to his image-making project. His resistance to exclusion is based on his simultaneous claims to a global Black subjectivity and a boundless Indianness vis-à-vis hip hop.

The comments found below the photo and its caption from a diverse set of friends in English, Somali, and Hindi reflect the ways in which they read his negotiations of racial subjectivity. For example, his Somali and West African friends, writing in English and Somali, highlighted their collective claim to a global form of Blackness in their comments that repeat *Nigga* (without *Desi*). There is a curious resistance in this partial recognition. African nationals might have persistent and indelible ties that connect them to India, yet not all of them claim these connections as a key part of their subjectivity. There is also an amplification of *nigga*, a testament to Blackness, as something that transcends nation.

Hanif's Nepali, Northeastern, and Bihari friends repeated *Desi Nigga* in the comments section of the Facebook post to reinforce their claim to his subjectivity. However, they never referred to Hanif as Desi *or* Nigga. This reiteration of *Desi Nigga* could be read as a gleeful celebration, a way to understand themselves through the moniker that they have created for Hanif as well as a way to cast their aspirations for a kind of transcendent subjectivity that exceeds the situated, the lived, the immediate. *Desi Nigga*, as it is circulated within the network of relations that this image and its caption reached, offered the promise of possibility of relationships beyond what was expected. Their use of *Desi Nigga* was also a way to recognize the need for a more complicated term to describe Hanif's subjectivity that did not fall back on oversimplification or appropriation. While a nuanced understanding of *nigga* (in relationship to *desi*) was evident in the way it was used among Hanif's circle of friends, this same sensitivity was not necessarily apparent in the larger, Delhi hip hop scene.

Nigga became a term of address used among hip hop–involved young people in Delhi to refer to one another. It manifested audibly within spoken Hindi phrases—"*Yo nigga, kya karta?* What are you doing?"—that I heard during hip hop events I attended in the city. In these moments, the ambient sound of the crowd, the porous murmurs, and the unintelligible conversations would give way to a two-syllable sound: *nigga*. I would hear it, wince, look up, and see a young (fifteen years old or so) b-boy who appeared Indian in the normative sense, smiling at the friend he was addressing, who also appeared Indian. Zanoor and I had many conversations about non-Black people in Delhi using the term. He was strongly opposed to anyone using *nigga* but felt especially affronted when kids in Delhi used the term. "They have no idea the racism that goes behind that word," he said. He recalled an instance where he called out an Indian American DJ and music producer, Sulu, for referring to him as *nigga* in a friendly conversation.

Zanoor said, "That guy, just because he grew up in America around Black people, he thinks he can use the word. It's offensive. I told him so and he pulled out his Zulu Nation medallion and said, 'I'm part of Zulu

Nation, bro,' as if that was going to justify it. We almost fought right then and there, but then he backed off and apologized. I still heard him using the word though, with other people. I don't know, bro. I think it's racist." Sulu, however, felt that as a self-identified low-caste Dravidian from the South of India, he had a claim to *nigga* that went beyond his diasporic experience. For Sulu, *nigga* referred to his status in the subcontinent, particularly as a dark-skinned southerner in Delhi.

Hanif's friends from Mizoram (in the Northeast), Nepal, and Kerala would, in the safe space Satpula provided, share their own stories of discrimination in Delhi through their poetics and in conversation in between rap exchanges. They also referred to Delhi as a racist place, drawing my attention to the violence committed against Northeastern and Nepali men and women in the city. For instance, they discussed with me the attack on an Arunachali student and his subsequent death in early 2014 (the same event K4 Kekho highlights in his video), pulling up their phones to show me the news coverage about the incident and the political response it generated, as it forced the issue of racial discrimination against Northeasterners in Delhi into the public eye. This incident against the Arunachali student subsequently sparked protests among Northeastern communities living in Delhi, who argued that the attack was an example of the racialized discrimination they faced regularly. This violent incident spurred Arvind Kejriwal, the chief minister of Delhi from the newly elected Aam Aadmi Party, to announce, "There is no place for elements trying to spread hatred against people belonging to any particular part of the country."[28]

In this context, Northeastern young men in Hanif's larger friend circle discussed the kinds of verbal abuse they faced on a daily basis. These conversations created equivalencies and connections between their various experiences of what they referred to as racism. "Chinky, that's what they call me," said Siddarth. "Madrasi, they call me Madrasi.[29] I am from Kerala but the stupid, racist bastards don't know anything," said Paul from Kerala. Hanif retorted, "Sometimes they call me Madrasi too, especially when I speak Hindi. They can't believe an African can speak Hindi." Everyone laughed.

While the first comment about being called chinky reiterates McDuie-Ra's research experiences of Northeasterners being identified and identifying as racialized subjects, as well as K4 Kekho's sentiments in the track I discussed earlier, Paul's and Hanif's responses offer a way to understand their shared articulation of racism as comparative and related. Chinky, in relationship to Madrasi, a term of derision used by Delhiites since the 1950s to describe South Indians when processes of urbanization and migration brought a significant influx of southerners to Delhi, created a means for Paul, Hanif, and Siddarth to tie their experiences together.[30]

These comparative ways of understanding how racism functions in Delhi as a structural system of exclusion and hierarchy that impacts regional and international migrants alike were inadvertently echoed in public discourse on particular occasions. In 2017 violence directed toward African nationals once again erupted in the capital city. A group of vigilantes attacked and viciously beat a Kenyan man in a mall in Noida as a response to the death of a teenager who had overdosed on drugs purportedly supplied to him by an African. Tarun Vijay, a politician and former MP, made a statement about this latest spate of violence against Africans not being rooted in racism. He argued, "If we were racist, why would we have all the entire south . . . Tamil, Kerala, Karnataka and Andhra . . . why do we live with them? We have black people around us."[31] Vijay's statement was an attempt to paper over the extreme discrimination that African nationals face, by making a claim that racism in India did not exist. Yet Vijay's statement creates an equivalence between Africans and South Indians based on color. The irony, of course, is that his statement highlights the virulent racism, colorism, and casteism that exists in India and that extends beyond the kinds of experiences that Africans in India face in the contemporary moment. Moreover, Vijay's statement gives credence to the kind of casual solidarity that Paul, Hanif, and Siddarth demonstrate. It perhaps also lends some context and credence to Sulu's claim to *nigga* in the South Asian context.

Soon after Hanif, Paul, and Siddarth finished their conversation, Paul pulled out his phone and put on a Kendrick Lamar track. I recognized it immediately as a song that Lamar released in 2011 called "Fuck Your Ethnicity." They began to recite some of the lyrics along with the song, although they were slightly off, not able to keep up with his cadence.

> Fire burning inside my eyes, this the music that saved my life
> y'all be calling it hip hop, I be calling it hypnotize
> yeah, hypnotize, trapped my body but freed my mind
> what the fuck are you fighting for? Ain't nobody gon' win that war
> my details be retail, man I got so much in store
> racism is still alive yellow tape and colored lines
> fuck that, nigga look at that line, it's so diverse.[32]

In his lyrics, Lamar argues that hip hop has freed his mind to recognize racism is still alive, even as he suggests hip hop traps him in a capitalist cycle of consumption. That Hanif and his Northeastern, Nepali, and South Indian friends mouthed these lyrics soon after joking about their shared experiences of everyday discrimination offers a view into how their conception of racism based on what they see, hear, and feel in Delhi relates to the (hip hop) media they consume. Racism becomes familiar. It is not only felt but narrated by others across the world in ways that are recognizable. Moreover, racism and consumerism are felt as inextricably linked. This produces a sense of solidarity across difference that is coupled with a bittersweet recognition that hip hop–endorsed diversity is good for business.

Yet this solidarity based on experiences of shared discrimination (and shared consumption) were shaken when state-sponsored acts of anti-Black violence offered a clear reminder of who Delhi's current hypervilified Other was. In 2014 Somnath Bharti, a law minister and part of the newly elected Aam Admi Party, began to listen to the complaints of his new constituency in Khirki and Malviya Nagar about the illegal African restaurants in the neighborhood. Rumors of cannibalism were mixed together with lurid tales of sexual deviance, substance abuse, and drug dealing linked to Africans and to the hospitality establishments associated with them. Bharti went on a public campaign to rid Khirki and its surrounds of African nationals. One evening, he rounded up a gang of vigilantes and raided several Congolese students' flats, looking for contraband and evidence of alleged prostitution. The raids became national news very quickly. On television Bharti defended his extrajuridical acts by claiming that the police were corrupt and would not address his constituents' concerns. He also justified his attacks on Africans by saying soon after the attacks, "Yeh hum aur aap jaise nahin hain. They are not like you or me."[33]

The bold and direct statement of Africans' radical alterity sits in stark juxtaposition to Kejriwal's statement calling for tolerance in relation to violence against Northeasterners. It offers a clear example of how the mobilization of the nation allows for a public discourse that makes opaque understandings of who can be included and who cannot in urban India. These statements, when taken together, also suggest how fragile solidarity might be between members of groups who describe their discrimination in the same language of racism when it comes to the possibility of state-sponsored violence.

Instances of violence against Africans, however, were not only instigated by the state. They also occurred during late-night parties across the city. These conflagrations were described to me as conflicts between men over women. I was told Northeastern men attempted to protect the "honor" of Northeastern women who were seen with African men by starting fights with the African men. This hypermasculine aggression no doubt evinces a persistent patriarchal assumption that women are not agentic, that they need protection from the power and influence of other men. It also indexes the ways in which Northeastern women have been perceived in Delhi as "loose" and available and the ways in which Northeastern men feel an obligation to subvert these assumptions.

When I spoke to some of the Northeastern men who were involved in these sorts of incidents, they suggested that the men they fought with were Nigerian and "aggressive" and that they were forced to fight. When I pushed them to recall what precipitated the fight in the first place, they told me that they asked the African nationals, "What are you doing here, anyway?"—a question that immediately reinscribes the bounded space of insiders and outsiders, a bordered, national space of inclusion.

The fissures and cracks that called into question solidarity between Northeasterners and African nationals also played out in less obvious ways. For instance, in the urban villages of Khirki and Humayunpur, I would hear of situations where apartments were rented to Northeasterners (as well as Tibetans and Nepalis) only after it became evident that the only other option for the landlord was to rent the flat to an African national. This sort of competition for inexpensive housing pitted everyone who experienced the brutal logics of everyday racism against one another when it came to basic needs.

The absence of young African nationals in the formalized spaces of hip hop cultural production also attested to the fragility of solidarity. I found it striking that, while I met aspiring rappers, singers, and dancers from Cameroon, Nigeria, Somalia, and Kenya in South Delhi's urban villages, these young people would never turn up at either the corporate-sponsored or underground jams that took place throughout the city (like the ones I described in the previous chapter). These young men had discovered the party scene and went to listen to DJs spin records in various locations around the city. Yet they had not been invited into the networks, by either Delhi-based practitioners or international hip hop emissaries, that put them into contact with the burgeoning hip hop milieu in the city, or, if they did find out about events, they felt it was not a space for them.

Roca, a Nigerian MC I met in Khirki, for instance, had witnessed in passing a few of the impromptu b-boy demonstrations that Sudhir and his crew put on in and around Khirki. When I asked him why he did not attend these jams, he said, "No, bredda, that's for these Indian kids. I wouldn't know what to do there. Anyway, I can't dance; I can only rap and sing." Part of the issue, as alluded to by Roca, was that in 2013–14 public-facing hip hop cultural production in Delhi was very much focused on dance. The jams that did take place in various locations around the city were opportunities for aspiring b-boys to practice together or to compete against each other. Only on a very rare occasion, as we saw in chapter 3, did it offer up a space for aspiring MCs to rap.

In the few instances where MCs could perform, only established rappers were given the opportunity. These opportunities to MC were offered to artists who could demonstrate they had a local following. Delhi-based MCs, like Zanoor but also, in subsequent years, MC Soni and MC Jay, utilized the music videos they posted on YouTube and the likes and comments they garnered as evidence of their growing fame. This social media–enmeshed economy placed MCs like Roca on the margins, precisely because it reproduced a local and national frame of recognition.

When I first met him, Hanif had not attended any underground events either. He only found out about the more visible Delhi hip hop scenes when he met MC Zanoor. Through Zanoor, Hanif was exposed to a world of hip hop in his city. He expressed surprise to me that this world existed as he told me stories of his first forays out with Zanoor to clubs and underground jams. He thought it was only his crew of friends that were interested in rapping and music production in Delhi.

Soon after I met Hanif, I began to introduce him to other MCs in Khirki as potential collaborators. I also began to bring Hanif and his crew to Singh's apartment to record tracks. Singh, the sociolinguist I met early on in my stay in Delhi, created a studio space located on the edge of Khirki, where it was easy to bring Hanif, Sudhir, and others together to play with writing and recording music. These meetings allowed for a different kind of dialogue around difference, inequality, and opportunity that did not center around race and racism or class discrimination but hinged on shared aspirations to produce lyrical stories of life in the capital city.

The Otherwise and the Fractures Therein

Singh's makeshift studio, located in Malviya Nagar, a well-to-do colony on the edges of Khirki, for a short while became a place to imagine an otherwise.[34] I use the term *otherwise* here purposefully, following Elizabeth Povinelli's suggestion that the otherwise is a sense of curiosity and that it is "not a curiosity to assimilate what is proper for one to know but that which enables one to get free of oneself."[35] While certainly the curiosity that drove these young men was a sense that they needed to have certain skills and products to participate in the hazy but promising world of youth cultural production

in Delhi and the perhaps even more ephemeral world of global hip hop, they also gravitated toward the studio to get free of themselves.

Part of getting free from themselves was losing—in the process of writing, rhyming, and recording—the feeling of weight that comes with the burden of categories. Race, class, and caste could dissolve in shared effervescence of creative play (even though the studio maintained itself as an exclusively male space). Of course, the irony is that in our capacity to get free by making signs to mark our experience of the world, in our ability to materialize feeling and point to the kinds of affective structures that make them, we often narrate that which binds us (recall Lamar's lyrics about hip hop, racism, and capitalism). In this sense, the notion of the globally familiar is a kind of trap that limits our capacity for seeking an otherwise that has not been imagined as yet. In this sense, the globally familiar reminds me of Berlant's idea that optimism, like curiosity, is cruel (or perhaps ambivalent, as I suggested in the introduction), particularly when it fixates on temporary freedoms and leaves aside the struggle for more enduring ones.[36]

Singh's studio, where Jay and I conspired to make a music video to bridge religious and ethnic difference for the sake of love, or where I sat with Hanif and helped him think through the lines with which this chapter began, was a space of curiosity, a place where an ephemeral sense of freedom could arise. Over time the studio also came to signify other things. As the years have passed, our makeshift studio has, for me, become an example of the fragile relations across difference that hip hop produces as it travels across contexts. It also became a starting point for several young people I met in Delhi in their continuing hip hop journeys: *pehle se track Jaspal Singh ke sath record kar diya*, I recorded my first track with Jaspal Singh. The studio also produced relations that endure. For instance, Hanif, even though he has since moved to Finland after his family gained asylum there, is still collaborating on a couple of tracks with a Khirki-based MC he met in the studio.

Yet aside from the hopefulness and the enduring networks it created, there is another reason, pertinent to the tack of this chapter, that I bring up the studio. Singh had rented out the barsati apartment in which he created the studio from an older couple who occupied the first and second floors of the building. To walk up to Singh's flat, one had to walk by the older couples' flat. In the several times I went to Singh's place, the couple sat just by the stairs at a table and would look at me as I passed by, not saying a word even as I greeted them, "Hello, *Uncleji, Auntiji, kese hain aap?* How are you?"

Over the course of a couple of months, after I had brought a few young people to Singh's place, Singh started to feel a bit wary of bringing too many

people through to the flat and told me I should take a break from bringing people and also limit the number of people I bring. One day I brought Hanif and his crew to Singh's place. I had brought Hanif over previously, but it was the first time I had invited Biggie, Amin, and some of the others. When we walked up, we all saw the older couple. All the boys said hello to them in respectful Hindi. We then proceeded to spend several hours at Singh's place. The next day, I had a conversation with Singh. He said the older couple had complained and told him he should not have guests over to the house again. Singh told me that for the short time that he had left in Delhi, maybe it was best to suspend the studio sessions or, at the very least, to keep them to a minimum and only invite a couple of people at a time.

I immediately responded that it must have been because I brought Hanif and his Somali friends over that the landlords responded in this way. Singh reacted strongly to that assertion, denying the plausibility that their complaint and request had anything to do with racism. We had several tense conversations about anti-Blackness in the days that followed, as there was a suggestion by Singh that my analysis was paranoid. And perhaps it was. My firsthand knowledge of anti-Black racism in the United States, coupled with Hanif, his friends, and other African nationals' stories of anti-Blackness in Delhi, made me quite sensitive. I immediately "saw" racism and responded to its coordinates of difference in the way I learned in the settler colonial context of the United States. My response, I think, is important to acknowledge and even linger on for a moment, as it is a small reminder that seeing racism as a familiar form of difference is a matter of sociohistorical perspective. My tendency to see and even look for implicit forms of racism come from my experiences as a man of color in the United States, an educator in US urban contexts, and a scholar working in US and UK institutions. For me, there was a certainty that the end of our studio time together was wound together with anti-Black sentiment. It was a kind of paranoia I had learned in North America that, as John Lester Jackson Jr. describes it, experiences events that ascribe racism to every action and intention one encounters in the world.[37]

My certainty that my ability to see the subtlety of interaction as a politics of difference related to more explicit forms of racism—state-sanctioned violence, housing discrimination, and so on—and to a history that centers a colonial logic of difference also points to another kind of distortion in my vision. That distortion produces a way of seeing that might miss other sociohistoric structures that animate the politics of difference in a city like Delhi. One could argue that the older couples' reaction to the young people, for instance, was class based and had less to do with the Somalis' presence

than the presence of the entire collective of class subordinate youth in their house. With that in mind, their response could have also been a more explicitly caste- *and* class-based reaction. That is, they could have felt the purity of their upper-caste house was being violated by the presence of those with unknown caste affiliations.

I have not discussed caste in a systematic or meaningful way in this book. This is mainly because the politics and everyday impact of caste consciousness did not explicitly rear their head in my time in Delhi *except* during discussions about racism. For instance, caste in relationship to racism emerged in a few conversations with Dhruv, the Dalit b-boy who offered his thoughts on the Delhi rape case. In one of our conversations, he explicitly discussed with me the discrimination he has faced in his life as caste based, offering me the analogy of race to explain his experience, as he thought that I, as an Indian American, might not understand what he meant by caste unless he explained it to me in terms of race: "Dalits are like Black people in India."

Dhruv was one of several young Scheduled Caste (sc) and Dalit men I had met in the scene who, when the Dalit PhD student Rohit Vemula died in 2016, circulated images of Dalit Lives Matter protests, with the hashtag #dalitlivesmatter.[38] In doing so, he (and others on my Twitter feed) linked the struggles of Dalits—those on the bottom rung of precolonial caste order in India—with the struggles of Black people everywhere. Dhruv's use of this hashtag echoed a twentieth-century discourse of solidarity between Dalits in India and Black Americans, which made explicit connections between the colonial chattel slave labor complex and the Dalit's history of subordinated labor in India.[39] In 2014 Dhruv also posted a Soundcloud track produced by the Mumbai-based rapper A-List (Ashwini Mishra) in 2013 called "Free Kabir Kala Manch."[40] The rap (in English) describes the plight of a group of activist poets from Pune, Maharashtra, who formed soon after the 2002 Gujarat riots and who were jailed for allegedly being Naxalites in 2011.[41]

Even in the cities, you see caste still exists
You think not but the dream won't last
You get shot for saying "*Jai Bhim* Comrade"
You think not, but the dream won't last
Let's get to the point. This is the crunch
Let's dedicate this joint to Kabir Kala Manch
They are poets, they say what the facts are like
But the state is calling them Naxalites.

This track, while it did not get much circulation when it was released, is an example of how rap has been harnessed in India to draw attention to the ongoing struggles against caste discrimination. In each of these examples, Dhruv reminds us of a different version of race as familiar, one that begins from a decidedly subcontinental sociohistorical perspective where caste endures and generates the structural conditions for discrimination, dispossession, and the political responses to these conditions.

Dhruv argued, during our one explicit conversation on caste, that hip hop allowed young people in Delhi not only to express their experiences about caste discrimination but to build relationships that cut across caste difference. "Look, caste doesn't matter in hip hop. See how people from different backgrounds get into the cipha and shake hands, they touch? Those people are from different castes, but it doesn't matter." Dhruv's claim serves as a reminder of why young people gravitated to hip hop in Delhi: its forms offered a means not only to express one's experience but to create new relations that collectively reach toward a vague, effervescent otherwise that could unmake history. Dhruv's otherwise clearly imagined hip hop practice was a means to quite literally reach across difference and have vital contact with those who one could previously never encounter. These dreams of life-affirming possibility and alternate urban Indian futures it provided, as I have shown in the previous two chapters, attracted the interest of various outsider actors—whether international hip hop practitioners or Delhi-based activists—who sought out young men who could authentically stand for the gendered figure of "Indian youth" through their respective digitally enabled representational projects. This opportunity, located in producing the globally familiar, was not available to Hanif or Roca.

One day in 2018, as I sat on the top front row somewhat vacantly looking out the window of one of those iconic red double-decker buses in London, my phone buzzed, a short burst of sound and vibration that I felt more than heard. I had that feeling that I get when my phone buzzes: a melding of slight annoyance, vague uneasiness, and mild curiosity that lends itself to immediate action. Would it be a news update on Brexit, the run-up to the 2019 Indian general election, or the midterm elections in the United States? Or would it be more personal: a text or WhatsApp message from someone I knew? I pulled out my phone to check.

It turned out I had a private Facebook message from Dhruv. In the message, he told me that there was a b-boy opportunity in London that he was really interested in pursuing, but he needed a sponsor letter in order to get a tourist visa from the UK Home Office to make the journey. "Can you write me a letter?" A few weeks prior to receiving Dhruv's message, I heard from Soni, also through Facebook Messenger. He wrote to let me know things were going well for him in Delhi and that I should listen to his new track and, if I liked it, I should put it up on my Facebook page, maybe even tweet a link to the video.

In turn, I reached out to the young men I met in Delhi through social media over the several years since I moved out of my flat in Lajpat Nagar,

South Delhi. In some cases, I messaged them because it was the only way I knew I could get in touch with them when I returned to Delhi for short stints and wanted to see them. Phones, it turns out, are incredibly unreliable ways to stay in touch with young people in Delhi, as they keep changing their numbers when cheaper mobile plans are introduced or when they lose their phones or SIM cards. I also reached out on Facebook if I had a particular request relating to something I was writing about or at least pondering writing about. In one instance, I messaged Jay to ask him how he was doing and to see if he could send me the lyrics of a track he produced that I wanted to scrutinize more closely as a text. Jay immediately responded with a write-up of the track in romanized Hindi. He also shared with me how his life had been going since we last touched base a year prior.

I conclude this book by thinking through how the globally familiar, encoded in technologies that collapse the distance between here and there, have the potential to prolong the ties that anthropologists build long after we have left the proverbial "field." These prolonged connections point to the way the familiar is not only a representational ghost one can summon or let loose in the world to generate new relations but a link, a connection, a means to virtually connect with those elsewhere. The familiar, in this sense, is a mode and medium of communication, a multiplatform means to maintain, to use Mirca Madianou and Daniel Miller's term, "polymediated" relationships with friends, kin, or someone you just met online.[1] As such, the familiar complicates persistent ideas in the discipline about the field and fieldwork that suggest a delimited space/time, that make "over there" a strange and fascinating place for research, distinct from the "here."

Six years after leaving Delhi, I still hear from and about many of the young men I got to know during the years I lived in the city. They remind me, through personal messages and through posts on Facebook and Instagram, of their ongoing relationship with hip hop, their successes (and struggles), and their desires for the future. They share with me (and others, of course) images, sounds, and videos that capture the hopefulness of their endeavors. These messages, whether directed to me or for general consumption, are tangible reminders of life unfolding in the city of Delhi. The messages I receive, along with the unanticipated comments I receive from them on my Facebook timeline when I post something about my family or my interests (political, social, and so on), often take me by happy surprise, even when they should not. The surprise I feel is largely a result of a persistent notion I picked up while a student of anthropology that somehow the connections one makes when doing research either dissolve altogether or are one-directional and at the discretion of the anthropologist, who might or might not go back to talk to those they met in the proverbial field. The surprise that then turns into anxiety also has to do with the constantly receding horizon that social media produces in relationship to writing ethnography.

Indeed, my interlocutors' various hailings and interjections on social media—whether to share, comment, like, or argue about something I have shared—have pushed me to reflect on the ways in which the anthropologist's job of writing the present in the digital age, particularly if one is interested in centering the stories and engagements with the people one meets in the world, cannot allude to neat conclusions. Part of the aim of this epilogue (and the reason why I call it an epilogue rather than a conclusion), then, is to share the continued digital unfolding that I witnessed of several young men I have introduced in this book—Soni, Jay, Dhruv, Hanif, and Sudhir—and the ways in which I have been and continue to be pulled into their unfolding stories through social media. It is also an effort to show the ways, through their stories, in which "here" and "there" are entangled and to think through what sorts of productive possibilities there might be in maintaining and nurturing relationships that initially emerge during "fieldwork." In this sense, I also have another agenda for this epilogue, and that is to engage with the kinds of ethical dilemmas that emerge as a result of the persistent connection that social media creates.

Madianou, in a recent keynote she gave about her long-term ethnographic work with Filipina migrant domestic workers and their reliance on social media to maintain and even deepen their relationships with their children from afar, suggests that the persistent social media–enabled relationship she has had for several years with several pairs of mothers and daughters has blurred relational boundaries. These ongoing relationships have pushed her, in certain instances, to explicitly reinscribe her role as a researcher with those she now has a different sort of relationship with, one that could be described as friendship.[2] For instance, she shared that when the women she has gotten to know over a period of years share intimate details with her on social media about their lives, she feels compelled to remind them that although they are friends, she is also a researcher. She also mentioned in her talk that she stopped mining social media for textual or visual material once the official study was over, even though there was a temptation to use material she had been given access to as a "friend."

Similarly, Dhiraj Murthy discusses how ethnographers might have a deep temptation in the digital age to stalk and even surreptitiously mine the social media sites of interlocutors we meet in the flesh during research for juicy tidbits we can mull over and theorize in the comfort of our own homes.[3] He argues that we should be conscious of this armchair temptation to take "data" in the form of images or text without permission, and either refrain from doing so or ask for explicit permission. In each of these accounts regarding the slipperiness of ethnography in the age of social media, there is an ethical dilemma followed by a solution. These solutions—whether to continually remind those we meet that we are researchers, to refrain from taking "data" without consent, or more generally to curtail the lazy desire to know through the surfaces that social media creates—certainly ameliorate some of the ethical issues that persistent digital connectivity creates. However, they do not eliminate them. It seems evident that if we are connected through social media with people we met and developed relationships with during fieldwork, our encounters with the materials they post on their social media sites, even if we do not use this specific material (photos, videos, text fragments) as evidence on which to hang our theoretically nuanced arguments, still influence how we write. I would take this argument one step further and suggest that attempts to eliminate ethical risk foreclose on the possibility of long-term relations with those we meet in the proverbial field. This possibility, in my estimation, is what makes the discipline of anthropology and the method of ethnography vibrant and exciting.

During my final year in graduate school, as several of my peers were gearing up to go to the "field," there were discussions among us about how and if we would use social media in our fieldwork. Should we accept the Facebook friend requests of those we meet in the field? If we do, do we open ourselves up to the possibility of our interlocutors in the field doing research on us? Do our friends and our family members, equally, need to be protected from the potential harm of cultivating a single social media persona? Should we then, anticipating those requests, set up "dummy" Facebook (and other social media) accounts for research purposes? Amusingly, the conversations I had with my peers in graduate school started in real space but continued in several Facebook threads and have been iterated on over the course of several years.

The discussions were productive and the resulting decisions on how to proceed were multiple. For instance, several of my peers who had projects that involved young people decided to create pseudonym social media personas that they would use for fieldwork. This decision reflects the practices of youthful social media users who create multiple accounts or use multiple platforms for different social groups or types of social engagement (certainly something I witnessed among the young people I met in Delhi). The move to make profiles with these pseudonyms created a contained space for on-line social media interaction, a space that could be explicitly imagined and articulated as a place for research. The taking on of pseudonyms, one could argue, also modeled a representational act of what was to come in the writing that followed. If I can take on a pseudonym to index my social media persona, it is not so shocking I would give you one when I write you into my book, or so the logic might go.

Some of my other anthropology graduate student peers decided not to engage in the use of social media at all, either arguing that digital access was limited in their respective field sites (there really is a persistent digital divide) or that it was too complicated to open up the tangle of tricky questions that would emerge if they did become "friends" with their interlocutors. In the end, I decided not to create a separate Facebook persona but let my one singular profile accrete friends/interlocutors from the field. My logic was simple. It seemed rather strange to me if I accepted friend requests from young people in Delhi in an account that was unpopulated, aside from other young people in Delhi. If one of the main reasons why young people in the scene engaged with hip hop was to extend their networks, both literally and as an imaginative possibility, it seemed unethical to not allow them to experience and connect with people in my networks.

It came to pass that Facebook enabled me to link a few MCs in Delhi to DJs and producers I knew in the United States who showed interest in collaborating. There was also an instance where one of the young MCs I met in the Delhi scene tried to set up a date with an environmental justice worker I met in Delhi—a young British Indian woman named Preethi—who was also my friend on Facebook.[4] He had met Preethi one night when I had invited her along to a club event where he was performing. I introduced them to each other at the end of the evening. The next day, he found her profile on my Facebook account and private messaged her. Preethi immediately texted me that he reached out to her but was quick to reassure me that he had not said anything unseemly and told me that she had the situation well under control. The next time I saw him, I told him to refrain from messaging women on my Facebook page, even if he met them in the flesh previously. He was apologetic but not sure what he had done wrong. Whatever it was, he promised not to do it again. The experience posed a warning that I took very seriously: the young men I met in Delhi might use the network of friends I had given them access to for unsolicited flirtation and even harassment. I ended up deciding to perform a heteronormative joking exchange with every male I met in Delhi who I became friends with on Facebook, an exchange that warned them not to approach any of my female friends on Facebook without their explicit consent or there would be hell to pay.

I will wager that the sorts of discussions I had with my anthropologist peers around how and whether we should incorporate social media into our ethnographic practice (and the decisions each of us came to and the challenges they produced) have been happening among graduate students in anthropology and related disciplines for the last decade. These conversations point to the changing terrain of ethnographic research and the complicated ways in which relationships, whether ambivalent or intimate, have a way of persisting well beyond what we go into our research engagements expecting. That these discussions concerning the relevance and ethics of social media relations during and after ethnographic fieldwork happened informally, among graduate students, also point to the ways in which ethnography is taught in the contemporary moment.

While there certainly has been an emerging body of literature on the digital that spells out methodological possibilities and problems of ethnography in a social media landscape—for example John Postill's work on the digital as a technological instantiation of the network, a means to study movement and (social) movements in a way that creates opportunities to see expansion and the aesthetic vocabulary that makes it possible; or Sarah Pink and John Postill's theorization of digital anthropology as an opportunity to straddle the online and offline worlds of others—these ideas are still often delimited to a conversation about digital anthropology rather than to anthropology writ large.[5] Anthropology departments have either not embraced, grasped, or contended with the sorts of complications and opportunities that the digital as a not-going-anywhere-soon familiar generates or they have relegated these sorts of theoretical-methodological-ethical discussions to the next generation of "digital" anthropologists. As a result, the ethics, politics, and possibilities of social media relations have been left to the bumbling discretion of anthropologists in the field and their peers from whom they ask for advice (on social media). Or worse, their actions are determined by the bureaucratic processes that come with institutional review boards, the lowest common denominator that might be used to sort out the messy continuities and potential ethical conundrums that social media generates in our fieldwork.

The notion that we can avoid the complicated and confounding ethical (and political) predicaments that social media entanglements generate if we just avoid social media relationships with our interlocutors altogether, or if we contain our engagements on social media into discrete, manageable sites of contact, misses the ubiquity of space-time collapse in the digital age such that those we research can, in turn, research us. Indeed, the digital and the familiars that it releases force us to contend with a collapse between there and here, academic and nonacademic, and so on, in ways that extend far beyond whether and how we decide to use social media in our ethnographic pursuits. John Lester Jackson Jr., for instance, writes about how his interlocutors in an Israel-based Black Hebrew community would find out when and how he was speaking about them through a simple Google search and then email him about the details of his talk or simply show up to his talk.[6] He argues that the possibility that we are being researched by those we met when we did research should push us to rethink our assumptions about the duration, quality, and ethical imperatives of our fieldwork.

Jackson also argues that we should pay close attention to how the digital, as it shapes the possibility for us to be seen, heard, and read (and even mobilized) by our interlocutors long after we have left the field, should push us to consider carefully how and what we write counts as "thick" description. In his call to pay more attention to the effects of the digital, there is a reversal of the Geertzian conceit that we generate knowledge by straining to look over the shoulder of those we seek to know.[7] Rather than looking over the shoulders of others, it is our shoulders that are being looked over and our casual thoughts, ideas, and even our more formal engagements with writing anthropology that are potentially being (mis)read.

Indeed, our writing circulates further than what was previously imaginable through networks of connection and connectivity. If anything, the digital moment has made arguments about academia being a bubble only true for those who choose to inhabit it as such. The possibility that we will be read more widely *and* more likely be read by those whom we spent time researching has increasingly become the case, as open source publishing gains traction, as institutions create digital public repositories of our writing, and as we are encouraged by our institutions to write as public intellectuals (in the UK, for instance, anthropologists need to be mindful of "research impact"). Ed Simpson argues (and I agree) that while having our work read is a good thing, something to celebrate, it does create some interesting dilemmas.[8]

For one, our anthropological writing is usually, as Kirsten Hastrup has argued, reaching for a truth beyond the truths we have observed.[9] It often, in turns of phrase and in its (contemporary) orientation toward the theoretical, signals a move away from the prosaic ethnographic experience of the field. This might mean that those whom we made friends with in the field, if they read our work, will feel betrayed by an account where they find somebody resembling themselves used to make a point that flattens, erases, or, worse, exemplifies their experience as generalizable. This danger of being accused of misrepresentation or betrayal in one's writing, of course, emerged well before the digital intensified circulation and potentiality for access. Simpson, for instance, writes in passing about these sorts of anguished encounters between anthropologists and those they write about as a segue to discussing his own experiences of being read as someone who has betrayed confidence.[10] He suggests, I think rather provocatively and productively, that these misunderstandings are an exciting opportunity as they challenge our complacency as scholars. They push us to remember that what we are doing goes beyond the lecture theaters where we give talks (or hope to give them) and the relatively small circulation that our books generate. The dilemmas that Simpson touches upon are magnified in the digital age, as the formal texts we write are enmeshed with our tweets, our Facebook updates, information about our public talks, and our other writerly engagements that present our research and our thinking in more accessible terms.

In 2017 I reached out on Facebook to Saj, an MC I met while in Delhi. Saj and I had met through Javan early on in my time in Delhi. Saj lived in Gurgaon and came from a privileged background; both his parents were doctors and he was at the time getting ready to go to pharmacy school in the Caribbean. When we first met in Delhi in 2012, he got very excited when he found out I was Indian American. "I was born Virginia, bro!" he told me. I shared with him that my mom, brother, and sister lived in northern Virginia and in the course of our conversation we figured out that both of our moms had worked in a hospital in Fairfax County, Virginia—the hospital he was born in—back in the late 1990s. "What a crazy coincidence," he said. "We are from the same place and our moms worked together." "Not together," I quickly said. "My mom worked in childcare. She probably took care of you because your parents worked long hours in the hospital as doctors."

I had initially reached out to Saj through Facebook to see if he was interested in contributing a short verse for this book. In a moment of inspiration, I had envisioned breaking the chapters with unexamined verses from several MCs in the scene who are currently getting some fame in India and beyond, as a way to offer a more layered textuality to the book and channel the affect of the familiar without my analysis attached. I agonized over whom to ask, precisely because of the kinds of authenticity struggles that hip hop brings with it as it travels, an authenticity debate that plays out in conversations like the one I had with Saj, where I positioned myself as a class other in relation to Saj's story of South Asian transnational mobility and success. Do I only include MCs from the working-class and migrant communities I spent the majority of my time in, or do I also include those from more privileged backgrounds, who are also important actors in the Delhi hip hop scene? In the end, I decided to skip including anyone's verses because I was not prepared to deal with the risk of leaving people out or making anonymous MCs who wanted to be named.

While I was catching up with Saj (and wondering if I should include a verse of his), he told me that he and his friend were coediting a website called desihiphop.com. As he shared the history of the website and its growing success promoting hip hop produced by South Asians across borders, he asked if he and his partner could interview me for desihiphop.com as the first academic writing about hip hop in India. I was a bit nervous. While it was true that I was interested in and wrote about hip hop, it certainly was not the central object of focus in this project, or at least not in the way I think he imagined it would be. I had an inkling that whatever I said would be read not only by the English-speaking young people I met in the Delhi hip hop scene but by hip hop heads across India and a youthful diasporic South Asian community that had gotten wind of the website.

A quick search on their website revealed that desihiphop.com got approximately ten thousand hits per article and thirty thousand hits per video upload. If I did this interview, I thought, I would certainly reach far more people than I ostensibly could through an article or even this book. I also thought that the interview would create potential trouble down the line, once this book came out. In addition to the problems of expectation around my engagement with Indian hip hop as some sort of "object" of study, there would be a mismatch in the register in which I spoke about Delhi. Also, I had done the social science move of making (almost) everyone in this book anonymous.[11] What would Soni, for instance, think when he read the interview and realized that he would be made anonymous in the book (which he probably would not read anyway)? Would he feel cheated that he had not been revealed as the hip hop version of himself, forever embedded in my book as a key figure in the history of an emergent Delhi hip hop scene? Finally, after a lot of thought, I decided to do the interview.[12] The questions Saj and his partner sent to me as prompts were sharp and not so easy to answer. For instance, they asked me about ethnography.

From what I understand, you have used ethnography for some parts of the book. Could you shed some light on how exactly have you utilized it in your book?
Sure. Ethnography is often described as writing that becomes possible as a result of hanging out with people for a long period of time. I hung out with a

few MCs, b-boys, and graf writers in Delhi for about eighteen months. Most of what I learned was while I was in conversation with these MCs and dancers or came from what I observed when I hung out with them. The book is full of stories that emerged during this time. For instance, I write about the music videos I made with a few MCs in the scene or about the underground and commercial battles and jams I attended. I also write about the metro system and going shopping for snapbacks and T-shirts in Palika bazaar. I write about clubs in Hauz Khas, Gurgaon, and other parts of Delhi that I visited. I also write about just sitting around with the young homies and just listening (and talking as best as I could with my imperfect Hindi). I use these stories to raise questions regarding the politics of hip hop, hip hop and its ability to describe and create social worlds, the unequal social reality of urban India, and so on.

It is always an interesting experience when people who are not anthropologists ask me to describe ethnography. It becomes a somewhat uncomfortable experience when I am asked to describe ethnography for an audience that I am ostensibly, at least in their eyes, analyzing in the book. Revealingly, in this version of ethnography that I provided Saj (and desihiphop.com readers), I leave out social media as a site of analysis. It was not a conscious choice when I responded, but in hindsight it seems to evidence something of the blurring complexity of doing ethnography in the digital moment.

What motivated you to actually write the book and what exactly should one expect out of it?

Well, I started writing about Delhi's hip hop scene for my PhD in anthropology. I started my PhD late—when I was thirty-five years old. I decided to try and go back to school after working for several years doing arts programming—theater, poetry (rap), dance—for young people who had been in jail or involved with the criminal justice system in New York City. I needed to take a break from doing that kind of work. I had seen too much growing up in NYC and working with young men in these kinds of jobs. I thought going back to school might offer me a chance to think, reflect, and write about what I had experienced. When I got into graduate school on a full scholarship (which was a huge and pleasant surprise because my grades in college were terrible and I didn't have enough money to fund an education) my mentors encouraged me to think beyond the United States for my final dissertation research project. I started to contemplate traveling back to India to do my ethnographic research but wasn't sure what I was going to do. I didn't want to write about things I had no idea about or wasn't a part of in any way. *Adi-*

vasi land rights, rural social movements, farmer suicides—these were topics that I was interested in but couldn't see myself authentically connecting with. In 2010 I heard about the growing Indian hip hop scene. I decided to visit Delhi in 2011 and decided to write about the scene. I think some of the things I learned with the homies I met in Delhi are important for people to read, particularly the people who think they know what urban India is about. What should one expect from the book? That's a great question. The easy answer is a lot of stories, stories that paint a picture of what it means to grow up in Delhi in the second decade of the 2000s. However, I also do a lot of thinking through big ideas in book—ideas about capitalism, gender, race, and what a city is and could be. I write in a way that I hope anyone can read but, to be real, I think parts of the book might get a bit heavy and philosophical for someone who is not fully invested in theoretical writing.

The initial part of my response is a legitimating narrative, one that casts me as an authentic voice, a voice capable of writing about hip hop and about urban India coherently. I mobilize, like I did in the "field" with prospective participants, my lived experience in the United States, my work experience, my diasporic experience, and even my age (which marks the hip hop era I come from) to demonstrate legitimacy and to limit potential critique. I also preempt the legibility of the book ("to be real") as a response to Saj's inquiry about expectations, to index the abstraction that the book will encompass. It is a move that is meant to prepare a potential reader in the public that desihiphop.com creates for the impossibility of the text in the book, this book.

Once the interview was published, I saw that it had appeared as a post on a few of my interlocutors' Facebook pages. I was not sure what that meant for this book but realized, on some level, that it was already out of my hands. To theorize the globally familiar is to recognize that you, too, are subsumed in its wake. The anthropologist can also become a media citation in this regard, something to draw on when necessary.

And what of the young men who have been introduced in this book, young men who were in a particular moment in their lives when I arrived in Delhi to do fieldwork? Soni is now one of the biggest rap names in India, a development that would not have been possible had the hip hop scene in India stayed static in the years since I left. Indeed, hip hop went from being a kind of everyday, aspirational practice just under the threshold of visibility—as I believe I have captured in this book in some small way—to an embodied aesthetic that promised and delivered its adherents imminent potentiality through its commodification. Soni was a clear example of this. In 2013 Soni began to produce his own music videos (after working on a couple with me). He slowly accumulated the money to build a small studio in his flat and started to produce tracks for himself and his friends. Early on, while I was still in Delhi, he began doing shows around the city. As his name spread through the circuitry of the web, he began to get bookings in Mumbai, Chandigarh, Bengaluru, and eventually in every corner of the country. He now regularly tours around India, and I think it is just a matter of time before he begins to tour around Asia and Europe. He recently signed for a new record label started by a British Indian entrepreneur and based in Delhi that has the resources to promote new music in the country and a vision for distribution and shared costing that is equitable to the musicians they represent. Soni has been on the radio in London (on a special BBC program) and continues to produce new music. Soni's story of humble beginnings—a young Sikh man from a working-class community in West Delhi who tells gritty stories about the everyday in his community through his Punjabi raps (what gets labeled gully rap in the emergent popular music scene in India)— and his rise to fame all too closely coheres to the kind of aspirational narrative of success that hip hop has created in its travels over the last thirty years.

Soni's ascendance, no doubt, generates a whole new set of aspiring young Delhi rappers, ready to try their luck with the rap game. If Soni is not enough, there was a Bollywood movie released in 2019, *Gully Boy*, about a rapper from the slums of Mumbai and his rise to fame—which is sure to propel hip hop, and DIY rap music production in particular, across India.[13] What is more, both major parties, Congress and BJP, commissioned some of the heavy hitters in Delhi and Mumbai's underground rap scene to do promotional music videos in the run-up to the 2019 election.[14] Each of these developments signals the enormous potential for the commodification and incorporation of digital hip hop and the working-class men who produce its aesthetics across India.

Soni (and Bollywood's and the politicos' interest in gritty, street hip hop) is a reminder of how fast things change. As I write this epilogue, 2012, when I first started fieldwork, feels like a long time ago. This feeling of the recent past as a distant one, I believe, is part and parcel of what the familiar produces. As Paul Virilio argues, our orientation—to time, to place, to experience—is distorted by the speed that digital circulation produces.[15] For anthropology, this distortion in time—that what we write is already behind what we see unfolding in the collapsed space-time of social media—creates anxiety and a desire to catch up, to rewrite the past in light of the present. The discipline has dealt with this anxiety either by becoming more abstract in its theorizations or turning to history to ground the shaky, amnesiac present. The globally familiar, in this sense, can also be read as an invitation to stay in the present as it leaks into the future and embrace the anxiety of speed and collapse as part of our contemporary condition.

Dhruv continues to b-boy, throw underground b-boy jams, and write raps in Delhi. He and I are in regular contact as he wants to come to London to do an internship with the Rain Crew, a b-boy dance community in East London. I am currently struggling to figure out how, as a noncitizen in the UK myself, I can sponsor his visit. Dhruv regularly posts photos online about his life. I see photos of him and his new girlfriend, a White American woman he met in the Delhi scene. He is ambitious and ready to leave India for new horizons. For him, producing the familiar in/as Delhi is no longer enough. He wants the lived familiar of elsewhere. I am surprised that there are only a few whom I met in Delhi who explicitly voice their desire to travel the networks they have generated through their creative production of the familiar, to find new homes, new places to be.

In this sense, Dhruv's desire to depart matches many of the young Somali men who are still waiting for asylum elsewhere. Hanif is one of the few who has gained asylum and now lives in northern Finland. He has set up a small recording studio in his tiny flat. He has a new set of Finnish, Somali, Kurdish, and Kosovan friends whom he makes music with and for. I went to his small town in Finland to visit him recently, to see him in his new home. We listened to the tracks he has been producing with his new friends, raps in English and Finnish. We also listened to the ongoing projects he has with MCs in Khirki. Delhi is always on his mind. He aspires to return to India one day but on his own terms: no longer as a refugee but as a Finnish national and a businessman.

Several others I keep in regular contact with are firmly grounded in Delhi. It is the place, they say, where they derive their energy and have durable relations. For instance, Jay has formed a new collective. The collective is composed of young men and a few young women, some from his old crew who we met in chapters 1 and 3, and some new: young people from fairly well-off backgrounds who have gravitated to Jay's authentic portrayal of the street in South Delhi. Jay has no incentive to leave a place where he is seen as an ambassador of real hip hop and the center of a decidedly Delhi scene. He has shaped a rap image that is located and locatable and yet one that signifies elsewhere. He now has short dreadlocks and instead of trying to dress up, as he did in the video for his now former girlfriend's parents, he dresses down in sweat pants, a T-shirt, and a custom snapback hat with his crew name emblazoned on the front. I recently saw on Facebook that he married a new member of his collective, a young woman from an agrarian village outside Delhi who is a singer and who has been collaborating with him on his new album. He and his collective also recently got a record deal with a major international label. In exchange for a regular salary stipend, the record label has charged them with the responsibility of producing a certain number of new music and dance videos every month. This development marks the continued transformation of labor in the globally familiar, a development that quantifies creative outputs for social media circulation in return for payment.

Sudhir and his Khirki crew also continue to creatively hustle in Delhi. They have started, with the help of Aarthi, a T-shirt business that celebrates Khirki village. In 2016, continuing over a decade of work engaging with and supporting Khirki through its public arts projects, Aarthi brought in a screen print designer from London to help them create the designs. In a recent article, Aarthi wrote about Khirki and its many changes and about the T-shirt enterprise. She also included a discussion with Sudhir on his plans for the future and how he saw his artistic pursuits embedded in these plans. Sudhir's response was simple: "No big cars or big life, just enough to get by."[16]

After tapping a quick response to Dhruv about coming to London, my two thumbs moving expertly on the surface of my cracked iPhone screen, I moved to put away the phone but hesitated. I had five more minutes before the large red bus I was ensconced in arrived at my destination. I decided to scan my Facebook feed one last time for an article, a video, a comment, a thread of conversation, anything that might inspire or provoke me to think of an elsewhere or an otherwise that cloys at the edges of my experience, to consume the familiar I can grasp with one touch of the screen.

Preface

1 Moonis Zuberi, "The Rise of the Aam Admi: A New Season for Indian Politics?," *Wall Street International*, May 30, 2015. See also Webb, "Short Circuits," for a more detailed account of the links between AAP and its links to the anticorruption movement, which started a few years prior to the formation of the party.

2 Kapur, *Makeshift Migrants and the Law*.

3 Atluri, "Young and the Restless," 362. See also Rupa Subramanya, "The Perils of Unfulfilled Indian Youth," *Wall Street Journal* (blog), February 28, 2013, https://blogs.wsj.com/indiarealtime/2013/02/28/the-perils-of-unfulfilled-indian-youth/, which offers an interesting view into the popular discourse on youth in India as at once a promise and a peril to the nation's future.

4 Rohit Dasgupta and Debanauj Dasgupta discuss the discursive production of the "monstrous" working-class male subject in urban India in relation to emergent Indian queer publics. Dasgupta and Dasgupta, "Introduction: Queering Digital India." Sareeta Amrute argues that the Delhi rape case offers a way to look at gender in relationship to spatialized labor in the ambivalent postliberalization era and argues for an attention to the discourse of "immobility" that surrounds men from the urban and peri-urban working class. Amrute, "Moving Rape," 334.

5 The expansion of the city was in part demographic, the result of tremendous in-migration as people from near and far sought out opportunities in the city. It was also topographic, as the borders of what constituted the city expanded outward, swallowing rural peripheries into the fold of what is now called the National Capital Region (NCR). For a historical account of Delhi's growth and development, particularly from the late colonial period to the present, see Hosagrahar, *Indigenous Modernities*. For a more recent account of the ways Delhi has transformed through simultaneous processes of dispossession and accumulation that expand the perimeters of the city, see Searle, *Landscapes of Accumulation*.

6 Ritty Lukose discusses the popular discourse of the Zippie, the middle-class child of liberalization who literally zips about from one consumer experience to the next. Lukose, *Liberalization's Children*.

7 For detailed accounts of India's transition into an actor in the global market and its impacts on public culture and social life, there are several wonderful books to choose from. See, for instance, one of the first books to capture India's postliberalization transformation of public life: Breckenridge, *Consuming Modernity*.

8 Since the late 1990s, several scholars of South Asia have focused on the ways in which economic liberalization created the possibility for what Lukose has aptly termed *consumer citizenship*. This project looks at consumption in relationship to audiovisual production for social media circulation as a key force shaping subjects in urban India today. Lukose, *Liberalization's Children*; Leichty, *Suitably Modern*.

9 Jeffrey, *Timepass*.

10 Sanjay Srivastava rightly suggests that this mediatized discourse that offers a binary opposition between tradition and modernity is not grounded in history. Srivastava, "Masculinity of Dis-Location."

11 For a detailed engagement with the world-class city discourse in relationship to urban India, and Delhi more specifically, see DuPont, "Dream of Delhi as a Global City," which I engage with more directly in the introduction.

12 Atluri, "Young and the Restless."

13 In India there are approximately six hundred million people under the age of thirty. The majority of this demographic already live in or will eventually move to the larger cities and towns of the nation as they come of age. "Population Enumeration Data," Census of India, 2011, http://www.censusindia.gov.in/2011census/population_enumeration.html.

14 Anand Taneja has compellingly argued for an attention to present-day Delhi as a city of *jinns* (spirits) tied to the city's Mughal past. In this book I think with the young men I met in Delhi about the city's present and future as it is imagined in and through hip hop and its evocation of urbanity and masculinity elsewhere. Taneja, *Jinneology*.

Introduction

1 In the Indian context, urban villages are preexisting agrarian settlements that have been subsumed by the expansion of the city and have absorbed migrants who have come to the city to find work and life. Urban villages, importantly, fall outside the jurisdiction of city planners due to legal precedents from the colonial era and thus take on a unique development trajectory. In the period just after independence, the Delhi Development Authority (DDA) continued to use colonial *lal dora* (redlining) practices to demarcate urban villages as exceptional (from a planning and development perspective) in the city. These redlining policies continue to the present day. I discuss urban villages and their relationship to a Delhi hip hop scene in some detail in the chapters ahead. For detailed discussions of urban villages and their political economic histories, see Govinda, "'First Our Fields, Now Our Women.'" See also Mehra, "Urban Villages in Delhi."

2 Joseph Schloss writes about New York b-boys as "intense and yet totally in control" and constantly in "battle mode" in their movements across the city. I witnessed a similar self-orientation in Delhi. Schloss, *Foundation*, 70–71.

3 Stories about hip hop in India's slums have been published by national and international news conglomerates like *The Hindu*, the *Times of India*, and the BBC as well as newer online players, such as *India Times*, since 2011. Many of the publications feature short videos that offer a space for young men to showcase their talent and share their hopeful aspirations. The videos, in particular, played a role in why I wound up in Delhi doing fieldwork on hip hop in the first place. Some of the videos (and articles) are discussed in the chapters ahead as analytic fodder for thinking through the ways in which the *globally familiar* is produced and circulated.

4 While I heard skepticism from some parents, I also met parents who were very supportive of their children's creative zeal and saw an (economic) future in it (see chapter 1). The more cynical responses on the street by elders and from some of the parents I met, as Jaspal Singh (a sociolinguist I met in the "field" who played an important part in my fieldwork, my thinking, and my writing) and I discussed one day, were reminiscent of the representation of hip hop cynicism and competing conceptions of masculinity in the classic hip hop film *Wild Style*. In the film, Zoro, the protagonist, is confronted by his older brother, who has just returned to his family's apartment in the Bronx from military duty. When he enters Zoro's apartment, he sees spray cans, sketches, and tagged-up walls and says, "You're just sittin' at home doin' this shit? Stop fucking around and be a man. There ain't nothing out here for you." Zoro replies, "Yes, there is! This!" He turns his head to gaze at a graffiti-painted wall. In Nas's music video "The Genesis," which samples Zoro's dialogue with his brother, we see the expansive landscapes of the Bronx and its above-ground trains open up in front of us as we hear their voices. Charlie Ahearn, dir., *Wild Style* (Los Angeles: Rhino, 1983); Nas, "The Genesis," *Illmatic* (New York: Columbia, 1994).

5 Ghertner, *Rule by Aesthetics*. See also A. Roy, "Blockade of the World-Class City."

6 Economic liberalization marks a historic moment in India's postcolonial history. In the early 1990s, the state, in fiduciary crisis, decided to open its protected markets to foreign investment. In so doing, it ushered in a period of tumultuous change that has subsequently and profoundly reshaped the nation. Much of the contemporary scholarship on India begins with this watershed historical moment as a starting point from which to think about changing political, economic, and social conditions in the nation.

7 "Delhi Master Plan 2021," accessed February 6, 2013, http://delhi-masterplan.com /about-delhi-masterplan-mpd-2021/.

8 Llerena G. Searle uses the phrase *internationally familiar* landscapes to engage with the real estate developments that have reconfigured urban space in the NCR of Delhi since the 1990s. This phrase works well when thinking through the ways that media of and about urban life elsewhere evoke new imaginaries and, in so doing, materially shape urban landscapes. Searle, "Constructing Prestige and Elaborating the 'Professional,'" 271.

9 By evoking infrastructure in relation to the media, I draw on Rahul Mukherjee's work on infrastructural imaginaries that "lie at the intersection of structured state

policy/corporate initiatives and lived experiences/affective encounters of ordinary citizens." Mukherjee, "Jio Sparks Disruption 2.0," 177. See also Larkin, "Politics and Poetics of Infrastructure." Amit Rai makes a related argument with regard to digital media bricolage and its potential to create rupture even as it reinforces contemporary discourses of entrepreneurship in India. He argues for an attention to *jugaad*, a Hindi term he glosses as a "hack," a way to creatively make a life in a system that is otherwise exclusionary. Rai, *Jugaad Time*.

10 I borrow the term *affective economy* from Sara Ahmed, who argues for an attention to how emotions "play a crucial role in the 'surfacing' of individual and collective bodies through the affective relationships that link bodies and signs." For Ahmed, "surfacing" has everything to do with the ways in which the internet links embodied experience and circulating discourses of how and who to be in the world in ways that generate value. Ahmed, "Affective Economies," 117. *Structures of aspiration* was a phrase that was eloquently deployed by one of my anonymous reviewers to remind me to think through the ways ongoing processes of development linked to liberalization have reshaped how young people think/feel about their present and future. The term is a bit of a play on Raymond Williams's phrase *structure of feeling*, which he used to describe and analyze historical ruptures that make visible the way otherwise silenced or unattended subjects see and respond to their political, social, and economic realities. Williams pushed against Antonio Gramsci's notion of hegemony as a totalizing sphere of influence, offering instead a way to think about how multiple and simultaneous understandings of the past and future that float in the public sphere structure the present. In the Indian context, Sareeta Amrute uses the term *postliberalization* to describe the kinds of ambivalent multiplicities of experience, affect, and mobility—what could easily be glossed *as* structures of aspiration—that have been unleashed since the early 1990s in urban India. See Williams, *The Long Revolution*; and Amrute, "Moving Rape."

11 In her recent book, Purnima Mankekar looks at the affective links that Indian diaspora creates between the United States and India and that rely on the circulation of images, texts, and objects. She argues that these affectively charged and image-mediated links unsettle the idea of India. In this book I am less interested in unsettling the national as I am in thinking through how digital consumption and production shape gendered subjects and produce different opportunities for participation in the city. However, I suspect that by starting not with the category "India" but with masculinity and urban space, the possibility to unsettle the national might be more realizable. Mankekar, *Unsettling India*.

12 What I am marking here are the ways in which the "global turn" offered a way for anthropology to rethink its objects of study. For instance, William Mazzarella argues that the global—exemplified in the movement of media forms—creates opportunities for anthropologists to shift the increasingly tenuous burden of representation back onto those we meet in the field who are reflexively assessing and representing their relationship to a politics (and political economy) of cultural practice. Mazzarella, "Culture, Globalization, Mediation." See also Hegde, "Disciplinary Spaces and Globalization."

13 Louis Althusser coined the concept *interpellation* to explain how ideology shapes individuals into subjects with normative ideas about the world that fall in line with state and other forms of power. For Althusser, subjects are always subject to power but are also a locus of agency. See Althusser, *Lenin and Philosophy and Other Essays*. In the mid-twentieth century, Theodor Adorno, having witnessed the power of mass media in Hitler's Germany, argued that mass media played a crucial role in interpellating individuals into a state-supported capitalist apparatus. For Adorno, mass media was the ultimate tool in producing docile citizen-consumers by subjecting them to the "humiliating conditions" of their lives—thereby reproducing their subordination. Adorno, *Culture Industry*, 282. Hall, working in the postcolonial Atlantic world context of the United Kingdom in the 1980s and 1990s, recovers Althusser's theorization of the subject who is at once a product of structure and agentic force, arguing for a more complex understanding of mass mediation that accounts for reception, contestation, and reformulation. See Hall, *Representation*; and Hall, "Notes on Deconstructing 'the Popular.'" Appadurai takes up a similar argument in the late 1990s, arguing for an attention to the twin axes of media and migration as way to understand the world beyond established boundaries of subjectification. Appadurai, *Modernity at Large*. We might also think with Radha Hegde, who recently has argued for an attention to media consumption "from below" to think through unanticipated processes of globalization linked to media circulations. Hegde, "Disciplinary Spaces and Globalization," 60. Mazzarella offers a lovely way to think about mass media as an interpellating discourse *and* site of agentic reformulation, arguing for an attention to *encounter*. An (ethnographic) engagement with encounter—that moment where media is received, produced, interpreted, and cited—opens up the possibility of seeing the subject in relation to media circulations anew, in tension between the past and the future, between structure and agency. The *globally familiar* takes up this call and looks at digitally enabled media in the moment it is consumed/produced and the affects and embodiments that it constitutes as social performance. Mazzarella, *Mana of Mass Society*, 5–7.

14 The concept of (the) "prosumer," since critiqued as ahistorical and overly celebratory, attempted to capture this collapse in distance between what we consume as media and what we produce as digital content. See, for instance, Jenkins, *Convergence Culture*.

15 While the move to think about media production and consumption simultaneously is linked to digital processes of mediation, I also borrow from Juan Flores, who argues (in a predigital moment) that Hall's invocation to engage with media as a site of contestation and negotiation often prefigures media engagement as a site of consumption rather than production. Flores encourages us to think with underground musicians and media producers in addition to those who consume the popular. Flores, *From Bomba to Hip-Hop*.

16 Haraway, *Simians, Cyborgs, and Women*, 164. See also Miller and Horst, "Introduction."

17 See, for instance, Partridge, "Occupying Black Bodies and Reconfiguring European Spaces." For a broader take on globally circulating forms of Blackness and their effects, see Clarke and Thomas, *Globalization and Race*.

18 Neves and Sarkar, "Introduction," 6.

19 For examples of powerful work on gender, queer subjectivities, and hip hop, see Perry, *Prophets of the Hood*; J. Morgan, *When Chickenheads Come Home to Roost*; Rose, *Black Noise*; and Shange, "A King Named Nicki."

20 Much of the work on global hip hop has focused on how hip hop shapes linguistic practice and localized debates around authenticity among young people. For instance, some of the scholarship has focused on how the introduction of English or the American racial schema shapes the way young people think about their local contexts. See Alim, Pennycook, and Ibrahim, *Global Linguistic Flows*, for a good example of the kind of attentive scholarship that has been produced as hip hop has traveled across contexts. For an exception, see Pardue, "Getting an Attitude."

21 In the early twenty-first century, a wave of scholarship on the new South Asian middle class emerged as way to specify liberalization's effects in the urban centers of India (adjacent to ongoing rural or village studies). The new scholarship deployed the category "middle class" to think through the emergence of an aspiring urban consumer citizen as the driver of cultural, social, and political change in India and, indeed, in the region. The category of the "middle class" was utilized as a way to track the ways in which this growing demographic with disposable incomes and newfangled aspirations—a demographic that cut across traditional lines of caste demarcation and upended classical definitions of class in relationship to property—negotiated their subject positions. See, for example, Fernandes, *India's New Middle Class*; Leichty, *Suitably Modern*; and Brosius, *India's Middle Class*. In this book I steer clear from using the fuzzy logics of the "middle class" as an analytical category to describe the gendered and economic positions of the young men I met in Delhi. I think this category, even if useful as an index of shared consumption and desire in contemporary urban India, obfuscates the economic, social, and political lives of my interlocutors as spatially, economically, and racially marginalized subjects. As Amrute has argued, there is a lacuna in the literature of South Asia regarding the "ill-defined place of urban and peri-urban working classes in everyday life." Amrute, "Moving Rape," 337. See also Agarwala, "From Work to Welfare."

22 For examples of historical and anthropological scholarship on "Indian," "Hindu," and "South Asian" masculinities (which are often conflated), see McClintock, *Imperial Leather*; Krishnaswamy, *Effeminism*; Alter, *The Wrestler's Body*; Alter, *Moral Materialism*; and Hansen, *Wages of Violence*.

23 For contemporary scholarship on masculinity in postliberalization India, see Nakassis, "Youth Masculinity"; Osella and Osella, *Men and Masculinities in South India*; Srivastava, "The Masculinity of Dis-Location"; Srivastava, "Modi-Masculinity"; and Dwyer and Pinney, *Pleasure and the Nation*.

24 The notable exception is Sanjay Srivastava's work, which, while it mobilizes the category of middle class to engage with masculinity and sexuality in Delhi, also punctures its categorical sameness. See, for instance, his discussions of working-class male same-sex sexual relations—where he credits Stacy Pigg for reminding him that working-class subjectivities mediate same-sex intimacies. Srivastava, "Semen, History, Desire, and Theory."

25 The limited (and relevant) scholarship on working-class (heterosexual) masculinities in urban India has offered insights into how young working-class men are

directed toward particular forms of labor, say, in construction or security, while young women from similar backgrounds find themselves in "pink collar" service work. See, for instance, Gidwani and Sivaramakrishnan, "Circular Migration and the Spaces of Cultural Assertion"; Roychowdhury, "'The Delhi Gang Rape'"; and Ramamurthy, "Why Is Buying a Madras Cotton Shirt a Political Act?" In chapter 3, I discuss how working-class masculinities are shaped as a result of the new opportunities for work that emerge in India's burgeoning creative and culture industries.

26 I have found it productive to think with Mikhail Bakhtin's concept of chronotope as it is picked up by media and linguistic anthropologists alike. For Bakhtin, chronotopes are narrative devices that locate the relationship between otherwise seemingly disparate times, spaces, and histories. Kathryn Hardy argues for an attention to chronotopes "as mass mediated representations of space allow images and sounds of places that do not otherwise exist to emerge into social imaginaries . . . [and] produce sketches of futures and pasts alike." Hardy, "Introduction," 7. Asif Agha extends the chronotope as a traveling space-time configuration to argue for its capacity to produce subjects. He argues, "A chronotopic depiction formulates a sketch of personhood in time and place." Agha, "Recombinant Selves in Mass Mediated Spacetime," 321. For the young men I got to know in Delhi, space-times elsewhere and otherwise (hip hop in 1990s New York, for instance) allowed them to produce a different understanding and representation of the space-time they inhabited in Delhi as well as fashion a different subject position.

27 I argue that an ethnographic engagement with mediatized masculinities in Delhi also opens up the way to see how notions of racial and ethnic difference play out in relationship to gender formation in Delhi as it relates to an urban American past and present. Formulations of gendered difference in contemporary Delhi draw from India's colonial history, which used precolonial caste and religious logics to differentiate racialized, gendered types according to laboring needs so that men from some groups were discursively produced as virile and martial while others were seen as effeminate and fit for cognitive labor. These systems of classification prevail in South Asia and, in the experiences of the young men I met in Delhi, become enmeshed with the processes of racialization in the United States (and elsewhere) that are depicted in circulating media forms. In this sense, I am writing against accounts that seek to essentialize a regional "South Asian" masculinity or masculinities. Rather, I push for an attention to the ways in which masculinity coarticulates with race, caste, ethnicity, and class at different spatiotemporal scales. For an example of "South Asian masculinities literature," see Chakraborty, "Mapping South Asian Masculinities." To engage with the ways in which ethnicity, race, and caste shape male experiences in Delhi, I draw from scholar Kimberlé Williams Crenshaw's conceptualization of intersectionality. See Crenshaw, "Mapping the Margins." By evoking intersectionality, I do not wish to suggest that preformulated categories of experience (such as caste, race, class) shape lives. I think with intersectionality, rather, to signal an attentiveness to multiplicity of sociohistoric factors that shape how subjects are made and make themselves and the ways in which these factors come together, in motion, in their performative self-representations in space. Here I draw from Amanda Lock Swarr and Richa Nagar, who argue that

to deploy intersectionality as a useful analytic in contexts outside the United States requires "that we reconceptualize difference as constituted and (re)configured in relation to place-specific struggles over rights, resources, social practices, and relationships." Swarr and Nagar, "Dismantling Assumptions," 514. See also the work of Jasbir Puar, who suggests that recent intersectional approaches attempt to "still" the otherwise disruptive force of perpetual motion that an explicit deployment of a multiplicity of subject positions creates. Instead she deploys the Deleuzian-inspired method-theory of assemblage to get at the kinds of fluid, ephemeral, and performative subjectivities that circulate in the present moment. Puar, *Terrorist Assemblages*.

28 *Cipha* is a hip hop term that indexes the improvisational space-time for sharing experience and demonstrating skills. See Spady, Meghelli, and Alim, *Tha Global Cipha*. I draw from scholarship on urbanity and urban infrastructure in South Asia that calls for an approach to the city that takes as its starting point the kinds of popular understandings that emerge from the street. See Chattopadyay, *Unlearning the City*, which pushes for an attention to the conjunctural spaces "where pleasure and politics might come together to create performative anchors and enlarge the imagination of public space" (xxi).

29 Larkin, *Signal and Noise*, 125–26.

30 Here I am thinking with Setha Low, who argues for an attention to the person as a "mobile spatial field—a spatio-temporal unit with feelings, thoughts, preferences, and intentions" so we might see place differently, from the perspective of people who socially create the spaces they inhabit. Low, "Claiming Space for an Engaged Anthropology," 393.

31 The idea (and heuristic) of the global city was originally developed by sociologist Saskia Sassen, whose careful scholarship revealed how certain cities—New York, London, Tokyo—emerged as key nodes in the circulation of finance capital in the post–Bretton Woods era. For Sassen, the global city is marked not only by capital's influx and the development of links between global cities but by the kinds of global scalings that produce uneven and unexpected laboring opportunities and social subjects. Sassen, *Global City*. The world-class city, in contrast, is a popular imagistic discourse of urban comparison used to drive development initiatives in India and elsewhere. See A. Roy, "Blockade of the World-Class City"; Brosius, *India's Middle Class*.

32 See, for instance, *Demonic Grounds*, Katherine McKittrick's intersectional work on gendered geographies that argues for an attention to place as dialectically constituted through intersections of subjectivity. In their introduction to *Culture, Power, Place*, Akhil Gupta and James Ferguson argue for an attention to "social and political processes of place making conceived less as a matter of ideas than of embodied practices" (6).

33 Ananya Roy discusses this either/or split in urban studies—where the global city is imagined as the creation of the elite while the megacity is seen as the inheritance of the urban poor (and the problem for developmentalists to solve)—in her article on subaltern urbanism. For Roy, the term *subaltern urbanism* suggests a different orientation to the city, one that starts from the bottom up and accounts for the self-representational projects that imagine the "slum" "as a terrain of inhabitation, live-

lihood and politics." Roy uses subaltern, a Gramscian concept that has a particular intellectual history in South Asia, as a means to interrogate dominant epistemologies and methodologies in urban studies that privilege simple binaries. The *globally familiar* recognizes the digital popular culture as a site where an aestheticized subaltern urbanism can be imagined as global. A. Roy, "Slumdog Cities," 224. For an example of research on Delhi that places an emphasis on the dilemmas of the megacity and the disconnect of the urban poor, see Bhan, "'This Is No Longer the City I Once Knew.'"

34 For a popular account of how the elite/subaltern division is represented, see Dasgupta, *Capital*. For a scholarly account, see Brosius, *India's Middle Class*. Writing about a decade ago, Brosius explains that "the lower middle class and the urban poor (in Delhi) are at the receiving end of globalization and urbanization" and suggests a focus on the "new upper middle classes and Indian diaspora to engage with the mediatized concept of world-class in Delhi" (ii). For a critique of this sort of tendency to describe Asian cities in terms of their sharp schisms, see Neves and Sarkar, "Introduction." For an exception to this sort of binaried approach, see Srivastava's exploration of Delhi and "the ties that bind the city, simultaneously, as they appear to produce self-contained realms." Srivastava, *Entangled Urbanism*, 7.

35 Sundaram, *Pirate Modernity*, 5.

36 Ortner describes dark anthropology as an anthropology that focuses on the "harsh dimensions of social life" and the totalizing effects of governmentality. Ortner, "Dark Anthropology and Its Others," 47. Dean argues that digital communications technology pushes us to perform our politics in ways that channel and tame its affects so that we become more deeply ensconced in capitalism. Dean, *Democracy and Other Neoliberal Fantasies*.

37 *Racial capitalism* is a term coined by Cedric Robinson to complexify Karl Marx's universalizing history of capital. Robinson argued that as capitalism emerged in Europe and spread across the world, it did not break from the feudal order that supposedly preceded it but used its logics to reproduce a racialized and class hierarchy during colonial and imperial expansions that exist to the present day. Robinson, *Black Marxism*. Hip hop artists have, since the early days of its practice in New York, pointed out the racial underpinnings of capitalism and subverted its exclusionary logics to produce (aesthetic) value. In so doing they have, ironically, contributed to its project. Yet these contributions to capital cannot be seen as totalizing, as hip hop also offers a possibility for embodied freedom.

38 I reference Abu-Lughod's germinal article on resistance as a diagnostic of power rather than a subversion of it. Abu-Lughod, "Romance of Resistance."

39 For recent engagements with youth, aspiration, and gendered becoming, see Chua, *In Pursuit of the Good Life*; Nakassis, *Doing Style*.

40 Lukose, *Liberalization's Children*; Chua, *In Pursuit of the Good Life*; Nakassis, *Doing Style*; Sancho, *Youth, Class and Education in Urban India*.

41 Osella and Osella, *Men and Masculinities*; Dickey, *Cinema and the Urban Poor in South India*.

42 Desai-Stephens, "Singing through the Screen."

43 Snighda Poonam's recent book offers a snapshot of the youthful structures of aspiration linked to India's emergent digital infrastructures. However, while its ethnographic material is captivating, it does not theorize the digital (or differentiated aspiration) in any meaningful way. Poonam, *Dreamers*.

44 Manuel, *Cassette Culture*. See also Liang, "Porous Legalities and Avenues of Participation"; and Udupa and McDowell, "Introduction."

45 "India: Number of Facebook Users," Statista, accessed February 6, 2020, https://www.statista.com/statistics/268136/top-15-countries-based-on-number-of-facebook-users/.

46 Mukherjee, "Jio Sparks Disruption."

47 Poonam, *Dreamers*.

48 Since 2012 there has been an explosion of YouTube-hosted media produced in India. For instance, All India Bakchod (AIB), a comedy collective out of Mumbai, started broadcasting their skits on YouTube. By 2018 they had more than three million subscribers to their YouTube channel before they stopped producing new work as a result of sexual harassment allegations.

49 For a discussion of networked media consumption, see Deuze, "Participation, Remediation, Bricolage." See also Uricchio, "Peer-to-Peer Communities." Networked media consumption pushes against the analytic "mass media" that suggests a singular, perhaps national, public. Rather, it asks us to think about the astonishing variety of user-generated and mass media content that circulates in and through networked publics such as algorithmically curated platforms like YouTube. The *globally familiar* picks up on these circulations and pushes us to think about the effects of networked media consumption and production, specifically on the lives of young working-class men living in Delhi.

50 In "Youth Masculinity," Constantine Nakassis rightly argues that debates in globalization studies have often framed the local in relationship to an amorphous global in ways that do not account for the complexities of how new meaning is made that exceeds both constructs. In "Global Situation," Anna Tsing argues against the binary of local places and global forces and suggests that we should think instead of place-making and force-making projects as at once global and local.

51 Vinay Gidwani and K. Sivaramakrishnan discuss how consumption becomes a site by which young Dalit and tribal men can reject caste hierarchies. Consuming and producing hip hop allowed the young men in the margins of Delhi to recognize and recalibrate their relationship to localized and global forms of hierarchical difference. Gidwani and Sivaramakrishnan, "Circular Migration and the Spaces of Cultural Assertion." Halifu Ousumare discusses how hip hop offers a way to recognize and articulate what she describes as *connective marginalization*, a way to recognize shared conditions of impossibility across difference and thus create new relations. Ousumare, "Beat Streets in the Global Hood." I discuss Ousumare's work in detail in chapter 6.

52 See, for instance, *Signal and Noise*, Larkin's account of Hindi cinema in northern Nigeria. See also Gopinath, "Bollywood Spectacles," in which the author shows how the increasing popularity of Bollywood among American audiences in the post-9/11 era signals the ways in which "popular culture becomes the contested terrain for consolidating ideologies of nation, race, gender, and sexuality" (160).

53 *Aam Aadmi*, "ordinary man," is a term coined by and for a political party that emerged in Delhi in late 2012. The party has since come to national prominence. Jay's play on the term where he referred to himself as a strange man was something I heard repeated by several young people in the scene, who felt the politics of the Aam Aadmi (or the Congress and BJP, for that matter) had very little to do with them or their families.

54 For a US history of hip hop, see Chang, *Can't Stop, Won't Stop*; and Rose, *Black Noise*. For a global history, see Spady, Meghelli, and Alim, *Tha Global Cipha*.

55 Mbembe, *Critique of Black Reason*, 6.

56 In "Linguistic Techniques of the Self," which focuses on on Brazilian MCs and their claims to American Black subjectivity, Jennifer Roth-Gordon pushes for an engagement with linguistic refashionings of racial subjectivity. In this book, I am interested in the multimodal refashionings of gender, race, ethnicity, caste, and class in Delhi.

57 To think of hip hop and media production as entrepreneurial closely aligns with the Modi-era Make in India, Shining India, and jugaad discourse that has sought to mobilize the enormous youth demographic in the country to fuel economic growth and sidestep the social upheaval that would undoubtedly come with youth unemployment. Rai, *Jugaad Time*; Poonam, *Dreamers*.

58 I am referring to Lauren Berlant's well-cited concept of cruel optimism, which, to quickly gloss, suggests that we often want what will do us harm. Ambivalent optimism suggests a kind of bittersweet knowing that the objects or subjects of our desire might provide us something that we need—recognition, relationship, connection—but will also, ultimately, fail to fulfill their full promise. Ambivalent optimism is necessarily aware of its classed, racialized, and gendered affective and material position. Berlant, *Cruel Optimism*.

59 *Capitalist realism* is a term Mark Fisher coined to describe the feeling that there is no alternative but to work within capitalism's framework and no future outside it. Fisher, *Capitalist Realism*.

60 See, for instance, Deuze, "Participation, Remediation, Bricolage"; and Jenkins, *Convergence Culture*.

61 The (transnational) hashtag #dmforcollab exploded in the Delhi scene (and across India) in 2016, a couple of years after I left the city. The hashtag makes explicit the aspiration that images or videos one posts can lead to unexpected collabs—opportunities to make with others but also, more implicitly, unexpected sexual encounters. While this hashtag had yet to come into being when I lived in Delhi from 2012 to 2014, its prelinguistic affect was palpable.

62 Marwick, "Instafame."

63 Stewart, *Ordinary Affects*, 3.

64 For a discussion on the analytical purchase of citation as a way to understand social performativity and media's role in shaping particular deployments of concept, gesture, and so on, see Nakassis, *Doing Style*.

65 Lampert, "Imitation," 380. See also *The Gay Archipelago* for Tom Boellstorf's discussion of dubbing culture as a way to understand the familiar or "not quite." Dubbing, where a linguistic concept moves from one sociocultural context to another but is rendered differently in its usage, bears a resemblance to how I am conceptualizing

the (globally) familiar. I extend the linguistic focus of dubbing, however, to think about how images and sounds in the digital age also become sites of translation.

66 There has been a growing interest in the ways that media forms, as they connect disparate contexts, create persistent relations through the migration and adoption of linguistic concepts, what Agha has called enregisterment. Media-enabled enregisterment, when accompanied by the potential for commodification, is what Agha has called processes of mediatization and is a very relevant concept to think with when we engage with the *globally familiar*. Agha, "Meet Mediatization"; Agha, *Language and Social Relations*.

67 For an engagement with "street art," social media, and processes of commodification, see Molnár, "Street Art and the Changing Urban Public Sphere."

68 James G. Spady, "Looplinking the Outlawz to the History of Mass Based Black Cultural Consciousness in the 21st Century," *Philadelphia New Observer*, December 13, 2000, 16.

69 Jaffa in Rose, *Black Noise*, 52–56.

70 Ismaiel-Wendt and Stemmler, "Playing the Translations."

71 Chang, "It's a Hip-Hop World," 60.

72 The presentation is now a book chapter. See Dattatreyan, "Small Frame Politics."

73 Spady, Meghelli, and Alim, *Tha Global Cipha*; Dattatreyan, "Critical Hip Hop Cinema." See also Jesse Shipley's film, *Living the Hiplife* (New York: Third World Newsreel, 2007).

74 I am thinking with David Graeber, who discusses how economic, social, and cultural value are inextricably entangled with one another, even if economics in the market fundamentalist view of contemporary capitalism says otherwise. What we come to understand as valuable constructs the world we live in and how we inhabit it. Graeber, *Towards an Anthropological Theory of Value*.

75 Rai, *Jugaad Time*.

76 Willis, *Learning to Labour*.

1. Friendship and Romance

1 A barsati is a top-floor apartment in a building consisting of three to four flats. It usually has a large outdoor space and a very small, sheltered indoor space. A barsati, while I was living in Delhi, was spoken of as fashionable; it was the accommodation of choice for cool, young urban professionals and creatives. There was also a sense of nostalgia regarding barsatis among well-educated, well-to-do Delhiites in their late twenties and early thirties: a feeling that their time as spaces of refuge, creativity, and alternate possibility had already passed. I would hear that "just a few years ago" one could find a barsati for under 10,000 rupees a month. Now, they would say, you cannot find one for under 15,000 rupees.

2 Ahearn, *Invitations to Love*.

3 Manuel Castells theorizes "portfolios of sociality," the potential for online relationships to translate into offline relationships and the offline relationships to continue in perpetuity long after face-to-face contact ceases to be a possibility. Castells, *Rise of the Network Society*.

4   See Miller, "Ideology of Friendship in the Era of Facebook," for a discussion of how the category of friend subsumes previous kin relationships and equalizes them with other kinds of relations. In other words, you can be friends with your mother, the neighbor down the street, or someone you met once on a trip.

5   See Marar, *Intimacy*, for a discussion of social media and the quest for intimate connection through the public articulation of emotion.

6   Bourriaud, *Relational Aesthetics*, 32.

7   For a discussion of how anthropology has had a tendency to discuss reciprocity as if it can be disentangled from public affect and felt emotion, see Povinelli, "Anthropological Fixation with Reciprocity."

8   Humayunpur is a small urban village adjacent to Green Park and Safdarjung Enclave in South Delhi.

9   Siva, or Shiva, is a deity in the Hindu pantheon.

10 The 1990 Mandal Commission report recommended reservations for other backward castes (OBCS) and Dalits in public universities and government jobs and resulted in mass public demonstrations by upper-caste young people across India. The right-wing Hindutva subsequently have appropriated elements of the argument I have made to make a case for reservations for economically marginalized upper-caste groups. For a discussion on the overlaps and disjunctures between caste and class, see Deshpande, *Contemporary India*. See also Amrute, "Moving Rape."

11 "India—Urbanization 2017," Statista, accessed March 3, 2016, https://www.statista .com/statistics/271312/urbanization-in-india/; "2011 Census Data," Census of India, http://www.censusindia.gov.in/2011-Common/CensusData2011.html.

12 See the India Census, 2011 for the most recent data on Delhi's growth. http:// censusindia.gov.in/2011-prov-results/data_files/delhi/3_PDFC-Paper-1-tables_60 _81.pdf. See also the India Online Pages for unofficial tally of Delhi's population as of 2020: http://www.indiaonlinepages.com/population/delhi-population.html/.

13 For accounts of Delhi's development as a migrant city in postindependence India, see Hosagrahar, *Indigenous Modernities*.

14 Appadurai, *Modernity at Large*, 16.

15 See, for instance, Searle, *Landscapes of Accumulation*.

16 Osella and Osella, "Friendship and Flirting."

17 Tupac Shakur, "Never Had a Friend like Me," *Gridlock'd* (Los Angeles: Death Row Records, 2002).

18 Nietzsche, *Thus Spoke Zarathustra*.

19 *Gully* is a globally circulating slang term that refers to the rough, unpolished, masculinist street ethos that emerges in ghettos across the world. Gully rap is a phenomenon that took off in India in 2015. Rappers like Soni, Jay, and Harish in Delhi and Divine and Naezy in Mumbai wrote lyrics in vernacular Hindi and Punjabi about their raw, everyday experiences growing up poor in crime-ridden, neglected sections of their respective cities—in distinction to the kind of glamorous party rap that had become popular in the years prior. They uploaded their music online, which subsequently went viral and attracted the culture industry and journalists. See Hannah Ellis-Peterson, "Poverty, Corruption, and Crime: How India's Gully Rap Tells the Story of Real Life," *The Guardian*, May 16, 2016.

20 Wacquant, *Body and Soul*, 26.

21 Hallam and Ingold, *Creativity and Cultural Improvisation*.

22 Nietzsche, *Thus Spoke Zarathustra*, 88.

23 Nakassis argues that efforts to establish status within youthful male groups often spur particular citational performances. This was certainly true in the Delhi hip hop scene. However, over time, status in the friendship group became inevitably tied to one's personal status within the larger Delhi hip hop community and to a kind of more ephemeral potential for national and even global fame. In the digital age, status in relationship to masculinity is shaped in multiple scales of sociality. Nakassis, "Youth Masculinity."

24 Rahul Roy, *When Four Friends Meet* (Mumbai: Magic Lantern, 1997).

25 Jeffrey, *Timepass*.

26 For an account of hip hop's hyperlocal tendencies, see Foreman, *The 'Hood Comes First*.

27 The predominantly Punjabi Sikh neighborhood that Soni lives in witnessed some of the worst violence in the 1984 riots, after then prime minister Indira Gandhi was killed by her Sikh security detail after ordering an attack on the Sikh Golden Temple in Amritsar. See Axel, *Nation's Tortured Body*, for a detailed history of these events and their impact on Sikhs in India and its diaspora.

28 Elizabeth Povinelli uses the term *autological society* to discuss how Western postenlightenment thought has created the fiction of a sovereign subject who is capable of willfully creating intimacy against the subject making force of the genealogical society—which dictates who one can be in intimate relations when using the logic of tribe, caste, custom, and so on. Jay's desire to make a video shows the complex ways in which the autological is braided with the genealogical in contemporary urban India. Povinelli, *Empire of Love*, 191–93.

29 M. Morgan, *The Real Hip Hop*.

30 Kama is Jay's second cousin.

31 A pound is a slapping together of the hands, sometimes followed by a snap. I was always taken aback at how softly Delhi hip hop practitioners who had origins in the subcontinent performed the physical reaffirmation of masculine belonging that the pound offered. It was in sharp distinction to the pounds I would receive, for instance, from Nigerians I met in the city—where a forceful clap and snap and subsequent sting on the hands viscerally reminded participants of their connection.

32 I discuss various forms of labor in the globally familiar in chapter 3. What is important to mark in this passage is the rapidly shifting sensibility around music production. When I first met Jay, it was a fun project one did with friends. Very quickly, it became a business opportunity.

33 Rai, *Jugaad Time*. *Jugaad* is a Hindi word that can be glossed as a hack or hacking—a strategy that poor people engage in to survive and thrive in India. Rai argues that jugaad has been taken up by capital. With policy initiatives like Make in India, jugaad has become an entrepreneurial catchphrase—one that might make Jay's dad see the economic potential of his musical play.

34 Lukose, *Liberalization's Children*, 98.

35 Chua, *In Pursuit of the Good Life*.

36 Mir, *Social Space of Language*.

37 For an account of the ways (digital) transnational jobs create new ideas about romance and intimacy, see Patel, *Working the Night Shift*, on gendered labor in the call centers of urban India.

38 "Eight out of Ten Millennials Support Inter-Caste Marriage in India: Survey," *Times of India*, June 29, 2018.

39 Annie Gowan, "A Muslim and a Hindu Thought They Could Be a Couple. Then Came the 'Love Jihad' Hit List,'" *Washington Post*, April 26, 2018.

40 Jackson, "On Ethnographic Sincerity," 279.

41 Riles, *The Network Inside Out*.

42 Rutherford, "Kinky Empiricism," 465.

2. The Materially Familiar

1 Kumar, "Perceiving Your Land."

2 Sulu is one of many Indian diasporic figures I met in Delhi's hip hop scene. I write about these figures and the ideologies they bring with them to Delhi in chapter 4.

3 Adidas put out the Stan Smith model in the 1960s. See Unorthodox Styles, *Sneakers*, for a fascinating history of collectible sneakers.

4 The urban poor, just like those with more resources, are pressured to accumulate things. However, the accumulation practices of the poor are often deemed a moral failure in public discourse.

5 Chua, *In Pursuit of the Good Life*.

6 Connell, *Masculinities*.

7 Govinda, "'First Our Fields, Now Our Women.'"

8 Alim, "Straight Outta Compton, Straight Aus München."

9 Miller, "Introduction," 8.

10 Rancière discusses dissensus in relationship to art and its capacity to reveal power dynamics in the social order and, potentially, rupture them. Rancière, *Dissensus*.

11 In "Small Frame Politics," I write in more detail about the ways in which the mall becomes a site of hip hop performance and aspiration precisely because of its role in producing value.

12 I spent several afternoons with Harish helping him with his exams on Émile Durkheim and Max Weber.

13 Taneja argues that Delhi's Islamic heritage sites are, for the most part, unused except for the random group of young men furtively playing cards. Taneja, *Jinneology*, 184–92. My time in the Delhi hip hop scene suggests that the Khirki masjid and Satpula dam were vital spaces for creative exchange and masculine becoming. I will return to Khirki and discuss the village in detail in chapter 5.

14 *Singh*, "Delhi to Bronx."

15 Luvaas, "Material Interventions."

16 Siegel, *A New Criminal Type in Jakarta*.

17 Luvaas, "Material Interventions," 133.

18 Tarlo, *Clothing Matters*.

19 La Tarde, *Laws of Imitation*.

20 Taussig, *Mimesis and Alterity*, iii.

21 Hebdige, *Subculture*, 12.

22 Burgin, *In/Different Spaces*, 142.

23 Benjamin, *Arcades Project*, 120–23.

24 For an interesting discussion on culture studies' relationship with resistance to and co-optation of capital, see Burgin, *In/different Spaces*.

25 Greene, *Punk and Revolution*.

26 Partridge, "Occupying Black Bodies," 42.

27 Boo, *Behind the Beautiful Forevers*, 8.

28 Derek Ide, "How Capitalism Underdeveloped Hip Hop: A Peoples' History of Political Rap," Hampton Institute, June 4, 2013, http://www.hamptoninstitution.org/capitalismhiphoppartone.html#.WgtnG4ZpGCQ.

29 Jay-Z, "Show You How," *Blueprint* (New York: Roc-A-Fella Records, 2001).

30 Mbembe, *Critique of Black Reason*.

31 Luvaas, "Material Interventions," 133. See also Nakassis, "Brands and Their Surfeits," for a more rarefied account.

32 Newell, *Modernity Bluff*. The dandies that Newell did his ethnography with in Abidjan had an interest in genuine brand-name items rather than genuine fakes and, according to Newell, spent considerable amounts of money acquiring brand-name gear to pull off their "modernity bluffs." My participants, however, saw their hip hop practice as the means to legitimize them and the gear they wore, whether real or genuine fakes.

33 Nakassis, *Doing Style*, 23.

34 Nakassis, *Doing Style*, 23–24. See also Peirce, *Peirce on Signs*, 5–17.

35 See, for instance, Chang, *Can't Stop, Won't Stop*.

36 Nakassis, *Doing Style*, 4–5.

37 Magical and Raxxo, "Swag Anusar," YouTube, March 10, 2017, https://www.youtube.com/watch?v=ACYHYJxYikM&feature=youtu.be.

38 *Singh*, "Delhi to Bronx."

39 Dhinchak Pooja, "Swag Wali Topi," YouTube, May 19, 2017, https://www.youtube.com/watch?v=dHGUvkYwES8.

40 Marwick, "Instafame."

41 Merleau-Ponty, *Phenomenology of Perception*.

42 DJ Kool Herc quoted in Chang, *Can't Stop, Won't Stop*, xi.

43 Goffman, *Frame Analysis*.

44 Voyce, "Shopping Malls in India.'" See also Brosius, *India's Middle Class*; and Srivastava, *Entangled Urbanism*.

45 Lukose, *Liberalization's Children*.

46 Kumar, "Perceiving Your Land."

47 Augé, *Anthropology for Contemporaneous Worlds*; see also Favero, "Phantasms in a Starry Place."

48 Ganti, *Producing Bollywood*.

49 Pratt, "Arts of the Contact Zone."

50 Pratt, "Arts of the Contact Zone."

51 Lukose, *Liberalization's Children*.

52 Adiga, *White Tiger*, 151.

53 For a longer discussion, see Dattatreyan, "Small Frame Politics."

54 Sundaram, *Pirate Modernity*.

55 Sundaram, *Pirate Modernity*, 91.

56 Soni was referring to the small boutique shops run by Northeastern youth that have sprung up in the small urban village of Humayunpur on the edges of Safdarjung.

57 Soni originally put the video up on YouTube and, in an earlier version of this chapter, I included a link to the video. Soni has since purged some of the videos on his channel—making available only his very slick productions that match his current (very successful) style.

58 Northeastern youth in the city, as Duncan McDuie-Ra argues, gravitate toward East Asian popular culture because they identify with and are identified as East Asians. Northeastern youth, whether they associate themselves with hip hop or not, thus become style bearers in the city for other young people. McDuie-Ra, *Northeast Migrants in Delhi*.

59 Adorno, "Culture Industry Reconsidered," 12.

3. Labor and Work

1 The urban village of Humayunpur appears in *Northeast Migrants in Delhi*, McDuie-Ra's ethnography on Northeastern youth in Delhi. My ethnographic work in Humayunpur no doubt traces some of the same physical geographies that McDuie-Ra did during his fieldwork in Delhi. However, rather than focusing solely on the experience of those within the synthetic category "Northeastern youth," I focus on the relationships across difference that hip hop produces in Humayunpur and in the city more broadly.

2 Hauz Khas Village makes its appearance in chapter 5, when I discuss how urban villages have become sites to imagine and enact a new urbanism discourse that valorizes a European aesthetic of scaled-down urban space.

3 S. M. Mustafi, "Is a Youth Revolution Brewing in India?," *India Ink* (blog), *New York Times*, August 27, 2012, http://india.blogs.nytimes.com/2012/08/27/is-a-youth -revolution-brewing-in-india/?_php=true&_type=blogs&_r=0.

4 "2011 Delhi Census," Census of India, http://www.censusindia.gov.in/2011-prov -results/prov_data_products_delhi.html. See also the India Online Pages for unofficial tally of Delhi's population as of 2020. http://www.indiaonlinepages.com /population/delhi-population.html/.

5 Jeffrey, *Timepass*.

6 Ong, "Please Stay," 84.

7 Duffy, "Romance of Work"; Terranova, "Free Labor"; Mazzarella, "Shoveling Smoke," 4.

8 Spence, *Stare in the Darkness*.

9 Gilroy, *Black Atlantic*.

10 My account of gendered laboring opportunities for the young men I met in Delhi coincides with discussions of the limited laboring possibilities that young migrant men have in the cities of India in comparison with their female working-class peers, who are able to access "pink collar" work. See, for example, Amrute, "Moving Rape"; Roychowdhury, "'The Delhi Gang Rape.'"

11 Duffy, "Romance of Work," 450.

12 Kelley, *Yo' Mama's Disfunktional!*

13 Kanye West, "Diamonds from Sierra Leone," YouTube, June 16, 2009, https://www.youtube.com/watch?v=92FCRmggNqQ.

14 Luvaas, "Material Interventions," 129.

15 The branding agents I met in Delhi were young and often practicing artists in their own right. The two I refer to in this chapter are from Delhi and New York and, I argue, are exemplars of the kinds of creative workers that are being brought in to manage the production of an Indian urban popular subcultural scene.

16 Hardt, "Affective Labor," 96.

17 Massumi has recently written a book that moves his previous theorizations of affect into the realm of the experiential and the social and, therefore, the economic and political. See Massumi, *Politics of Affect.*

18 Terranova, "Free Labor."

19 Hardt, "Affective Labor"; Hardt and Negri, *Empire*; Lazzarato, "Immaterial Labor."

20 Hardt, "Affective Labor," 96.

21 Lazzarato, "Immaterial Labor."

22 Haug, *Critique of Commodity Aesthetics*, 24.

23 Rajagopal, "Commodity Image in the (Post)Colony."

24 Blommaert and Varis, "Life Projects."

25 Mazzarella, *Shoveling Smoke.*

26 Arvidsson, "Creative Class or Administrative Class."

27 Virno, *Grammar of the Multitude*, 9.

28 See Wilson, "Anthropology and the Radical Philosophy."

29 See, for instance, McRobbie, "Clubs to Companies."

30 See Ong, "Introduction."

31 Honey Singh is one of the few famous rappers in India who was born and resides in the country. He is often deployed as a symbol of inauthenticity in online and offline conversations about hip hop in India by the youth in the Delhi scene.

32 Lathis are wooden batons that police are issued as standard gear. Lathi charges refer to the tactic used by police in urban India when they wish to disperse a crowd. They quite literally charge at the gathering with their batons drawn. *Goonda raj* is a Hindi term used to describe corrupt government regimes.

33 Anna Hazare is the Indian activist who garnered public support by performing a hunger fast to protest corruption in the Indian government. Sonia Gandhi is the erstwhile leader of the Congress Party and the widow of Rajiv Gandhi, son of Indira Gandhi.

34 See also Mumbai rapper Divine's 2018 video and track "Rape Roko," which draws attention to rape as a social problem and references the 2012 case in Delhi. Divine, "Rape Roko," YouTube, April 16, 2018, https://www.youtube.com/watch?v=uBo-CeDKWoo.

35 Atluri, "Young and the Restless."

36 *Dance India* is a contemporary popular reality TV show that features young dancers from all over India competing to claim the status of India's best dancer(s).

37 Graeber, *Towards an Anthropological Theory of Value.*

38 For a discussion of aging b-boys and imagined futures, see Fogarty, "Each One Teach One."

4. Hip Hop Ideologies

1 Nehru Place became an important destination for me during my time in Delhi as it was the place where one could make, for instance, hip hop "mixtapes" in mass quantities for a cheap price or buy the necessary equipment that I left behind in the United States for video production. While I do not go into the techno-material relationship between hip hop and copy culture in Delhi in this book, it is worth noting that the relationship between technology and cultural production in the twenty-first century makes places like Nehru Place central in the mapping of a changing youth culture in the city.

2 A *piece* refers to a long-form work of graffiti art. Pieces are differentiated from throw ups, which are quick but large character references to pieces, and tags, which are small writings of one's graffiti name, usually with a marker.

3 Café Coffee Day is the brainchild of V. G. Siddartha, an Indian businessman who wanted to replicate in India the Starbucks and Costa model from the United States and the United Kingdom, respectively.

4 Dhiraj Murthy writes about the electronic music scene in Mumbai and the ways in which postliberalization middle-class youth linked with the Indian diaspora to complicate nationalistic impulses back home. Delhi's early hip hop scene seems to have functioned along the same logic—where diasporic Indians and their well-to-do Indian counterparts played American hip hop for small audiences in exclusive clubs. Murthy, "Nationalism Remixed?"

5 The notion of hip hop *as* German culture in India is fascinating, and the subject of an article Jaspal Singh and I authored on soft diplomacy through hip hop. See Singh and Dattatreyan, "Cultural Interventions"; "Indo-German Hip Hop & Urban Art Project 2011–2012," Littlei, accessed March 11, 2020, http://littlei.in/indo-german-hip-hop-urban-art-project-26-28-april-2012/.

6 Begumpur, located in the south of Delhi, is another historic urban village where hip hop visual culture makes its appearance.

7 Singh and Dattatreyan, "Cultural Interventions."

8 See, for instance, Alim, "Hip Hop Nation Language," for a discussion of African American English-language circulation through hip hop and its role in the formation of an Anderson-like nation of hip hop practitioners. For Alim, like Anderson, nation signifies a feeling of connection to a collectivity, and that feeling requires the circulation of media to sustain itself. The concept of nation in relation to hip hop has also been critiqued by Jared Ball, who argues that the metaphor of nation carries problematic colonial, imperial, and, of course, nationalist residuals. See Ball, *I Mix What I Like.*

9 Lyric from Boogie Down Production track "I'm Still #1," *By All Means Necessary* (New York: Jive Records, 1998).

10 Hall, "Notes on Deconstructing 'the Popular,'" 448.

11 Hall, "Notes on Deconstructing 'the Popular,'" 449.

12 For a theorization of sincerity (rather than authenticity) as an analytical frame, see Jackson, "On Ethnographic Sincerity." See also Dattatreyan, "Diasporic Sincerity."

13 This is a somewhat gratuitous citation of a Dead Prez song titled "Hip Hop" from their album *Let's Get Free* (New York: Loud Records, 2000).

14 Marx, "A Critique of the German Ideology," 6.

15 MacLeod, "Authenticity within Hip Hop."

16 This debate, of course, exceeds hip hop. Theories of value, and debates around what makes a work of art valuable, have been going on in the art world for some time.

17 KRS-One, "KRS One Explains the Fifth Dimension along with the Innerspace and the Innerman," YouTube, posted July 17, 2017, https://www.youtube.com/watch?v=5MiT-_XZgEQ. See also Zulu Nation website on knowledge-science, accessed April 3, 2017, http://www.zulunation.com/knowledge-science/.

18 I draw on Sharma, *Hip Hop Desis*; and Huq, *Beyond Subculture*, to suggest that there is a reemergence of Blackness as a tentative political category in multiple contexts around the world, even as there is a retrenchment of anti-Blackness within diverse communities of color in the United States, Canada, and the United Kingdom.

19 See Ousumare, "Beat Streets in the Global Hood."

20 Rudraniel Sengupta, "Mandeep Sethi: Homeland Hip Hop," *LiveMint*, May 25, 2013, http://www.livemint.com/Leisure/diUw2k1tTkbPWmIg9cVwxL/Mandeep-Sethi—Homeland-hip-hop.html.

21 Brown, in this South Asian sense, is not to be confused with what José Esteban Muñoz theorized in US-based Latinx contexts as a specific kind of racialized melancholia. See Muñoz, "Feeling Brown, Feeling Down."

22 Desi, originally a Sanskrit word meaning "of the homeland," formulates a pan–South Asian identity among dispersed youth. See Maira, *Desis in the House*.

23 For a discussion of how 'hoods, ghettos, and slums have become the spatial locus for "real" hip hop, see Foreman, *The 'Hood Comes First*.

24 Smita Mitra, "The Slum of All Parts," *Outlook India*, March 28, 2011, https://www.outlookindia.com/magazine/story/the-slum-of-all-parts/270932.

25 Sunil Mehta, "Building a Scene: The Indo-German Hip Hop Project," Insider.in, April, 26, 2012, http://nh7.in/indiecision/2012/04/26/building-a-scene-the-indo-german-hip-hop-project/.

26 Spady, Meghelli, and Alim, *Tha Global Cipha*.

27 "Indo-German Hip Hop & Urban Art Project 2011–2012."

28 Mignolo, *Darker Side of Western Modernity*.

29 Riles, *Network Inside Out*; Clifford, *Routes*.

30 Ananya Roy uses the Mumbai-based NGO Pukar's critique of Danny Boyle's film *Slumdog Millionaire* (Century City, CA: Fox Searchlight, 2008) to demonstrate a "native" refusal of the kind of poverty narrative the film trafficked in. She argues that in Pukar's refusal lies a different narrative of the slum, one that paints it as a site of creative entrepreneurship aligned to capital and the project of the global city. A. Roy, "Slumdog Cities." Hip hop emissaries use a similar logic by promoting hip hop as a way for Dharavi's youth to reimagine the "slum" and thus depict Mumbai as a global city or, perhaps, a *familiar megacity* not in spite of but *because of* its 'hoods.

31 Some of the young men, Soni and Jay for instance, were able to transform themselves from b-boys into highly successful rappers who produced a gritty and authentic hip hop sound that reflected the challenges they and their families faced in Delhi.

32 Mauss, *The Gift*.

33 We could read Javan's paternalism as just that: a literal attachment to these young men that does not allow him to let go and let them make their own decisions. Mary Fogarty develops the concept of a hip hop family and discusses the dilemmas that emerge between the kin that hip hop practice creates. Fogarty, "Each One Teach One."

34 Dattatreyan, "Diasporic Sincerity."

35 Jackson, "Ethnography Is, Ethnography Ain't."

5. Urban Development

1 "Big man" refers to a male figure who has status sometimes, but not always, connected to wealth.

2 My arrival at this translation of our dialogue in Hindi and English happened well after it transpired, after I had heard about the Aap Ki Sadak project from several others who were involved.

3 Hansen and Verkaaik, "Introduction."

4 Hansen and Verkaaik, "Introduction," 12.

5 Mazumdar, *Bombay Cinema*.

6 Appadurai, "Right to Research," 174.

7 See Gupta and Ferguson, *Culture, Power, Place*.

8 Lewis and Lewis, *Delhi's Historic Villages*.

9 Mehra, "Urban Villages in Delhi"; Delhi Development Authority, "Master Plan Delhi, 1962."

10 Founded in 1946, DLF Group touts itself as the largest real estate company in India. The largest commercial and retail hub in South Delhi is DLF Saket, which opened in 2010 and consists of five malls, three hotels, and several office buildings.

11 Mehra, "Urban Villages in Delhi."

12 A piece wall is a designated "legal" wall space for graffiti writers or street artists to produce work.

13 Khoj International Studios held several art festivals in the public-private parks around Khirki during the years I lived in the city. They paid a nominal fee to the RWA council to use the space, inviting the b-boys of Khirki to perform there.

14 Jeffrey and McFarlane, "Guest Editorial."

15 Rutheiser, "Beyond the Radiant Garden City Beautiful."

16 Certeau, *Practice of Everyday Life*.

17 Bernroider, "Dynamics of Social Change."

18 Smith, "New Globalism, New Urbanism." See also the work of Ruth Glass, who coined the term *gentrification* in 1964. Glass, *London*.

19 Tarlo, *Clothing Matters*.

20 Rutheiser, "Beyond the Radiant Garden City Beautiful."

21 For an engagement with the category of "professional" as a discursively produced mobile class type in Delhi, see Searle, "Constructing Prestige."

22 The cinema chain PVR was founded in 1978 in South Delhi and now has branches across the country. Sudhir is referring to the Saket branch where he worked.

23 "Project Space: Word. Sound. Power," Tate Modern, July 12–November 3, 2013, http://www.tate.org.uk/whats-on/tate-modern/exhibitionseries/project-space/project-space-word-sound-power.

24 Rita Halder, "Road Design to Unclog Malviya Nagar," *Hindustan Times*, December 21, 2013.

6. Race and Place

1 Hauz Rani sits just adjacent to Khirki and across from the DLF shopping mall.

2 Tupac Shakur's "Changes" was recorded in 1992 but remixed and released in 1998. It sampled Bruce Hornsby's "The Way It Is." Tupac Shakur, "Changes," *Greatest Hits* (Los Angeles: Amaru, Death Row, Interscope, 1998); Bruce Hornsby and the Range, "The Way It Is," *The Way It Is* (Los Angeles: RCA, 1986).

3 Clarke and Thomas, "Globalization and Race."

4 Mullings, "Interrogating Racism," 668.

5 Gilroy, *Darker than Blue*. See also Burton, *Brown over Black*.

6 See Singh, "Loudness Registers." Singh and I have discussed race, ethnicity, and class at great length while we lived in Delhi and since we have left. These discussions continue to shape my thinking and writing about masculinity and difference in urban India.

7 McDuie-Ra, *Debating Race in Contemporary India*.

8 Trayvon Martin became a national and international symbol of the legacy of racism in the settler colonial reality of America.

9 K4 Kekho, "I Am an Indian," YouTube, May 8, 2018 (first produced 2015), https://www.youtube.com/watch?v=VMDhNLzKSFk.

10 For an engagement with the public theater and politics of eating in South Asia, see Parama Roy's wonderful book, *Alimentary Tracts*. For more on beef bans and cow vigilantism, see Gundimeda and Ashwin, "Cow Protection in India." Sambaiah Gundimeda and V. S. Ashwin offer a historical perspective on the latest mobilization of moral and economic arguments regarding cow protection by the Hindu right, which systematically targets Muslims, Dalits, and other minority groups. I mention the fact that men in particular are targeted because the majority of violent attacks by vigilante *gau rakshaks* ("cow protectors") have been directed at men who have been accused of trafficking in cows for slaughter.

11 Ousumare, "Beat Streets in the Global Hood," 172. See also Jennifer Roth-Gordon and her work on how American racial binaries of Black and White are brought over to new contexts through the circulation of hip hop, what she calls racial trafficking. Roth-Gordon, "Conversational Sampling, Racial Trafficking."

12 The Ministry of External Affairs is a government branch charged with creating relationships between India and other nations. During my time in Delhi, there was an initiative to celebrate the postcolonial relationships between India and Africa. Ironically, as these celebrations went on, there were several attacks on students and entrepreneurs from different African nations living in Delhi.

13 Zanoor became an older brother figure for Hanif and some of the other MCs in his crew. For a discussion regarding the ways hip hop creates new kin, see Fogarty, "Each One Teach One."

14 Dattatreyan, "Waiting Subjects."

15 Cissé, "South-South Migration"; Norman Lauzon and Mohamed Ibn Chambas, "Migration," Atlas on Regional Integration in West Africa, OECD, August 2006, https://www.oecd.org/migration/38409521.pdf.

16 Burton, *Brown over Black*.

17 The Satpula dam is another Mughal-era landmark in South Delhi. Anand Vivek Taneja wrote about this landmark in *Jinneology*, describing it as a place where very little sociality occurs. In my experience, the tunnels of Satpula were creative oases for young rappers and beatboxers from the area.

18 Trouillot, "Anthropology and the Savage Slot."

19 Munasinghe, *Callaloo or Tossed Salad*, 43.

20 Das, *Life and Words*.

21 Katyabaaz are self-trained electricians who are often called upon by residents in informal colonies in northern Indian cities to set up illegal electric connections to houses by pulling power from the main grid. *Powerless*, a film released in 2014 and directed by Deepti Kakkar and Fahad Mustafa, details the role katyabaaz play in the constantly shifting and changing topos of urban India.

22 Naija pop is a popular dance music currently being produced in Lagos, Nigeria.

23 Vivian Chenxue Lu discusses the impact of racialized tropes linked to Nigerian traders and merchants in her work. Lu, "Identifications." See also Pierre, *Predicaments of Blackness*, for an account of how the politics of race plays out among African nationals.

24 Susan Gal and Judith Irvine call this sort of ideological shifting around higher and lower scales "fractual recursivity." Gal and Irvine, "Language Ideology and Linguistic Differentiation," 38. Fractal recursivity is a useful linguistic concept that helps sheds light on the ways in which difference manifests across time and space.

25 In "Waiting Subjects," I discuss the global umma, the idea in Islam of a worldwide community of Muslims, and the way it braids together with hip hop for Hanif and his crew.

26 For discussions of the term *Desi*, see Maira, *Desis in the House*; and Shukla, *India Abroad*.

27 Neale, "Nigga," 557.

28 "NE Students Protest Arunachal Boy's Death," *Hindustan Times*, February 1, 2014.

29 *Madrasi* is a term used to describe someone from the city of Madras, now formally known as Chennai, which is the capital of Tamil Nadu.

30 My family lived in Delhi in the late 1970s. We had uncles and aunts who had lived in the city since the 1950s. All the elders in my family have stories to share about being derisively referred to as Madrasi while living in the city.

31 Dhrubo Jyoti, "Tarun Vijay Sparks Racism Row: 'We've South India . . . We Live with Black People,'" *Hindustan Times*, April 9, 2017.

32 Kendrick Lamar, "Fuck Your Ethnicity,'" *Section 80* (Carson, CA: Top Dawg Studios, 2011).

33 Kavita Srivastava, "Diffuse the Ugly Racism," *Outlook*, January 22, 2014, https://www.outlookindia.com/website/story/diffuse-the-ugly-racism/289247.

34 Malviya Nagar was one of several residential colonies developed in the 1950s to accommodate the expanding population of the city.

35 Povinelli, "The Will to Be Otherwise," 453. We could also think productively with Dead Prez's album *Let's Get Free* (New York: Loud Records, 2000).

36 Berlant, *Cruel Optimism.*

37 Jackson, *Racial Paranoia.*

38 Other Backwards Caste (OBC) and Scheduled Caste (SC) are state categories (among others) developed at the time of Indian independence to identify groups who had been systematically marginalized, ostensibly to offer them opportunities to succeed in the new state of India through job and higher education quotas, and other state schemes.

39 See, for instance, Rawat and Satyanarayana, *Dalit Studies,* for a series of powerful essays that link historical struggles of the African diaspora and Dalits in India.

40 A-List, "Free Kabir Kala Manch," accessed March 11, 2020, https://soundcloud.com /alistrap/free-kabir-kala-manch-produced.

41 For a closer look at the activism of Kabir Kala Manch, see Anand Patwardhan's 2011 documentary, *Jai Bhim Comrade.*

Epilogue

1 Madianou and Miller, *Migration and New Media.*

2 Madianou, "Smart Ethnography."

3 Murthy, "Digital Ethnography."

4 Preethi is a pseudonym.

5 Postill, "Remote Ethnography"; Pink and Postill, "Social Media Ethnography."

6 Jackson, *Thin Description.*

7 Geertz, "Balinese Cockfight."

8 Simpson, "Is Anthropology Legal?"

9 Hastrup, "Getting It Right."

10 Simpson, "Is Anthropology Legal?" For an analog-era discussion of similar dilemmas, see Brettell, *When They Read What We Write.*

11 There are a couple of key actors in the book who have not been given a pseudonym (Jaspal Singh, for instance) or, if they have, are easy to trace if I have provided a citation that names them.

12 For a full transcript, see "First Book on Desi Hip-Hop Culture Is in the Pipeline!," Desi Hip Hop, November 7, 2017, http://desihiphop.com/ first-book-desi-hip-hop-culture-pipeline/551443.

13 Zoya Akhtar, *Gully Boy* (Mumbai: Excel, Tiger Baby, 2019).

14 The MCs I got to know in Delhi distanced themselves from this political project— even going so far as to publicly call out some of their friends that did party promotion videos for Congress or the BJP. Indeed, the period leading up to the elections pushed Soni, Jay, and others to articulate macropolitical commentary and critique—a register I had not seen them take up prior to the run-up to the 2019 election.

15 Virilio, *Speed and Politics.*

16 Chauhan, "Pay as You Go."

Abu-Lughod, Lila. "The Romance of Resistance: Tracing Transformations of Power through Bedouin Women." *American Ethnologist* 17.10 (1990): 41–55.

Adiga, Aravind. *The White Tiger*. New York: Simon and Schuster, 2008.

Adorno, Theodor W. *The Culture Industry: Selected Essays on Mass Culture*. Edited by J. M. Bernstein. London: Routledge, 1991.

Adorno, Theodor W. "Culture Industry Reconsidered." *New German Critique* 6 (1975): 12–19.

Agarwala, Rina. "From Work to Welfare: A New Class Movement in India." *Critical Asian Studies* 38.2 (2006): 419–44.

Agha, Asif. *Language and Social Relations*. Cambridge: Cambridge University Press, 2007.

Agha, Asif. "Meet Mediatization." *Language and Communication* 31.3 (2011): 163–70.

Agha, Asif. "Recombinant Selves in Mass Mediated Spacetime." *Language and Communication* 27.3 (2007): 320–35.

Ahearn, Laura. *Invitations to Love: Literacy, Love Letters, and Social Change in Nepal*. Ann Arbor: University of Michigan Press, 2001.

Ahmed, Sara. "Affective Economies." *Social Text* 79.22 (2004): 117–39.

Alim, H. Samy. "Hip Hop Nation Language: Localization and Globalization." In *The Oxford Handbook of African American Language*, edited by Jennifer Bloomquist, Lisa J. Green, and Sonja L. Lanehart, 1–14. Oxford: Oxford University Press, 2015.

Alim, H. Samy. "Straight Outta Compton, Straight Aus München: Global Linguistic Flows, Identities and the Politics of Language." In *Global Linguistic Flows: Hip Hop Cultures, Youth Identities, and the Politics of Language*, edited by H. Samy Alim, Alastair Pennycook, and Awad Ibrahim, 1–24. New York: Routledge, 2008.

Alim, H. Samy, Alastair Pennycook, and Awad Ibrahim, eds. *Global Linguistic Flows: Hip Hop Cultures, Youth Identities, and the Politics of Language*. New York: Routledge, 2008.

Alter, Joseph. *Moral Materialism: Sex and Masculinity in Modern India*. New Delhi: Penguin, 2011.

Alter, Joseph. *The Wrestler's Body: Identity and Ideology in North India*. Berkeley: University of California Press, 1992.

Althusser, Louis. *Lenin and Philosophy and Other Essays*. New York: Monthly Review Press, 1971.

Amrute, Sareeta. "Moving Rape: Trafficking in the Violence of Postliberalization." *Public Culture* 27.2 (2015): 331–59.

Appadurai, Arjun. *Modernity at Large: The Cultural Dimensions of Globalization*. Minneapolis: University of Minnesota Press, 1996.

Appadurai, Arjun. "The Right to Research." *Globalisation, Societies, and Education* 4.2 (2006): 167–77.

Arvidsson, Arvon. "Creative Class or Administrative Class: On Advertising and the Underground." *Ephemera* 7.1 (2007): 8–23.

Atluri, Tara. "The Young and the Restless: Gender, 'Youth,' and the Delhi Rape Case of 2012." *Sikh Formations* 9.3 (2013): 361–79.

Augé, Marc. *An Anthropology for Contemporaneous Worlds*. Stanford: Stanford University Press, 1999.

Axel, Brian Keith. *The Nation's Tortured Body: Violence, Representation, and the Formation of a Sikh Diaspora*. Durham, NC: Duke University Press, 1984.

Ball, Jared. *I Mix What I Like: A Mixtape Manifesto*. Chico, CA: AK Press, 2011.

Benjamin, Walter. *The Arcades Project*. Translated by Howard Eiland and Kevin McLaughlin. Cambridge: Cambridge University Press, 1999.

Berlant, Lauren. *Cruel Optimism*. Durham, NC: Duke University Press, 2011.

Bernroider, Lucie. "Dynamics of Social Change in South Delhi's Hauz Khas Village." *SOAS South Asia Institute Working Papers* 1 (2015): 1–16. https://www.soas.ac.uk/south-asia-institute/publications/working-papers/file108721.pdf.

Bhan, Gautam: "'This Is No Longer the City I Once Knew': Evictions, the Urban Poor, and the Right to the City in Millennial Delhi." *Environment and Urbanization* 21.1 (2009): 127–42.

Blommaert, Jan, and Piia Varis. "Life Projects." *Tilburg Papers in Culture Studies*, no. 58 (2013). https://research.tilburguniversity.edu/en/publications/life-projects.

Boellstorf, Tom. *The Gay Archipelago: Sexuality and Nation in Indonesia*. Princeton, NJ: Princeton University Press, 2005.

Boo, Katherine. *Behind the Beautiful Forevers: Life, Death, and Hope in a Mumbai Slum*. London: Portobello, 2012.

Bourriaud, Nicolas. *Relational Aesthetics*. Paris: Les Press du Reel, 2006.

Breckenridge, Carol, ed. *Consuming Modernity: Public Culture in a South Asian World*. Minneapolis: University of Minnesota Press, 1995.

Brettell, Caroline, ed. *When They Read What We Write: The Politics of Ethnography*. Westport, CT: Bergin and Garvey, 1993.

Brosius, Christiane. *India's Middle Class: New Forms of Urban Leisure, Consumption and Prosperity*. London: Routledge, 2010.

Burgin, Victor. *In/different Spaces*. Berkeley: University of California Press, 1996.

Burton, Antoinette. *Brown over Black: Race and the Politics of Postcolonial Citation.* New Delhi: Three Essays Collective, 2012.

Castells, Manuel. *Rise of the Network Society.* The Information Age: Economy, Society, and Culture 1. Oxford: Blackwell, 2000.

Certeau, Michel de. *The Practice of Everyday Life.* Berkeley: University of California Press, 1984.

Chakraborty, Chandrima. "Mapping South Asian Masculinities: Men and Political Crises." *South Asian History and Culture* 5.4 (2014): 411–20.

Chang, Jeff. *Can't Stop, Won't Stop: A History of the Hip-Hop Generation.* New York: St. Martin's, 2005.

Chang, Jeff. "It's a Hip-Hop World." *Foreign Policy* 163 (October 12, 2009): 58–65. https://foreignpolicy.com/2009/10/12/its-a-hip-hop-world/.

Chattopadyay, Swati. *Unlearning the City: Infrastructure in a New Optical Field.* Minneapolis: University of Minnesota Press, 2012.

Chauhan, Aastha. "Pay as You Go: The Birth of South Delhi's Khirkee 17." Centre for Contemporary Asian Art, 4A Papers 2 (2017). http://www.4a.com.au/4a_papers _article/pay-go-birth-south-delhis-khirkee17/.

Chenxue Lu, Vivian. "Identifications: Notoriety and Diasporic Nigerian Life in China and Dubai." Paper presented at the Racialisation and Publicness in Africa and the African Diaspora Conference, Oxford, UK, June 27–28, 2019.

Chua, Jocelyn. *In Pursuit of the Good Life: Aspiration and Suicide in Globalizing South India.* Berkeley: University of California Press, 2014.

Cissé, Daouda. "South-South Migration and Sino-African Small Traders: A Comparative Study of Chinese in Senegal and Africans in China." *African Review of Economics and Finance* 5.1 (2013): 17–30.

Clarke, Kamari, and Deborah Thomas. "Globalization and Race: Structures of Inequality, New Sovereignties, and Citizenship in a Neoliberal Era." *Annual Review of Anthropology* 42 (2013): 305–25.

Clarke, Kamari, and Deborah Thomas, eds. *Globalization and Race: Transformations in the Cultural Production of Blackness.* Durham, NC: Duke University Press, 2006.

Clifford, James. *Routes: Travel and Translation in the Late Twentieth Century.* Cambridge, MA: Harvard University Press, 1997.

Connell, Raewyn. *Masculinities.* Berkeley: University of California Press, 2005.

Crenshaw, Kimberlé Williams. "Mapping the Margins: Intersectionality, Identity Politics, and Violence against Women of Color." *Stanford Law Review* 43.6 (1991): 1241–99.

Das, Veena. *Life and Words: Violence and the Descent into the Ordinary.* Berkeley: University of California Press, 2006.

Dasgupta, Rana. *Capital: A Portrait of Delhi in the Twenty-First Century.* New Delhi: 4th Estate, 2015.

Dasgupta, Rohit K., and Debanauj Dasgupta. "Introduction: Queering Digital India." In *Queering Digital India: Activisms, Identities, Subjectivities,* edited by Rohit K. Dasgupta and Debanauj Dasgupta, 1–45. Oxford: Oxford University Press, 2018.

Dattatreyan, E. Gabriel. "Critical Hip Hop Cinema: Racial Logics and Ethnographic Ciphas in Delhi." *Widescreen* 7.1 (March 2018): 1–27. http://widescreenjournal.org/index.php/journal/article/view/119/149.

Dattatreyan, E. Gabriel. "Diasporic Sincerity: Tales from a Returnee Researcher." *Identities: Studies in Culture and Power* 21.2 (2014): 152–67.

Dattatreyan, E. Gabriel. "Small Frame Politics: Public Performance in the Digital Age." In *Media as Politics in South Asia*, edited by Sahana Udupa and Stephen McDowell, 21–36. London: Routledge, 2017.

Dattatreyan, E. Gabriel. "Waiting Subjects: Social Media–Inspired Self-Portraits as Gallery Exhibition in Delhi, India." *Visual Anthropology Review* 31.2 (2015): 134–46.

Dean, Jodi. *Democracy and Other Neoliberal Fantasies: Communicative Capitalism and Left Politics*. Durham, NC: Duke University Press, 2009.

Delhi Development Authority. "Master Plan Delhi, 1962." https://dda.org.in/planning/mpd-1962.htm.

Desai-Stephens, Anaar Iris. "Singing through the Screen: *Indian Idol* and the Cultural Politics of Aspiration in Post-Liberalization India." PhD diss., Cornell University, 2017.

Deshpande, Satish. *Contemporary India: A Sociological View*. New Delhi: Viking, 2003.

Deuze, Mark. "Participation, Remediation, Bricolage: Considering Principal Components of a Digital Culture." *Information Society* 22.2 (2006): 63–75.

Dickey, Sarah. *Cinema and the Urban Poor in South India*. Cambridge: Cambridge University Press, 2007.

Duffy, Brooke Erin. "The Romance of Work: Gendered and Aspirational Labor in the Digital Culture Industries." *International Journal of Cultural Studies* 19.4 (2016): 441–57.

DuPont, Veronique. "The Dream of Delhi as a Global City." *International Journal of Urban and Regional Research* 35.3 (2011): 533–54.

Dwyer, Rachel, and Chris Pinney, eds. *Pleasure and the Nation: The History, Politics and Consumption of Public Culture in India*. Oxford: Oxford University Press, 2001.

Favero, Paulo. "Phantasms in a Starry Place: Space and Identification in a Central New Delhi Market." *Cultural Anthropology* 18.4 (2003): 551–84.

Fernandes, Leela. *India's New Middle Class: Democratic Politics in an Era of Economic Reform*. Minneapolis: University of Minnesota Press, 2006.

Fisher, Mark. *Capitalist Realism: Is There No Alternative?* Winchester, UK: Zero, 2009.

Flores, Juan. *From Bomba to Hip-Hop: Puerto Rican Culture and Latino Identity*. New York: Columbia University Press, 2000.

Fogarty, Mary. "Each One Teach One: B-Boying and Ageing." In *Ageing and Youth Cultures: Music, Style, and Identity*, edited by Andy Bennett and Paul Hodkinson, 53–66. London: Berg, 2012.

Foreman, Murray. *The 'Hood Comes First: Race, Space, and Place in Rap and Hip Hop*. Middletown, CT: Wesleyan University Press, 2002.

Gal, Susan, and Judith Irvine. "Language Ideology and Linguistic Differentiation." In *Regimes of Language: Ideologies, Polities, and Identities*, edited by Paul V. Kroskrity, 35–83. Santa Fe, NM: School of American Research Press, 2000.

Ganti, Tejaswini. *Producing Bollywood: Inside the Contemporary Hindi Film Industry*. Durham, NC: Duke University Press, 2012.

Geertz, Clifford. "Deep Play: Notes on the Balinese Cockfight." *Daedalus* 101.1 (1972): 1–37.

Ghertner, D. Asher. *Rule by Aesthetics: World-Class City Making in Delhi*. Oxford: Oxford University Press, 2015.

Gidwani, Vinay, and K. Sivaramakrishnan. "Circular Migration and the Spaces of Cultural Assertion." *Annals of the Association of American Geographers* 93.1 (2003): 186–213.

Gilroy, Paul. *Black Atlantic: Modernity and Double Consciousness*. Cambridge, MA: Harvard University Press, 1992.

Gilroy, Paul. *Darker than Blue: On the Moral Economies of Black Atlantic Culture*. Cambridge, MA: Harvard University Press, 2010.

Glass, Ruth. *London: Aspects of Change*. Centre for Urban Studies Report 3. London: MacGibbon and Kee, 1964.

Goffman, Erving. *Frame Analysis: An Essay on the Organizing of Experience*. Cambridge, MA: Harvard University Press, 1973.

Gopinath, Gayatri. "Bollywood Spectacles: Queer Diasporic Critique in the Aftermath of 9/11." *Social Text* 23.3–4 (2005): 157–69.

Govinda, Radhika. "'First Our Fields, Now Our Women': Gender Politics in Delhi's Urban Villages in Transition." *South Asia Multidisciplinary Academic Journal* 8 (2013). doi:10.4000/samaj.3648.

Graeber, David. *Towards an Anthropological Theory of Value: The False Coin of Our Own Dreams*. London: Palgrave, 2001.

Greene, Shane. *Punk and Revolution: Seven More Interpretations of Peruvian Reality*. Durham, NC: Duke. University Press, 2016.

Gundimeda, Sambaiah, and V. S. Ashwin. "Cow Protection in India: From Secularising to Legitimating Debates." *South Asia Research* 38.2 (2018): 156–76.

Gupta, Akhil, and James Ferguson. *Culture, Power, Place: Explorations in Critical Anthropology*. Durham, NC: Duke University Press, 1997.

Hall, Stuart. "Notes on Deconstructing 'the Popular.'" In *People's History and Socialist Theory*, edited by Raphael Samuel, 227–40. London: Routledge, 1981.

Hall, Stuart. *Representation: Cultural Representations and Signifying Practices*. London: SAGE, 1997.

Hallam, Elizabeth, and Tim Ingold. *Creativity and Cultural Improvisation*. London: Bloomsbury, 2008.

Hansen, Thomas Blom. *Wages of Violence: Naming and Identity in Postcolonial Bombay*. Princeton, NJ: Princeton University Press, 2001.

Hansen, Thomas Blom, and Oskar Verkaaik. "Introduction—Urban Charisma: On Everyday Mythologies in the City." *Critique of Anthropology* 29.1 (2009): 5–26.

Haraway, Donna. *Simians, Cyborgs, and Women: The Reinvention of Nature*. London: Routledge, 1991.

Hardt, Michael. "Affective Labor." *boundary 2* 26 (1999): 89–100.

Hardt, Michael, and Antonio Negri. *Empire*. Cambridge, MA: Harvard University Press, 2000.

Hardy, Kathryn. "Introduction." In "Production of Cinematic Space," special issue, *Widescreen* 7.1 (2018): 1–19.

Hastrup, Kirsten. "Getting It Right: Knowledge and Evidence in Anthropology." *Anthropological Theory* 4.4 (2004): 455–72.

Haug, Wolfgang Fritz. *Critique of Commodity Aesthetics: Appearance, Sexuality, and Advertising in Capitalist Society*. Minneapolis: University of Minnesota Press, 1986.

Hebdige, Dick. *Subculture: The Meaning of Style*. London: Routledge, 1979.

Hegde, Radha S. "Disciplinary Spaces and Globalization: A Postcolonial Unsettling." *Global Media and Communication* 1.1 (2005): 59–62.

Hosagrahar, Jyoti. *Indigenous Modernities: Negotiating Architecture and Urbanism*. London: Taylor and Francis, 2005.

Huq, Rupa. *Beyond Subculture: Youth and Pop in a Multi-Ethnic World*. London: Routledge, 2006.

Ismaiel-Wendt, Johannes S., and Susanne Stemmler. "Playing the Translations." In *Translating Hip Hop*, edited by Detlef Diedrichensen, Johannes S. Ismaiel-Wendt, and Susanne Stemmler, 67–85. Freiburg: Orange, 2012.

Jackson, John Lester, Jr. "Ethnography Is, Ethnography Ain't." *Cultural Anthropology* 27.3 (2012): 480–97.

Jackson, John Lester, Jr. "On Ethnographic Sincerity." *Current Anthropology* 51.2 (2010): 279–87.

Jackson, John Lester, Jr. *Racial Paranoia: The Unintended Consequences of Political Correctness*. New York: Basic Civitas, 2008.

Jackson, John Lester, Jr. *Thin Description: Ethnography and the African Hebrew Israelites of Jerusalem*. Cambridge, MA: Harvard University Press, 2014.

Jeffrey, Craig. *Timepass: Youth, Class and the Politics of Waiting in India*. Stanford: Stanford University Press, 2010.

Jeffrey, Craig, and Colin McFarlane. "Guest Editorial: Performing Cosmopolitanism, Environment and Planning." *Society and Space* 26.3 (2008): 420–27.

Jenkins, Henry. *Convergence Culture: Where Old and New Media Collide*. New York: New York University Press, 2006.

Kapur, Ratna. *Makeshift Migrants and the Law: Gender, Belonging, and Postcolonial Anxieties*. London: Routledge, 2012.

Kelley, Robin D. G. *Yo' Mama's Disfunktional! Fighting the Culture Wars in Urban America*. Boston: Beacon, 1998.

Krishnaswamy, Revathi. *Effeminism: The Economy of Colonial Desire*. Ann Arbor: University of Michigan Press, 2002.

Kumar, Sunil. "Perceiving Your Land: Neighborhood Settlements and the Haus-i-Rani." In *The Anthropology and Archaeology of Landscape: Shaping Your Landscape*, edited by Peter J. Ucko and Robert Layton, 159–74. London: Routledge, 1999.

Lampert, Michael. "Imitation." *Annual Review of Anthropology* 43 (2014): 379–95.

Larkin, Brian. "The Politics and Poetics of Infrastructure." *Annual Review of Anthropology* 42 (2013): 327–43.

Larkin, Brian. *Signal and Noise: Media, Infrastructure, and Urban Culture in Nigeria*. Durham, NC: Duke University Press, 2008.

La Tarde, Gabriel. *The Laws of Imitation*. 1903. Reprint, New York: Patterson, 2013.

Lazzarato, Maurizio. "Immaterial Labor." In *Radical Thought in Italy: A Potential Politics*, edited by Paulo Virno and Michael Hardt, 133–50. Minneapolis: University of Minnesota Press, 1996.

Leichty, Marc. *Suitably Modern: Making Middle-Class Culture in a New Consumer Society.* Princeton, NJ: Princeton University Press, 2003.

Lewis, Charles, and Karoki Lewis. *Delhi's Historic Villages.* London: Penguin, 2012.

Liang, Lawrence. "Porous Legalities and Avenues of Participation." In *Sarai Reader 05: Bare Acts.* Delhi: Sarai Media Lab, 2005. http://sarai.net/sarai-reader-05-bare -acts/.

Low, Setha. "Claiming Space for an Engaged Anthropology: Spatial Inequality and Social Exclusion." *American Anthropology* 113.3 (2011): 389–407.

Lukose, Ritty. *Liberalization's Children: Gender, Youth, and Consumer Citizenship in Globalizing India.* Durham, NC: Duke University Press, 2009.

Luvaas, Brent. "Material Interventions: Indonesian DIY Fashion and the Regime of the Global Brand." *Cultural Anthropology* 28.1 (2013): 127–43.

MacLeod, Kembrew. "Authenticity within Hip Hop and Other Cultures Threatened with Assimilation." *Journal of Communication* 49.4 (1999): 134–50.

Madianou, Mirca. "Smart Ethnography: Ethnography in Polymedia." Paper presented at the workshop Smart Ethnography? Goldsmiths, University of London, December 2016.

Madianou, Mirca, and Daniel Miller. *Migration and New Media: Transnational Families and Polymedia.* London: Routledge, 2012.

Maira, Sunaina Marr. *Desis in the House: Indian American Youth Culture in NYC.* Philadelphia: Temple University Press, 2012.

Mankekar, Purnima. *Unsettling India: Affect, Temporality, Transnationality.* Durham, NC: Duke University Press, 2015.

Manuel, Peter. *Cassette Culture: Popular Music and Technology in North India.* New Delhi: Oxford University Press, 2001.

Marar, Ziyad. *Intimacy: Understanding the Subtle Power of Human Connection.* London: Routledge, 2014.

Marwick, Alice. "Instafame: Luxury Selfies in the Attention Economy." *Public Culture* 27.1 (2015): 137–60.

Marx, Karl. "A Critique of the German Ideology." 1932. https://www.marxists.org /archive/marx/works/download/Marx_The_German_Ideology.pdf.

Massumi, Brian. *The Politics of Affect.* Cambridge: Polity, 2015.

Mauss, Marcel. *The Gift: Forms and Functions of Exchange in Archaic Societies.* 1922. Reprint, London: Routledge, 1990.

Mazumdar, Ranjani. *Bombay Cinema: An Archive of the City.* Minneapolis: University of Minnesota Press, 2007.

Mazzarella, William. "Culture, Globalization, Mediation." *Annual Review of Anthropology* 33.1 (2004): 345–67.

Mazzarella, William. *The Mana of Mass Society.* Chicago: University of Chicago Press, 2017.

Mazzarella, William. *Shoveling Smoke: Advertising and Globalization in Contemporary India.* Durham, NC: Duke University Press, 2003.

Mbembe, Achille. *Critique of Black Reason.* Durham, NC: Duke University Press, 2017.

McClintock, Anne. *Imperial Leather: Race, Gender and Sexuality in the Colonial Context.* New York: Routledge, 1995.

McDuie-Ra, Duncan. *Debating Race in Contemporary India*. London: Palgrave Macmillan, 2015.

McDuie-Ra, Duncan. *Northeast Migrants in Delhi: Race, Refuge and Retail*. Amsterdam: Amsterdam University Press, 2012.

McKittrick, Katherine. *Demonic Grounds: Black Women and the Cartographies of Struggle*. Minneapolis: University of Minnesota Press, 2006.

McRobbie, Angela. "Clubs to Companies: Notes on the Decline of Political Culture in Speeded-Up Creative Worlds." *Journal of Cultural Studies* 16.4 (2002): 516–31.

Mehra, Ajau K. "Urban Villages in Delhi." In *Urbanization and Governance in India*, edited by Evelin Hust and Michael Mann, 279–310. New Delhi: Manohar, 2005.

Merleau-Ponty, Maurice. *The Phenomenology of Perception*. London: Routledge, 2012.

Mignolo, Walter. *The Darker Side of Western Modernity: Global Futures, Decolonial Options*. Durham, NC: Duke University Press, 2011.

Miller, Daniel. "The Ideology of Friendship in the Era of Facebook." *HAU: Journal of Ethnographic Theory* 7.1 (2017): 377–95.

Miller, Daniel. "Introduction." In *Materiality*, edited by Daniel Miller, 1–51. Durham, NC: Duke University Press, 2005.

Miller, Daniel, and Heather Horst. "Introduction: The Digital and the Human." In *Digital Anthropology*, edited by Heather Horst and Daniel Miller, 3–35. London: Bloomsbury, 2012.

Mir, Farina. *The Social Space of Language: Vernacular Culture in British Colonial Punjab*. Berkeley: University of California Press, 2010.

Molnár, Virág. "Street Art and the Changing Urban Public Sphere." *Public Culture* 29.2 (2017): 385–414.

Morgan, Joan. *When Chickenheads Come Home to Roost: A Hip-Hop Feminist Breaks It Down*. New York: Simon and Schuster, 1999.

Morgan, Marcyleina. *The Real Hip Hop: Battling for Knowledge, Power, and Respect in the LA Underground*. Durham, NC: Duke University Press, 2009.

Mukherjee, Rahul. "Jio Sparks Disruption 2.0: Infrastructural Imaginaries and Platform Ecosystems in Digital India." *Culture, Media, and Society* 41.2 (2019): 175–95.

Mullings, Leith. "Interrogating Racism: Toward an Anti-Racist Anthropology." *Annual Review of Anthropology* 34 (2005): 667–93.

Munasinghe, Viranjini. *Callaloo or Tossed Salad: East Indians and the Cultural Politics of Identity in Trinidad*. Ithaca, NY: Cornell University Press, 2001.

Muñoz, José Esteban. "Feeling Brown, Feeling Down: Latina Affect, the Performativity of Race, and the Depressive Position." *Signs* 31.3 (2006): 675–88.

Murthy, Dhiraj. "Digital Ethnography: An Examination of the Use of New Technologies for Social Research." *Sociology* 42 (2008): 837–55.

Murthy, Dhiraj. "Nationalism Remixed? The Politics of Cultural Flows between South Asian Diaspora and 'Homeland.'" *Ethnic and Racial Studies* 33.8 (2010): 1412–30.

Nakassis, Constantine. "Brands and Their Surfeits." *Cultural Anthropology* 28.1 (2013): 111–26.

Nakassis, Constantine. *Doing Style: Youth and Mass Mediation in South India*. Chicago: University of Chicago Press, 2016.

Nakassis, Constantine. "Youth Masculinity, 'Style' and the Peer Group in Tamil Nadu, India." *Contributions to Indian Sociology* 47.2 (2013): 245–69.

Neale, Mark Anthony. "Nigga: The 21st-Century Theoretical Superhero." *Cultural Anthropology* 28.3 (2013): 556–63.

Neves, Joshua, and Bhaskar Sarkar. "Introduction." In *Asian Video Cultures: In the Penumbra of the Global*, edited by Joshua Neves and Bhaskar Sarkar, 1–35. Durham, NC: Duke University Press, 2017.

Newell, Sasha. *The Modernity Bluff.* Chicago: University of Chicago Press, 2016.

Nietzsche, Friedrich. *Thus Spoke Zarathustra: A Book for All and None.* 1883. Reprint, Cambridge: Cambridge University Press, 2008.

Ong, Aihwa. "Introduction: Worlding Cities, or the Art of Being Global." In *Worlding Cities: Asian Experiments and the Art of Being Global*, edited by Ananya Roy and Aihwa Ong, 1–26. London: Blackwell, 2011.

Ong, Aihwa. "Please Stay: Pied-a-Terre Subjects in the Megacity." *Citizenship Studies* 11.1 (2007): 83–93.

Ortner, Sherry. "Dark Anthropology and Its Others: Theory since the Eighties." HAU: *Journal of Ethnographic Theory* 6.1 (2016): 47–73.

Osella, Filippo, and Caroline Osella. "Friendship and Flirting: Micro-Politics in Kerala, India." *Journal of the Royal Anthropological Institute* 4.2 (1998): 189–206.

Osella, Filippo, and Caroline Osella. *Men and Masculinities in South India.* London: Anthem, 2006.

Ousumare, Halifu. "Beat Streets in the Global Hood: Connective Marginalities of the Hip Hop Globe." *Journal of American and Comparative Cultures* 24.1–2 (2001): 171–81.

Pardue, Derek. "Getting an Attitude: Brazilian Hip-Hoppers Design Gender." *Journal of Latin American and Caribbean Anthropology* 15.2 (2010): 434–56.

Partridge, Damani. "Occupying Black Bodies and Reconfiguring European Spaces—The Possibilities for Non-Citizen Articulations in Berlin and Beyond." *Transforming Anthropology* 21.1 (2013): 41–56.

Patel, Reena. *Working the Night Shift: Women in India's Call Center Industry.* Stanford: Stanford University Press, 2010.

Peirce, Charles Sanders. *Peirce on Signs: Writings on Semiotic.* Edited by James Hoopes. Chapel Hill: University of North Carolina Press, 1991.

Perry, Imani. *Prophets of the Hood: Politics and Poetics in Hip Hop.* Durham, NC: Duke University Press, 2004.

Pierre, Jemima. *The Predicaments of Blackness: Postcolonial Ghana and the Politics of Race.* Chicago: University of Chicago Press, 2012.

Pink, Sarah, and John Postill. "Social Media Ethnography: The Digital Researcher in a Messy Web." *Media International Australia* 145.1 (2012): 123–34.

Poonam, Snigdha. *Dreamers: How Young Indians Are Changing the World.* Cambridge, MA: Harvard University Press, 2018.

Postill, John. "Remote Ethnography: Studying Culture from Afar." *In Routledge Companion to Digital Ethnography*, edited by Larissa Hjorth, Heather Horst, Anne Galloway, and Genevieve Bell, 61–70. London: Routledge, 2017.

Povinelli, Elizabeth. "The Anthropological Fixation with Reciprocity Leaves No Room for Love." *Critique of Anthropology* 31.3 (2013): 210–50.

Povinelli, Elizabeth. *The Empire of Love: Toward a Theory of Intimacy, Genealogy, and Carnality*. Durham, NC: Duke University Press, 2006.

Povinelli, Elizabeth. "The Will to Be Otherwise / The Effort of Endurance." *South Atlantic Quarterly* 111.3 (2012): 453–75.

Pratt, Mary Louise. "Arts of the Contact Zone." *Profession* 1991 (1991): 33–40.

Puar, Jasbir. *Terrorist Assemblages: Homonationalism in Queer Times*. Durham, NC: Duke University Press, 2007.

Rai, Amit. *Jugaad Time: The Pragmatics of Everyday Hacking in India*. Durham, NC: Duke University Press, 2019.

Rajagopal, Arvind. "The Commodity Image in the (Post)Colony." May 18, 2010. http://tasveerghar.net/cmsdesk/essay/100/.

Ramamurthy, Priti. "Why Is Buying a 'Madras' Cotton Shirt a Political Act? A Feminist Commodity Chain Analysis." *Feminist Studies* 30.3 (2004): 734–69.

Rancière, Jacques. *Dissensus: On Politics and Aesthetics*. London: Continuum, 2012.

Rawat, Ramnarayan S., and K. Satyanarayana, eds. *Dalit Studies*. Durham, NC: Duke University Press, 2016.

Riles, Annelise. *The Network Inside Out*. Ann Arbor: University of Michigan Press, 2001.

Robinson, Cedric. *Black Marxism: The Making of a Black Radical Tradition*. Chapel Hill: University of North Carolina Press, 1983.

Rose, Tricia. *Black Noise: Rap Music and Black Culture in Contemporary America*. Hanover, NH: University Press of New England, 1994.

Roth-Gordon, Jennifer. "Conversational Sampling, Racial Trafficking, and the Invocation of the *Gueto* in Brazilian Hip Hop." In *Global Linguistic Flows: Hip Hop Cultures, Youth Identities, and the Politics of Language*, edited by H. Samy Alim, Alistair Pennycook, and Awad Ibrahim, 63–79. New York: Routledge, 2008.

Roth-Gordon, Jennifer. "Linguistic Techniques of the Self: The Intertextual Language of Racial Empowerment in Politically Conscious Brazilian Hip Hop." *Language and Communication* 32.1 (2012): 36–47.

Roy, Ananya. "The Blockade of the World-Class City: Dialectical Images of Indian Urbanism." In *Worlding Cities: Asian Experiments and the Art of Being Global*, edited by Ananya Roy and Aihwa Ong, 259–78. London: Blackwell, 2011.

Roy, Ananya. "Slumdog Cities: Rethinking Subaltern Urbanism." *International Journal of Urban and Regional Research* 35.2 (2011): 223–38.

Roy, Parama. *Alimentary Tracts: Appetites, Aversions, and the Postcolonial*. Durham, NC: Duke University Press, 2010.

Roychowdhury, Poulami. "'The Delhi Gang Rape': The Making of International Causes." *Feminist Studies* 39.1 (2013): 282–92.

Rutheiser, Charles. "Beyond the Radiant Garden City Beautiful: Notes on the New Urbanism." *City and Society* 9.1 (2008): 117–33.

Rutherford, Danilyn. "Kinky Empiricism." *Cultural Anthropology* 27.3 (2012): 465–79.

Sancho, David. *Youth, Class and Education in Urban India: The Year That Can Make or Break You*. London: Routledge, 2015.

Sassen, Saskia. *The Global City: New York, London, Tokyo*. Princeton, NJ: Princeton University Press, 2001.

Schloss, Joseph. *Foundation: B-Boys, B-Girls, and Hip-Hop Culture in New York.* Oxford: Oxford University Press, 2009.

Searle, Llerena G. "Constructing Prestige and Elaborating the 'Professional': Elite Residential Complexes in National Capital Region, India." *Contributions to Indian Sociology* 47.2 (2013): 271–302.

Searle, Llerena G. *Landscapes of Accumulation: Real Estate and the Neoliberal Imagination in Contemporary India.* Chicago: University of Chicago Press, 2016.

Shange, Savannah. "A King Named Nicki: Strategic Queerness and the Black FemmeCee." *Women and Performance: A Journal of Feminist Theory* 24.1 (2014): 29–45.

Sharma, Nitasha Tamar. *Hip Hop Desis: South Asian Americans, Blackness, and a Global Race Consciousness.* Durham, NC: Duke University Press, 2010.

Shukla, Sandhya. *India Abroad: Diasporic Cultures of Postwar America and England.* Princeton, NJ: Princeton University Press, 2003.

Siegel, James. *A New Criminal Type in Jakarta: Counter-Revolution Today.* Durham, NC: Duke University Press, 1998.

Simpson, Ed. "Is Anthropology Legal? Earthquakes, Blitzkrieg, and Ethical Futures." *Focaal: Journal of Global and Historical Anthropology* 74 (2016): 113–28.

Singh, Jaspal Naveel. "Delhi to Bronx: Transkulturelle Historizität als transformatives Potential." In *Textuelle Historizität: Interdisziplinäre Perspektiven auf das Diskursive Apriori*, edited by Heidrun Kämper, Daniel Schmidt-Brücken, and Ingo H. Warnke, 261–84. Berlin: de Gruyter, 2017.

Singh, Jaspal Naveel. "Loudness Registers: Normalizing Cosmopolitan Identities in Narratives of Ethnic Othering." *Journal of Sociolinguistics* (2019): 1–19. doi:10.1111 /josl.12364.

Singh, Jaspal Naveel, and E. Gabriel Dattatreyan. "Cultural Interventions: Repositioning Hip Hop Education in India." *Linguistics and Education* 36 (2016): 55–64.

Smith, Neil. "New Globalism, New Urbanism: Gentrification as a Global Urban Strategy." *Antipode* 34.3 (2002): 428–50.

Spady, James G., Samir Meghelli, and H. Samy Alim. *Tha Global Cipha: Hip Hop Culture and Consciousness.* Philadelphia: Black History Museum Press, 2006.

Spence, Lester. *Stare in the Darkness: The Limits of Hip Hop and Black Politics.* Minneapolis: University of Minnesota Press, 2011.

Srivastava, Sanjay. *Entangled Urbanism: Slum, Gated Community, and Shopping Mall in Delhi and Gurgaon.* Delhi: Oxford University Press, 2015.

Srivastava, Sanjay. "The Masculinity of Dis-Location: Commodities, the Metropolis, and the Sex-Clinics of Delhi and Mumbai." In *South Asian Masculinities: Change and Continuity*, edited by Radhika Chopra, Caroline Osella, and Filippo Osella, 175–223. New Delhi: Kali for Women, 2004.

Srivastava, Sanjay. "Modi-Masculinity: Media, Manhood, and Traditions in a Time of Consumerism." *Television and New Media* 16.4 (2015): 331–38.

Srivastava, Sanjay. "Semen, History, Desire, and Theory." In *Sexual Sites, Seminal Attitudes: Sexualities, Masculinities, and Culture in South Asia*, edited by Sanjay Srivastava, 1–24. New Delhi: SAGE, 2004.

Stewart, Kathleen. *Ordinary Affects.* Durham, NC: Duke University Press, 2007.

Sundaram, Ravi. *Pirate Modernity: Delhi's Media Urbanism*. London: Routledge, 2010.

Swarr, Amanda Lock, and Richa Nagar. "Dismantling Assumptions: Interrogating 'Lesbian' Struggles for Identity and Survival in India and South Africa." *Signs: Journal of Women in Culture and Society* 29.2 (2004): 491–516.

Taneja, Anand Vivek. *Jinneology: Time, Islam, and Ecological Thought in the Medieval Ruins of Delhi*. Stanford: Stanford University Press, 2017.

Tarlo, Emma. *Clothing Matters: Dress and Identity in India*. Chicago: University of Chicago Press, 1996.

Taussig, Michael. *Mimesis and Alterity*. London: Routledge, 1993.

Terranova, Tiziana. "Free Labor: Producing Culture in the Digital Economy." *Social Text* 18.2 (2000): 33–58.

Trouillot, Michel-Rolph. "Anthropology and the Savage Slot: The Poetics and Politics of Otherness." In *Recapturing Anthropology*, edited by Richard G. Fox, 17–44. Santa Fe, NM: School of American Research Press, 1991.

Tsing, Anna. "The Global Situation." *Cultural Anthropology* 15.3 (2000): 327–60.

Udupa, Sahana, and Steve McDowell. "Introduction: Beyond the Public Sphere." In *Media as Politics in South Asia*, edited by Sahana Udupa and Steve McDowell, 1–18. London: Routledge, 2017.

Unorthodox Styles. *Sneakers: The Complete Collectors Guide*. London: Thames and Hudson, 2005.

Uricchio, William. "Peer-to-Peer Communities, Cultural Citizenship, and the Limits of National Discourse." In *Media Cultures*, edited by William Uricchio and Susanne Kinnebrock, 61–88. Heidelberg: Universitätsverlag Winter, 2006.

Virilio, Paul. *Speed and Politics*. New York: Semiotext(e), 1986.

Virno, Paulo. *A Grammar of the Multitude*. Translated by Isabella Bertoletti, James Cascaito, and Andrea Casson. Cambridge, MA: MIT Press, 2004.

Voyce, Malcolm. "Shopping Malls in India: New Social 'Dividing Practices.'" *Economic and Political Weekly* 42.22 (2007): 2055–62.

Wacquant, Loïc. *Body and Soul: Notes of an Apprentice Boxer*. Oxford: Oxford University Press, 2004.

Webb, Martin. "Short Circuits: The Aesthetics of Protest, Media and Martyrdom in Indian Anti-Corruption Activism." In *The Political Aesthetics of Global Protest: The Arab Spring and Beyond*, edited by Pnina Werbner, Martin Webb, and Kathryn Spellman-Poots, 193–221. Edinburgh: Edinburgh University Press, 2014.

Williams, Raymond. *The Long Revolution*. 1961. Reprint, Cardigan: Parthian Books, 2011.

Willis, Paul. *Learning to Labour: How Working-Class Kids Get Working-Class Jobs*. 1977. Reprint, Oxford: Routledge, 2017.

Wilson, Ara. "Anthropology and the Radical Philosophy of Antonio Negri and Michael Hardt." *Focaal: Journal of Global and Historical Anthropology* 64 (2012): 3–15.

Page numbers in italics refer to illustrations.

East Asians, 165–66, 221n58

economic liberalization, 2, 3, 67–68, 206n8, 207n6

economic opportunities, 61–62, 215n57; b-boying, 80, 82, 93–94; branding agents and, 77; dialectic value between aspiration and labor, 88–89; DLF mall and, 142; #dmforcollab, 12, 215n61; Otherness and, 166; smart phones and, 72; urban development projects and hip hop artists, 151, 160. *See also* competition; entrepreneurship

education, 82

elites, 67–68, 212–13n33, 213n34

"elsewhere," xi, 2, 8, 142, 164–66, 169, 175, 192, 203, 211n26

embodied practices, xi, 1–7, 10–13, 17, 29, 85, 87, 92, 95, 112, 207n2, 213n37. *See also* body; clothing/fashion practices; friendship; romance; tattoos

emissaries. *See* hip hop emissaries

English, 173

enregisterment, 216n66

entrepreneurship: jugaad discourse, 40, 208n9, 215n57, 218n33; neoliberal valorization of, 83–84. *See also* economic opportunities

environmental issues, 153

ethical issues, 130–33, 193–95

European and Indian European hip hop emissaries, 108–11, 116, 118–21, 125–27, 126, 129–31, 223n5

Evisu jeans, 60

exchange value, 91–92, 95, 97

Facebook, 9, 16, 23, 28, 47, 63–66, 137, 217n4

face-to-face contact, 58, 112, 216n3

false consciousness, 52

familiarity. *See* globally familiar

female objectification, 34

Ferguson, James, 212n31

fetish, 17–18; commodity fetish, 51, 96–97; globally familiar indexed by, 66–67, 83; surpassing of, 65

Filipina migrant domestic workers, 193

Flores, Juan, 209n15

food politics, 168

foreign investment, 207n6

fractual recursivity, 227n24

frames, 53

freedom: expression of, 91–92; hustle as, 88; from oneself, 182–84

"Free Kabir Kala Manch" (A-List), 188–89

free labor, 83, 91–92, 103

French situationists, 147

friendship, 22; anthropology and, 19, 42–45; categories of, 217n4; in Delhi, 25–31, 33, 72; difference and, 21–23, 27–28, 41–42; embodied practices, 29; hip hop and, 24; homosocial, 30, 33, 53, 85, 96; international, 127–28; in rap, 34; other relationships and, 35; screens and, 27–28. *See also* romance

frontier logic, 120

"Fuck Your Ethnicity" (Lamar), 179–80, 184

futures, 18–19; aspirations for, 5, 8–9; of Delhi and India, xi, 2–3, 6, 63; imagined alternatives, 12, 35–36; limits on, x, 7, 10–12; potential, ix, 2–3, 12, 88; shared exchanges, 24, 30

Gal, Susan, 227n24

Gandhi, Indira, 218n27

Gandhi, Rajiv, 73, 222n33

Gandhi, Sonia, 222n33

Ganti, Tejaswini, 68

Garhwal district, 10, 25

gated communities, 70, 89, 144, 156

Gati (NGO), 144

Geertz, Clifford, 85, 197

gender: colonialism and, 4–5; DIY production, 24; fetish and, 51; hip hop and, 4, 8, 168; immaterial labor and, 18; South Asian, 31; style and, 18, 57, 60–62

genealogical society, 218n28

gentrification, 89, 132, 140, 147–48, 154–57, 225n18

"genuine fakes," 56, 61

Germany, 18, 108–11, 116, 118–21, 223n5

The Get Down (Netflix series), 59–60

Ghertner, Asher, 2

Gidwani, Vinay, 214n51

Gilroy, Paul, 83, 165

global capital, ix, 2, 12, 212n31. See also capital; capitalism

global cities, 212n31

global hip hop nation, 53, 110

globalization, 3, 7, 35, 52

globally familiar, 3–4, 207n3, 209n13; anthropologist as, 16; brand symbols, 2, 50–51; clothing and, 45, 53, 66–67; co-creation

subjectivities: autological society, 218n28; digitally enabled, 139; disciplining practices, 97; gendered, 4, 8, 168; global Black, 176; swag and, 53; techno-futuristic male, 23
Sundaram, Ravi, 7, 73
surveillance, 68–70, 72–73, 145, 157
sustainability: economic, 90
swag, 17–18, 51–53, 62–66, 82–83. *See also* clothing/fashion practices; style
Swarr, Amanda Lock, 211–12n27

Tamil (Brahmin) community, 26
Tamil Nadu, 8
Taneja, Anand Vivek, 55, 206n14, 219n13
tapori (vagabond/hustler), 138
tastemakers, 76, 89
Tate Modern Museum, 129
tattoos, 21, 22, 28, 51, 75
Taussig, Michael, 57
team symbols, 45, 47, 50, 56, 62
technological infrastructure, 3, 9
television, 8–9
Terranova, Tiziana, 83, 91–92
thick description, 197
Thomas, Deborah, 164
transgression, 23
transnational popular discourses, 13
transportation, 139
Trouillot, Michel-Rolph, 171
Tughlaq dynasty, 144

unanticipated audiences, 59
United Nations High Commissioner for Refugees (UNHCR), 157, 164, 170
United States, 59, 109–10, 186
universalist discourses, 99–100, 111, 118–20, 122
upper-caste youth, 89
urban charisma, 138
urban development, 135–61; Aap Ki Sadak project, 136–40, 146–61, 225n2; discourses of, 18, 146, 212–13n33; gentrification, 89, 132, 140, 147–48, 154–57, 225n18; Hauz Khas heritage area, 79, 221n2; Islamic heritage sites, 157, 219n13; political economy of, 148, 157–58, 166

urbanization, 117
urban poor and working class, 4–6, 58, 116–17
urban villages, 18, 26–27, 89, 140–49, 206n1.
    See also Delhi; *specific villages*
Uttar Pradesh, 136–37, 142

Varis, Piia, 95
Vemula, Rohit, 188
Verkaaik, Oscar, 138
Verma, J. S., viii–ix
videographers and photographers, 94
video shoots, 72–73
Vijay, Tarun, 179
violence: against African nationals, 170, 172, 178, 179; colonial legacy of, 5; against romantic partners, 41–42; sexual, viii–x; by state, 180; street, 35, 89–90; women and, 180–81
Virilio, Paul, 202
Virno, Paulo, 95

Wacquant, Loïc, 29
walkability, 137, 140, 146, 149
Washington Post, 42
West, Kanye, 88
West Africa, 61
West Africans, 144
West Delhi, 26, 34–35
When Four Friends Meet (film), 33–34
White Tiger (Adiga), 69
"Why Can't You Understand?" (Jay's solo production), 40–41, 43, 46
Wild Style (film), 207n4
world-class status discourse, x–xi, 2, 6–7, 11, 96, 147, 206n11, 212n31, 213n34

youth, 8, 9, 19, 33; and culture industry, 18, 29, 80, 82, 88, 90–91, 93–94, 166
YouTube videos, 10, 74, 182; fame from, 63–65; learning from, 14, 21, 29; "likes," 93, 182; public record, 46–47. *See also* music videos

zamindars (landlords), 142, 148, 172, 181
Zimmerman, George, 167
Zulu Nation, 115, 177–78